EAST ASIA
HISTORY, POLITICS, SOCIOLOGY, CULTURE

Edited By
Edward Beauchamp
University of Hawaii

A ROUTLEDGE SERIES

East Asia
History, Politics, Sociology, Culture
Edward Beauchamp, General Editor

PITFALL OR PANACEA

The Irony of US Power in Occupied Japan, 1945–1952

Yoneyuki Sugita

Routledge
New York & London

Published in 2003 by
Routledge
29 West 35th Street
New York, NY 10001
www.routledge-ny.com

Published in Great Britain by
Routledge
11 New Fetter Lane
London EC4P 4EE
www.routledge.co.uk

Routledge is an imprint of the Taylor & Francis Group
Printed in the United States of America on acid-free paper.

10 9 8 7 6 5 4 3 2 1

Library of Congress Cataloging-in-Publication Data

Sugita, Yoneyuki.
  Pitfall or panacea : the irony of US power in occupied Japan, 1945–1952 / by Yoneyuki
Sugita.
    p. cm. – (East Asia: history, politics, sociology, culture)
  Includes bibliographical references (p.   ) and index
    ISBN 0-415-94752-9 (hardcover)
    1. Japan–History–Allied occupation, 1945–1952. II. Title. II. Series: East Asia (New
York, N.Y.)
DS889.16.S85 2003
952.04'4–dc21   2003008828

For Shoko

Contents

Glossary

CCP	Chinese Communist Party
CFR	Council on Foreign Relations
CIA	Central Intelligence Agency
CUJEC	Committee on US-Japan Economic Cooperation
DLP	Democratic-Liberal Party
FEC	Far Eastern Commission
ECAFE	Economic Commission for Asia and the Far East
EROA	Economic Recovery for Occupied Area
ERPC	Economic Recovery Planning Committee in the Japanese government
ESB	Economic Stabilization Board
ESS	Economic and Scientific Section (of SCAP)
GHQ	General Headquarters
GS	Government Section (of SCAP)
HCLC	Holding Company Liquidation Commission
JCP	Japanese Communist Party
JCS	Joint Chiefs of Staff
JMFA	Japanese Ministry of Foreign Affairs
JSP	Joint Staff Planners

JSSC	Joint Strategic Survey Committee
KMT	Kuomingtang Party
LDP	Liberal Democratic Party
MCI	Ministry of Commerce and Industry
MDAP	Mutual Defense Aid Program
MITI	Ministry of International Trade and Industry
NAC	National Advisory Council on International Monetary Affairs
NSC	National Security Council
OCI	Overseas Consultants Incorporated
OIR	Office of Intelligence Research
PPS	Policy Planning Staff
PRC	People's Republic of China
PRF	Police Reserve Force
PTC	Peace Treaty Committee
PWC	Committee on Post-War Programs
RFB	Reconstruction Finance Bank
RSD	Research and Statistics Division (of the ESS)
SANACC	State-Army-Navy-Air Coordinating Committee
SCAP	Supreme Commander for the Allied Powers
SFE	Subcommittee for the Far East (of the SWNCC)
SWNCC	State-War-Navy-Coordinating- Committee
UN	United Nations
UNWCC	United Nations War Crimes Commission

Acknowledgments

Home sweet home. A stable and fun family life is the best environment for generating new ideas. Without Shoko, my dear wife, this would not have been possible. For this and more, she deserves my greatest affection. Without Gakuto (our 4-year old son) and Natsuki (our 1-year old daughter), I would not have had enough energy to finish this book.

First and foremost, I would like to extend my deepest gratitude to Professor Thomas J. McCormick, who served as my Ph.D. dissertation advisor at the University of Wisconsin-Madison. His patience, kindness, and advice made it possible for me to finish my dissertation in 1999. My special thanks go to Professor Aruga Tadashi, who was my MA thesis adviser at Hitotsubashi University, Professor Matsuda Takeshi at Osaka University of Foreign Studies, and Professor Edward Beauchamp, the editor of the East Asia dissertations series, who first encouraged me to publish my dissertation in book form.

Friendship and assistance from colleagues and friends are the best assets a student of history can have. There are many who deserve profound thanks, including Professors Nishimura Shigeo, Nakamura Masanori, Stanley Kutler, Brett Sheehan, Hasegawa Tsuyoshi, Ishii Osamu, Timothy McKeown, William Borden, Glenn Hook, Aaron Forsberg, Gordon Berger, Michael Barnhart, Roger Dingman, Howard Lentner, Richard Fry, Jon Davidann, Marie Thorsten, Robert Eldridge, Kan Hideki, and Richard Jensen.

Many individuals shared there precious collections of materials, sources, and information with me. In particular, Professor John Dower generously and unhesitatingly allowed me to use his enormous document collection gathered at his office at the Massachusetts Institute of Technology. He also gave me critical advice on US economic policies and regionalism.

Assistance from officials working at libraries and archives is indispensable for finishing the kind of book I have written. I tremendously appreciate the fantastic help received from the Osaka University of Foreign Studies Library, Hitotsubashi University Library, the Institute of Economic Research Library at Hitotsubashi University, Tokyo University Library, the Center for Pacific and American Studies at Tokyo University, the Graduate School of American Studies Library at Doshisha University, the National Diet Library (Japan), the Library of Congress, US National Archives and Records Administration, the University of Wisconsin-Madison Memorial Library, the Wisconsin State Historical Society Library, the Princeton University Seeley G. Mudd Manuscript Library, the Rutgers University Archibald S. Alexander Library, the Harvard University Widener Library, the Ohio State University William Oxley Thompson Memorial Library, the Columbia University Butler Library, the United States Naval Academy Nimitz Library, the Council on Foreign Relations Archives, the Detroit Public Library, the Harry S. Truman Library, the MacArthur Memorial Library and Archives, Public Record Office (Great Britain), the London School of Economics Library, the School of Oriental and African Studies (SOAS) Library (University of London), University of Oxford Bodleian Library, H-NET, and many others.

Research for my book received generous financial support from Osaka University of Foreign Studies, the Japanese Ministry of Education, the University of Wisconsin-Madison Graduate School, the University of Wisconsin-Madison History Department, the Fulbright Program, the Research Institute for Peace and Security (Tokyo), H-NET, the Japan Association of International Relations, the Japan-Philippines Study Forum, Flinders University (South Australia), and Old Dominion University.

I would like to thank Kimberly Guinta, associate editor, and John Shea, production editor, at Routledge, for their excellent handling of this project, and Mary-Alice Pickert, John Garside, and John McGlynn for their immensely capable English proofreading assistance.

> June 2003
> At home in Kawanishi City
> Hyogo Prefecture, Japan
> Yoneyuki Sugita

PREFACE

The United States began bombing Iraq a few days ago. Before the attacks began, American policy makers reportedly based plans to occupy Iraq on "successful" occupation reforms implemented in post-war Japan about six decades ago. In the literally thousands of books, articles, essays, and other writings on the US occupation of Japan, most writers blindly assume that occupation polices were highly "successful". However, if American "success" in occupied Japan eventually led the United States to get bogged down in an Asian quagmire, this "success" is nothing but an ironical outcome of America's preponderance of power.

When the United States acquired overwhelming power immediately after the end of World War II, it used that power unanimously, believing that it would use the power wisely to create a better and peaceful world. The United States used its prerogative to force Japan to adopt democracy and demilitarization. In order to maintain this democratic, demilitarized, and pro-Western Japan, the United States had to assume responsibility for Japan's economic prosperity as well as its security. The United States presumed that it would be impossible to implement an economic recovery in Japan without establishing solid regional economic linkages between Japan and Southeast Asia, which in turn forced Washington to undertake a series of campaigns to eliminate political instability in Southeast Asia. In other words, one intervention in Japan inevitably led the United States to make other interventions, causing Washington to eventually find itself stuck in an Asian quagmire.

The United States, as a hegemonic power, exercised its prerogatives to accomplish what it wished in occupied Japan, but, alas, this very success ironically led the United States to be pulled more and more deeply into Asian affairs, probably more deeply than it ever wished.

There is no such thing as absolute power. The United States eventually found itself reeling from the "success" of its occupation policies in Japan, refusing to pay attention to the negative consequences of using its hegemonic power to remold the country. Unfortunately, it seems clear today that the United States did not learn any lessons from its experience occupying Japan. The Bush administration started the war against Iraq, convinced that it could make real its dream of democratizing and demilitarizing Iraq, and using an expansion of its power in the Middle East to stabilize the entire region. History is likely to repeat itself. In the current situation involving Iraq, resorting to a preponderance of power might solve an imminent threat, but it also creates the potential for new problems. We all should take the time to study history seriously to learn the correct lessons. Power is truly a fruit that should be forbidden to the unwise.

Note on Transliteration

Japanese names appear in Japanese order, with family name first. However, names of authors of works in English follow English order, with given name first.

INTRODUCTION

The United States' occupation of Japan, which lasted from 1945 until 1952, was a grandiose experiment that had an extensive influence on Japanese society, on the United States' involvement in the Asia-Pacific region, and on US-Japan relations in the post-World War II era. The occupation and its effects continue to spark intellectual debate, and various, often contradictory, interpretations, of the occupation's historical significance abound.

US policy toward East Asia in the post-World War II era had two basic undercurrents. First, the United States assumed that Asians would respect powerful and authoritarian leadership. Consequently, Washington attached importance to the psychological elements of its policies, including authority, leadership, dignity, and prestige. Second, the United States also assumed that it was powerful enough to determine the future development of Asia.

The primary purpose of this book is to shed light on the limits and incongruities of the American hegemony in occupied Japan. Hegemony means a situation in which "one nation possesses such unrivaled supremacy, such predominant influence in economic power, military might, and political-ideological leadership, that no other power, or combination of powers, can prevail against it."[1] The United States exercised its hegemonic power to shape Asia's future; however, the United States also suffered greater burdens because of its continuous involvement in the region. Ironically, then, America's own policy of resorting to hegemonic prerogatives in Asia resulted in the gradual erosion of the United States' own power.

This book presents a new perspective based on the accumulation of previous scholarship concerning the US occupation of Japan. One group of scholars argues that the American occupation was a successful social experiment, accomplishing its primary goals of making Japan more democratic, more pluralistic, and more friendly to the United States.[2] Some scholars focus on the limited progressive aspects in the occupation.[3] Another group of scholars tends to employ structural explanations centered on the crisis of world capitalism and the onset of the cold war.[4] Still other scholars stress the coherency of the United States' goals and the continuity of its economic policy toward Japan during the occupation.[5] Most recently, John Dower introduces a new approach to occupation studies by describing the perspectives of ordinary Japanese in much more detailed ways than previous studies. Herbert Bix reveals the active role played by Emperor Hirohito in the Asia-Pacific War.[6]

Most of these previous studies share the assumption that the United States enjoyed a preponderance of power in managing the Japanese occupation and that it was in a strong position to shape postwar development in the Asia-Pacific region. In contrast, this book explains the limits of American hegemony in occupied Japan. In a similar approach to that of *Embracing Defeat*, this book emphasizes the significant influence that an occupied Japan exerted on the United States, an influence that encouraged America's deep involvement in Asia-Pacific affairs; however, unlike Dower's method, this book focuses on Japanese as well as on American elite perspectives in order to demonstrate the limits of American hegemony in occupied Japan.

Chapter one argues that Washington and the Supreme Commander for the Allied Powers (SCAP) had different attitudes toward Japan: In general, immediately after the end of the Asia-Pacific War, Washington had a more punitive attitude while SCAP employed more pragmatic policies toward Japan. Since General Douglas MacArthur had significant discretionary power, and Japan shared his political and pragmatic approaches concerning the issues of the Imperial institution, demilitarization, and economic deconcentration, their shared attitudes prevailed during the early occupation period.

Chapter two deals with shift in US occupation policies. A cold-war mentality began to prevail in Washington around 1947. An anti-communist perspective gradually replaced the punitive sentiment toward Japan. The punitive attitude toward Japan, which dominated the period immediately after the end of the Asia-Pacific War, was supplanted by more moderate approaches as in the case of economic deconcentration and reparations. Moreover, peace treaty negotiation issues indicated that there had been a transfer of policy initiatives from SCAP to Washington.

Chapter three discusses Japan's road to economic stability. The need for this stability finally led to the rigid implementation of the austerity program by Joseph Dodge (the Dodge Line). The Japanese financial community positively assisted Dodge in implementing his balanced-budget program in order to win its power struggle against those within the Japanese government who favored an inflationary, production-first strategy. The Dodge Line constituted a turning point in the occupation, establishing a solid basis for a new economic system monitored by the financial community. This program, however, precipitated a broad range of resistance in Japan. In order to contain Japanese frustration, Washington sought Japanese economic expansion by establishing a close and organic regional economic linkage between Japan and countries in the Asia-Pacific region. Successful implementation of the Dodge Line in Japan ironically induced more American commitment in Asia.

When Washington considered a peace treaty in 1949, Japan's security after the occupation loomed as the most critical problem. Chapter four focuses on this security issue. There was a basic consensus between Japan and the United States on gradual rearmament and on the retention of American bases in Japan prior to the outbreak of the Korean War. Both countries, however, recognized that security issues would impinge on sensitive sovereignty and constitutional matters, which would precipitate political problems in Japan. The emergence of communist China stimulated Washington's cold-war anxiety about China's impact on an unstable Asia, and increased Japanese bargaining power vis-à-vis the United States. Tokyo used its weakness to induce deeper US involvement in Asia. Assuming hegemonic responsibility to manage the world system smoothly, the United States gradually committed itself to Asia, where it had little direct significant security or economic concerns.

Chapter five treats the Korean War not as a watershed of US-Asian relations, but as a catalyst that accelerated and consolidated the processes Washington had already established in Asia. The war did not remilitarize the Japanese economy but strengthened a new Japanese economic structure instigated by the financial community. The Korean War psychologically solidified Washington's cold-war perspectives and over-inflated its sense of communist threat. The Chinese Communists' intervention in the war and their evenly matched fighting with the United States increased China's prestige in Asia, which forced Washington to demonstrate its intention and capability to maintain order in Asia. Japanese nationalists openly advocated rearmament as the path to becoming an autonomous power, raising Washington's fear of possible emergence of Japanese neutralism. The United States realized that Prime Minister Yoshida Shigeru, a pragmatic gradualist, was the best choice as a leader to make Japan a dependable and pro-American partner. The Korean War brought different consequences to Japan and the United States. Tokyo set a course of economic growth through peaceful means, while Washington became hypersensitive to the communist menace, which propelled its intense enmeshment in Asia.

Chapter six analyzes the Dulles-Yoshida negotiations of early 1951. Japanese post-occupation security constituted the most critical issue in these talks. Yoshida and John Foster Dulles shared a fundamental consensus as to gradual Japanese rearmament and American base rights after the termination of the occupation. The United States acquired what it wished, but as its achievements piled up, Washington's responsibilities also increased. Each commitment required another commitment, which made Washington's burden bigger and bigger. Japanese rearmament made it absolutely necessary to tie Japan to the West to prevent Japan from again becoming a menace to the world community. Moreover, its acquisition of bases forced the United States to act carefully in its relations with Japan in order to contain anti-American sentiment in Japan. In order to maintain a positive image, the United States had to provide security and economic prosperity to Japan, which required the establishment of a close regional linkage in Asia, which in turn demanded the pacification of Southeast Asia.

Although the United States was able to exercise its hegemonic power to shape Japan's future, the more the nation accomplished in Japan during the occupation, the greater the burdens it seemed to suffer for its continuous involvement. Ironically, American achievements restrained America's freedom of behaviors in Japan. The very conduct of resorting to hegemonic prerogatives in Japan resulted in the gradual erosion of its own power base.

CHAPTER ONE

SETTING THE STAGE
THE DEMILITARIZATION AND
DEMOCRATIZATION OF JAPAN

DIVIDED-CORE STRATEGY IN
THE POSTWAR ASIA-PACIFIC REGION

When Japan surrendered on 15 August 1945, nearly every major city in Japan lay in ruins. As colonists repatriated and babies boomed, the population growth on shrunken territory wreaked havoc on a nation already on its knees from incendiary damage, food deprivation, spiritual demoralization and physical exhaustion. Forfeiting the Greater East Asia Co-Prosperity Sphere, Japan lost access to raw materials and the market for Japanese goods. Price controls and rationing came to an abrupt halt, leaving a black market to flourish.

In contrast, World War II left the United States as the most powerful country in the world, and it set about establishing a new world-system backed up by military, economic, and ideological power. John Stuart, the American Ambassador to China, was concerned that with "Japan's elimination as a power, the USSR has re-emerged as a major element on the Far Eastern scene." He believed, "East Asia's present economic plight is attributed to the vacuum created by the elimination of Japanese shipping, Japanese management and Japanese trade." He also worried that China's disorganization made it a potential arena for rival ideologies and influences.[1] George Kennan, a career diplomat, considered Asia to be "going through [the] throes of a complete political, social, and economic revolution. Most of the people in the area are bewildered by the shattering of the age-old patterns of life."[2] The United States was the dominant influence directing the course of Japanese development, but at the war's end, American policy-makers had not yet formulated a coherent occupation scheme.

1

In 1944 and 1945, Washington began to realize that the country would have to play a major role in the Asia-Pacific region.[3] Joseph Ballantine, Deputy Director of the Office of Far Eastern Affairs, sent a memo to Secretary of State Cordell Hull stating: "Responsibility for future security and order in the Pacific will fall primarily upon the United States. That responsibility makes necessary a carefully integrated policy (economic, political, and military) for eastern Asia and the western Pacific area as a unit."[4] In the prewar era, Japan alone had dominated this area economically, politically, and militarily. Since Asia dominated by a single power was a dreadful picture for Washington, this region would require a strong US presence to help balance power against a resurgent Japan. In the region, only Japan had a modern industrial infrastructure, a reservoir of highly skilled labor, technical expertise, a banking system, and prewar economic ties with American businessmen. American officials assumed that Japan would rejoin the postwar international economic system. Ballantine insisted, "Any policy for Japan to be successful . . . must permit . . . [that country's] eventual participation in world trade."[5] The US goal for postwar reconstruction was to resuscitate the Japanese economy without reviving its military and political power. The United States, therefore, had to alter power relationships in the region.

In May 1942, President Franklin D. Roosevelt announced that China would become one of the four great powers that would maintain postwar world peace. He expected China to become a pro-American stabilizing force in Asia, and he promised to equip Chinese military forces. In short, China would become a major political and military power in Asia. China was, however, in deep crisis at the war's end. The Chinese Communist Party (CCP) considered the war as a means to implement a social revolution, and to establish a "new democracy," whereas the Kuomingtang Party (KMT) sought to strengthen its authority. Economically, China was suffering from a spiral of vicious inflation. The CCP made the best use of deteriorating socioeconomic conditions to attract a large number of supporters to its "egalitarian" and "democratic" programs. Facing the rapid expansion of the CCP's influence, the KMT focused on containing its adversary, neglecting more urgent, liberal reform.[6] In economic terms, China remained a backward country even though it had vast resources and the greatest potential market in the world. The United States did not expect China to become an industrialized nation in the near future, as it had neither the requisite economic infrastructure nor sufficient technical expertise. When the Chinese government asked Donald Nelson, the US special economic envoy to China, about the possibility of a postwar automobile industry in China, the American replied that such a possibility was at least ten years away because of China's lack of supporting industries.[7]

The United States anticipated political turmoil in a Southeast Asia whose people would demand political independence as former colonial powers returned home. Washington hoped to channel nationalist aspirations along a moderate course, so that the newly independent nations would augment a liberal, capitalist world-system based on multilateralism. However, since the United States had enjoyed little influence in this region before the Asia- Pacific War, it expected the former European colonial powers to deal with the situation.[8]

Thus, Washington faced three primary issues in postwar Asia: how to use Japan's great economic potential, how to establish a pro-American China as a stabilizing force in Asia, and how to channel the nationalist movements in Southeast Asia along an acceptable course. The United States developed a 'divided-core strategy' in which the power functions between China and Japan were divided in order to avoid the emergence of a single dominant power. China was to be Asia's political and military core while Japan its economic center. Consequently, Washington worked to transform the Chinese tutelage into a participatory coalition government and to get Japan back to multilateral, liberal capitalism.[9]

Because power would thus be divided, neither China nor Japan could seek regional hegemony. Congressman Walter Judd clearly expressed this vision of regional balance of power: "Withholding war materials so that there is no possibility of Japan's rearming, we should permit her to recover economically. ... [and] take every proper means to develop China as the great stabilizing bulwark in Asia." He goes on to argue that a strong China would prevent Japan from becoming a dangerous power in Asia. "Japan can never seriously threaten us as long as in her rear is a strong, independent China, friendly to the democracies."[10] In addition, the United States hoped that building China and Japan into modern, liberal democratic nations, would provide Southeast Asia with models to guide their nationalist movements.

GENERAL DOUGLAS MACARTHUR'S DISCRETIONARY POWER

As the world's most powerful country, the United States appeared able to implement the divided-core policy in Asia. The major obstacle, however, was resurgent domestic isolationism, which surfaced once the war ended. The American people demanded that its government bring the soldiers home for discharge. Washington reduced the number of servicepersons from 12 to 1.5 million in just two years. The federal government also had to make adjustments for the transition from a wartime to a peacetime economy, and fears of inflation prevented the maintenance of high-level military spending after the war.[11]

As a result, the limits of American power after the war prevented the diplomatic elite in Washington from making active commitments around the world. Decision-makers placed the top priority on Europe, while Asia received only peripheral notice.[12] The National Security Council (NSC) concluded, "Western Europe merits first consideration in terms of both urgency and potential value. . . . the Near and Middle East is of second priority . . . The Far East is of only third priority in this reckoning. . . ."[13] Even though the United States devised a divided-core strategy toward postwar Asia, it simply did not have enough resources to implement the program. Because Washington officials perceived severe limitations of American power and lacked the will to commit themselves to Asian affairs, they did not employ a coherent policy towards Asia. Thus, the policy remained in a state of flux during the early postwar period.[14]

Besides paying little attention to the wider Asia-Pacific region, Washington failed to formulate a clear occupation strategy in Japan. The State Department began postwar planning for Japan as early as the summer of 1942, but, at the war's end, had not yet reached a firm consensus, particularly about economic policies. Some officials insisted on the need for Japan's de-industrialization, severance of foreign trade, and its return to an agricultural economy. They desired to punish Japan and to demote it to the status of it as a third tier country. Others sought to eliminate Japan's heavy industries and the merchant marine, leaving only light industries. Still other planners advocated moderate change in the Japanese oligopoly in order to use the country's economic strength for the future development of Asia as a whole. Thus, different, often contradictory, ideas coexisted in the State Department.[15]

Moreover, because Japan surrendered earlier than the United States had expected, Washington had prepared only a general guide for major objectives: demilitarization, democratization, and the reintegration of Japan into the world community.[16] When the War Department showed the Basic Directive to General Douglas MacArthur in September 1945, he complained that it did not detail program implementation. The War Department replied that MacArthur had discretionary power to modify the generalization and add appropriate policies.[17] When the Joint Chiefs of Staff (JCS) issued the directive on 3 November 1945 as the general guidance SCAP should follow, it stressed the document's flexible nature: "This directive does not purport finally to formulate long-term policies concerning the treatment of Japan in the postwar world . . . . Those policies and the appropriate measures for their fulfillment will in large measure be determined by developing circumstances in Japan."[18] With Washington's peripheral priority paid to Asia and the flexible nature of occupation policy directives, General MacArthur possessed a relatively free hand to implement the occupation in Japan.

BACK TO NORMALCY

Wars often cause drastic transformation not only in social structures, but also in people's minds. Japanese civilian leaders, such as Yoshida Shigeru and Konoye Fumimaro, feared that the Asia-Pacific War would have a revolutionary impact on Japanese society, including its capitalist economic system, class structure, and Imperial system.[19] In February 1945, Konoye agreed, "What we must be most concerned about from the standpoint of preserving the *kokutai* [national polity] is the communist revolution which may accompany defeat."[20] Prince Konoye strongly recommended the preservation of feudal forces and Zaibatsu, the great family-controlled banking and industrial complexes, in order to prevent a communist takeover.[21] Between 1945 and 1947, the Japanese government was seriously afraid of a left-wing revolution.[22] Japanese civilian leaders considered that the best road to contain this revolutionary trend would be a quick return to "normalcy," which was to say, accepting Western institutions and becoming a junior partner of the most powerful Western power in Asia. Yoshida argued that Japan's future "was to be a global power, and the expansion as well as the security of the state was best guaranteed by close alliance with the dominant Western power in Asia and the Pacific."[23] Kagawa Takaaki, Yoshida's private secretary, recalled, "Yoshida once said to me that in diplomacy there are always active and passive powers. Europe and the United States had always been active, capable of influencing other countries. He said we should always deal first with those strong, active powers. . . . He would always say that since the Meiji period, Japan should have been with the strong maritime countries and that our failure to do that [during World War II] was our undoing." Yoshida was convinced that the United States would be the dominant, active, and maritime power in postwar Asia.[24] In February 1946, the Treaty Bureau of the Japanese Ministry of Foreign Affairs (JMFA) contended that since the United States would be the dominant country in the Far East, Japan would need to establish a close relationship with it. Consequently, the peace treaty should wipe out all unstable relationships between these two countries.[25]

There was, however, an immediate problem. Japanese and Americans had demonstrated vehement racial hatred toward one other during the war, much of the enmity having been inculcated through the formal channels of state propaganda. After half a decade of relentless hate-mongering, no one could accurately predict how the other would act during the occupation, an unprecedented encounter between national cultures as well as between the victor and the vanquished.[26] Americans expected at least sporadic, regional guerrilla resistance even after the official surrender; the Japanese anticipated brutal treatment by the occupation authorities. Both sides grossly overvalued mutual suspicions. The Allied Occupation of Japan, for all of its complications and shortcomings, proved to be one of the most unexpectedly successful feats of grand social engineering by victors over vanquished ever.

Contrary to American apprehensions, the Japanese readily cooperated with the occupation authorities and welcomed the new social "revolution from above." In October 1945, the JMFA recommended that all the other ministries swiftly draw up a concrete and voluntary package of political, economic, and social reforms based on progressivism, democracy, pacifism, and rationalism in order to head off extreme United Nations' demands and to launch Japan's recovery.[27] In January 1946, the Political Bureau of the JMFA also advocated a swift, complete, and voluntary democratization. It argued that this would be the most rational way to reform its political system including the constitution, to contain the Allied Powers' intervention, and to acquire a moderate peace treaty.[28]

Explaining Japan's volte-face requires clarification of at least three contexts: psychological, practical, and historical. First, according to many cross-cultural assumptions, the Japanese believed in situational ethics, regarding truth as changeable according to context rather than immutable.[29] During the war, it was right to obey the militarists and to despise the Western way of living. When Japan lost the war, however, it was appropriate to criticize militarists and to look to the West. Although most people's physical existence was desperate, Japanese society had become open to new ideas as the recovering population sought to define new values primarily in economic terms. While this new energy was generated indigenously by Japanese society, much of it would be shaped in deference to the demands of occupation authorities. The occupation authorities successfully channeled much of the new energy into peaceful economic-first orientation, one of the most important hallmark features of the Japanese postwar state: the Japanese policy of prioritizing its economic development, and at the same time, minimizing Japanese political and military influences in the global community.

The Japanese also had pragmatic reasons to change their frame of mind after their defeat. In 1949, *The Economist* argued that the "submissiveness and docility of the Japanese under American occupation so far has been due . . . to the feeling that American control and American bounty and protection have come to stay for a long time." Under this circumstance, "all sensible Japanese can see that nationalist agitation and gestures of defiance would merely make things more difficult for Japan without any prospect of regaining real national independence."[30]

Defeat in the Asia-Pacific War had a devastating impact on the Japanese economy. Japan forfeited all its colonies, which consisted of approximately 45 percent of land space of the former empire and all the assets there. As a result, Japan lost sources for a large percentage of its commodities: 92 percent of sugar, 79 percent of iron ore, 54 percent of coal, 58 percent of soybeans, and 45 percent of salt. The war also did damage to its domestic industries: 30.2 percent of its thermal power, 31.5 percent of its gas, 58 percent of its oil refineries, and 71.9 percent of its ship building industries.[31] Japan had also made little investment during the war into development of new industrial technologies, so in addition to be highly damaged its technology was also out-dated.[32] In October 1945, a Finance Ministry officer argued that since the Japanese fiscal recovery would require material assistance from the United States, Japan would have to regain its international credibility by strongly pro-moting political democratization.[33] In December 1945, the Research Bureau of the JMFA foresaw that the "world economy will be divided into a Soviet bloc and an Anglo-American bloc."[34] Since the latter controlled the advanced tech-nologies, Japan would have to accommodate to the Anglo-American bloc as a way of life.[35] In February 1946, the Treaty Bureau of the JMFA also argued that America's dominant position in Asia made it necessary for Japan to lean toward Washington.[36] Japan had to promote industrial development because "it is impossible for Japan to live on agriculture. . . . In order to feed a large population in a small country, Japan must expand employment opportunities through industrial development."[37] The Japanese Ministry of Commerce and Industry (MCI) recommended that the country focus on heavy and chemical industries to increase exports and return to the standard of living of the 1930s. Since advanced technology would be essential for economic recovery, eco-nomic deconcentration and the adoption of advanced technology had to go in tandem.[38] Isolated from the world-economy, Japanese leaders realized that outdated technology seriously decreased Japan's power and they emphasized the importance of "technology development" to sustain economic expansion.[39]

In addition to psychological and practical contexts, there was also a histor-ical background for the United States and Japan to reestablish a congenial rela-tionship swiftly. Japanese democratic and pro-American liberal forces had sur-vived the war. The US leaders regarded the 1920s as the most harmonious decade of US-Japan cooperation, when "liberals" such as Shidehara Kijuro, Prime Minister, and Inouye Junnosuke, Governor of the Bank of Japan, led Japan. The United States and Japan then shared the idea of a multilateral world economy, and both countries had a common interest in the mainte-nance of open-door policies in China.[40]

Even during the war, when US officials tended to focus on the military elites who controlled policymaking, some within the US government recog-nized that business interests in Japan did not always agree with the political elite. For example, a State Department memo of November 1944 discussed liberal elements in Japan who could restore the cooperative relations of the 1920s.[41] Another memo from July 1945 to the Secretary of State indicated "strong groups [in Japan] who believe in the capitalistic system of economic society. . . . [and] such groups must be supported as a core of the future Japanese economy."[42] In August 1945, De Forest Van Slyke, an Army officer, suggested the "strong probability that the Japanese will be ripe, if permitted to direct it themselves, for a genuine democratic movement." He understood, "the democratic elements in Japan were increasing in strength [prior to 1931] and, with the military discredited, could probably be [revived]."[43]

Secretary of War Henry Stimson passed Van Slyke's memo to President Harry Truman, US Army Chief of Staff General George Marshall, Assistant Secretary of War John McCloy, Undersecretary of State Joseph Grew, and Secretary of State James Bynes. They all agreed to revive Japanese 'liberal elements' by eliminating militarists, purging feudalistic officials, and restructuring the oligarchic Zaibatsu-controlled economic system.[44] General MacArthur expected that progressive reforms would induce Japanese 'liberal elements' to provide SCAP with voluntary cooperation.[45] James Lee Kauffman, a prominent attorney and student of the Japanese economy, predicted, "Japan would return to her policy of the twenties" with an economy led by "financial leaders . . . who did not favor war, but sought economic penetration through peaceful means."[46]

At his meeting with General MacArthur in October 1945, Prince Konoye claimed, "the combination of the military clique and leftists led Japan into today's disaster."[47] In an address to the House of Representatives in November 1945, Prime Minister Shidehara argued that the reactionaries had interrupted the development of Japan's modern democracy that had started with the Meiji Restoration. He insisted that the Japanese people eliminate the militarists and return the country to democratic forces.[48] Idealizing the 1920s, he tried to return to that decade by criticizing the military forces for distorting Japan's normal course of development.[49]

It is debatable whether Japan truly had liberals and democracy in the 1920s, but the destruction wrought by the ultra-nationalists and militarists in the 1930s and 1940s made it easy for American policy-makers to remember the friendly decade and idealize it. They came to regard the period between the Manchuria Incident of 1931 and the end of the Asia-Pacific War as a "great aberration" in Japanese history. Emphasizing the importance of eliminating those unwanted forces in Japan, the JCS insisted, "No nationalistic or military clique or combination should again be able to dominate that country and lead it into a war of aggression."[50]

Changes in those three contexts, namely, psychological, practical, and historical, constituted the necessary conditions for the successful implementation of social reforms. The sufficient condition was the insulation of Japan's economy after 1945, so it was able to develop without having to face international competition. Since SCAP controlled Japan's foreign trade, Japan was exempted from the heavy burden of its huge trade deficit, much of which was covered by American aid. The assistance amounted to $404 million and $461 million in 1947 and 1948 respectively and accounted for 92% of Japanese imports in 1947 and 75% in 1948.[51] Because Japan's trade, in real terms, had constantly declined since 1937, the country actually performed much better after SCAP took over control of its foreign trade. Japan's commodity exports increased by 69 percent, 48 percent, 94 percent, and 61 percent in 1946-47, 1947-48, 1948-49, and 1949-1950 respectively.[52] In a sense, Japan was in an economic greenhouse. In addition, since it was under Allied military occupation, Japan enjoyed a cost-free military shield against external attacks. In the mid-1930s, Japan spent over 40% of governmental expenditure for military purposes and the proportion increased after 1937. After the war, the military expenditure greatly decreased. The Government Section of SCAP (GS) pointed out, "During the first and most difficult years of Japanese democracy there will be little, if any, concern over the problems of external and internal security, problems which have plagued many young governments and have been the cause of democracy's undoing in many countries."[53] GS also indicated, "The government will not be concerned with the problem of military security, which means that it will be able to concentrate on internal questions."[54]

Under these protected circumstances, it was much easier for SCAP to experiment with radical reforms and for the Japanese government to digest the occupation reforms. Although the economic and security greenhouse enabled Japan to accept many of SCAP's reforms without too much difficulty, the future of the Emperor constituted one of the most critical issues in which Japan and the United States would have to compromise in order to bring the occupation to a successful conclusion.

THE IMPERIAL INSTITUTION

As the holder of supreme power under the Meiji Constitution, the Emperor could not escape major, if not entire, responsibility for the Asia-Pacific War.[55] Nevertheless, on 29 December 1943, Joseph Grew, Special Assistant to the Secretary of State, made a speech entitled "War and Post-War Problems in the Far East." In his speech, he implied that the Emperor would be necessary to stabilize Japanese society in the postwar era.[56] Grew's speech stirred a heated public discussion about the postwar Imperial system. Four days later, the *New York Times* bluntly criticized Grew's defense of the Emperor.[57] Edward Hunter, a journalist, asserted that once the Allies abolished the Imperial system, Japan would naturally lean toward a republic.[58] According to a Gallup Poll, the majority of responses supported a harsh punishment of the Emperor–including execution, imprisonment, or exile. Only three percent of replies suggested that the Allies could use the Emperor in the postwar era. Based on the results of this poll, Director of the Office of Far Eastern Affairs, Joseph Ballantine, warned Grew that it would be politically questionable to support the Imperial system.[59] Two Assistant Secretaries of State, Archibold MacLeish and Dean Acheson, had already clarified their positions: that Congress, the Press, and public opinion would not accept any proposal for maintaining the Imperial system.[60] In September 1945, the United States Senate adopted a resolution, "It is hereby declared to be the policy of the United States to try Hirohito, Emperor of Japan, as a war criminal."[61] In September 1945, a *New York Post* editorial stated that if the Japanese people were willing to use force to overthrow the feudalistic institutions, the US occupation authorities should not intervene.[62]

There was strong support in Asia to punish the Emperor as a war criminal. In October 1943, Sun Fo, a liberal politician in China, had published an article in the *National Herald* entitled "The Mikado Must Go," indicating that Japan would have to abolish the Imperial system in the postwar era.[63] In July 1945, the People's Political Council in China made a resolution that the Emperor was a war criminal.[64] The Australian and New Zealand governments shared China's opinion that the Allies should put Hirohito at the disposal of the Allies.[65] Joseph Stalin was of the opinion that the Allies should abolish the Imperial system.[66] The Chinese Communist's paper insisted that the Emperor Hirohito assume responsibility for this war.[67] In November 1945, Antonio Araneta, President of the National Executive Council of the Philippine Lawyers Guild, pleaded to President Harry Truman that Hirohito be put on trial.[68]

Although the Japanese were clearly fighting a losing war after their defeat at the Battle of Midway in June 1942, they only became increasingly fanatical to die for the Emperor. *Kamikaze Tokkotai* (suicidal attack) and the Japanese diehard resistance at Iwojima and Okinawa indicated that the Japanese were willing to fight until the very last man. The US government anticipated that the invasion of *Honshu* (the mainland) would be long and bloody. Acting Secretary of State Grew explained to Truman: "We must remember that the Japanese are a fanatical people and are capable, if not likely, of fighting to the last ditch and the last man. If they do this, the cost in American lives will be unpredictable."[69] Because the US policy makers failed to reach a consensus among themselves concerning the Imperial system, they could not submit a list of war criminals to the United Nations War Crimes Commission (UNWCC). Lord Wright, head of the UNWCC, was so irritated that he said the United States was responsible for the absence of major war criminals.[70]

President Franklin D. Roosevelt preferred personal diplomacy, using a non-bureaucratic, ad hoc envoy to have direct contact with foreign leaders. He also emphasized the importance of China, paying less attention to Japan in the postwar Asia-Pacific region. Roosevelt's style of diplomacy allowed State Department bureaucrats and experts on Asia to formulate postwar policies regarding Japan without interference from above. They engaged in heated discussion concerning the Emperor. Because they had such diverse opinions, they could not make coherent suggestions. There were roughly three attitudes toward the treatment of the postwar Emperor. First, there was a group of people who considered social stability as the top priority. In order to achieve this goal, they insisted that the United States use the influence of the Emperor. This group included Joseph W. Ballantine, served as Director of the Office of Far Eastern Affairs in 1944, George H. Blakeslee, professor at Clark University, and Isaiah Bowman, president of the Johns Hopkins University. A second group, led by Hugh Borton, a first-rate Japan specialist at Columbia University, maintained that the United States should link the Emperor with liberal elements in Japan. Using the Emperor's influence, Japan could make liberal reforms. The third group believed that Japan would have to abolish the Imperial system in order to become a republic. Progressive intellectuals such as Thomas A. Bisson, Nathaniel Peffer, Army Vandenbusch, and Hamilton Fish Armstrong held this punitive position.[71]

On 15 January 1944, the Committee on Post-War Programs (PWC)–consisting of top-level officials such as Cordell Hull, Edward Stettinius, Adolf Berle, Dean Acheson, G. Howland Show, Green Hackworth, and other high-ranking officials in the State Department–was established. The postwar status of the Emperor, however, was such a controversial issue in the PWC that it could not formulate a coherent policy.[72]

Immediately after the war, there was a high probability that the United States would abolish the Imperial system in Japan. The Subcommittee for the Far East (SFE) of the State-War-Navy Coordinating Committee (SWNCC) made two important decisions in September 1945: first, that the Emperor "should be removed from office and arrested for trial as a war criminal," and second, that the United States should inspire Japan "to seek abolition of the institution of the Emperor."[73]

The "United States Initial Post-Defeat Policy" approved by President Truman in September 1945, however, recognized the usefulness of the Emperor: "In view of the present character of Japanese society and the desire of the United States to attain its objectives with a minimum commitment of its forces and resources, the Supreme Commander will exercise his authority through Japanese governmental machinery and agencies, including the Emperor, to the extent that this satisfactorily furthers United States objectives." Washington, however, permitted General MacArthur to "act directly if the Emperor . . . does not satisfactorily meet the requirements of the Supreme Commander in effecting the surrender terms."[74] In short, it was up to the attitude of the Emperor and MacArthur's judgment whether SCAP would maintain or abandon the monarch. In this situation, General Douglas MacArthur, who was immediately in charge of the Japanese occupation, exerted great influence on both the formulation and implementation of US policy toward the Emperor. MacArthur held the straightforward idea that he would use the Emperor to facilitate the Japanese occupation.[75]

In October 1945, Brigadier General Bonner Fellers, Military Secretary to the Commander-in-Chief and the chief of MacArthur's psychological-warfare operations, analyzed the critical position of the Emperor in Japanese social psychology: "Hanging of the emperor to them [the Japanese] would be comparable to the crucifixion of Christ to us." Unlike Christians, he warned, "the Japanese have no God with whom to commune. Their emperor is the living symbol of the race in whom lies the virtues of their ancestors. He is the incarnation of national spirit, incapable of wrong or misdeeds. Loyalty to him is absolute." He argued for exploiting the imperial authority for the purposes of the occupation – "The emperor can be made a force for good and peace" – and he argued for not including the emperor in the punitive treatment of the military clique.[76]

In October 1945, SFE recommended: "All available evidence of Hirohito's participation in and responsibility for Japanese violations of international law should immediately be assembled with strict security safeguard." SFE believed that SCAP could only spare Hirohito "if it were evident that Hirohito had gained the confidence of the genuinely democratic elements in Japan and that he was committed to basic democratic reforms and the complete alteration of the institution of the Emperor to place it in a position of 'innocuous desuetude.' . . ."[77] SWNCC 55/6 of October 1945 suggested that the choice was either "the abolition by the Japanese themselves of the institution of the Emperor or its complete alteration. . . ." It decided to ask General MacArthur "to recommend as to conditions which may warrant or permit proceedings against Hirohito as a war criminal."[78] In November 1945, the JCS ordered General MacArthur to collect evidence concerning Hirohito's involvement in the war.[79]

General MacArthur perceived that this was a signal from Washington that he held the key for the US decision on the treatment of the Imperial institution. In order to conciliate anti-Emperor forces, he tried to create an image of a democratized Emperor. General MacArthur praised Hirohito because the Japanese military forces and people obeyed the Emperor's directive to surrender in an orderly fashion. MacArthur said that nobody else knew Japan and the Japanese better than the Emperor, and he was willing to listen to the monarch's opinion and advice at anytime.[80] In October 1945, Fellers advised General MacArthur that indicting the Emperor would definitely cause nation-wide resistance, precipitating confusion and bloodshed. It would require Washington to dispatch thousands of civil administrators and a large armed force.[81] SCAP told George Sansom, the British representative in Japan, that it would be disastrous to indict the Emperor, whose presence was necessary to carry out the occupation policies smoothly.[82]

In December 1945, SCAP advised the Imperial Household Agency that it would be quite helpful if the Emperor declared publicly that he was not a living god. The Japanese Emperor faithfully followed this advice and in his New Year's Day Rescript of 1 January 1946 stated: "The ties between us and our people have always stood upon mutual trust and affection. They do not depend upon mere legends and myths. They are not predicated upon the false conception that the Emperor is divine and the Japanese people are superior to other races and fated to rule the world."[83] General MacArthur praised this example of the Emperor playing a leading role in democratization.[84] It was Hirohito himself and his close advisers who were flexible enough to liberalize the imperial system in order to survive during the occupation period.[85] George Atcheson, the Political Adviser to SCAP, recommended to President Truman that the "speedy demobilization of our military forces is already creating hand-icaps." In order to carry out reforms, "there is no question that the Emperor is most useful." He considered it inadvisable to pursue "any trial of the Emperor as a war criminal . . . [because] the overwhelming majority of the Japanese people wish to retain the Imperial system in some form."[86]

On 18 December 1945, the JCS, supporting MacArthur's opinion, wrote a memorandum for SWNCC stating, "the implementation of the proposed reforms [including the abolition of the Emperor institution] may foment unrest in Japan."[87] The Acting Political Adviser in Japan George Atcheson orig-inally had advocated a punitive policy toward the Emperor. He believed that "the Emperor is a war criminal . . . I have not altered my opinion that the Imperial system must disappear if Japan is ever to be really democratic." However, having firsthand experience of Japan, he modified his attitude: "A number of circumstances seem to make . . . more cautious policy the best for us to follow at this time. . . . there is no question that the Emperor is most useful [for the administration of Japan and the carrying out of reforms]." Consequently, he suggested to Truman in January 1946: "if we decide to con-tinue to use the Emperor, he should be given some sort of immunity from arrest."[88] On 7 January 1947, SFE revised its original position that: "The Japanese should be encouraged to abolish the Emperor Institution or reform it along more democratic lines." Since the SFE assumed that retention of the Imperial system would be inevitable, it focused on the reduction of the Emperor's power, insisting, "The Emperor shall act in all important matters only on the advice of the Cabinet; The Emperor shall be deprived of all military authority . . . [and] the Cabinet shall advise and assist the Emperor."[89]

On 29 November 1945, the JCS gave a top-secret directive to MacArthur to collect evidence concerning Hirohito's involvement in the war.[90] In January 1946, in his response to this JCS inquiry, General MacArthur concluded that the Emperor was innocent: "No specific and tangible evidence has been uncovered with regard to his exact activities which might connect him in varying degree with the political decisions of the Japanese Empire during the last decade." SCAP alerted the JCS that since the Emperor's indictment would "unquestionably cause a tremendous convulsion among the Japanese people," a dramatic expansion of the occupation forces would be necessary. MacAurthur estimated that "a minimum of a million troops would be required which would have to be maintained for an indefinite number of years. In addition, a complete civil service might have to be recruited and imported, possibly running into a size of several hundred thousand."[91] This report became the critical factor for the US decision not to indict Hirohito.[92] After visiting Japan between December 1945 and February 1946, George E. Blakeslee, the US representative to the Far Eastern Commission (FEC), reported that the occupation found "the Emperor to be a great asset in its task of disarming and administering Japan."[93]

Until it formulated a firm policy, the US government prevented other Allied powers from putting Hirohito on the war criminal list. On 18 February 1946, Secretary of State Byrnes sent an urgent message to John Winant, US Ambassador to the United Kingdom: "Should [the War Crimes] Commission . . . vote to proceed to prepare and adopt list of major Japanese war criminals . . . you are instructed to state [that the]USGov[ernment] considers position of Emperor as war criminal should not be discussed. . . ." Byrnes clearly understood that the Emperor issue had "far-reaching political implications." Consequently, it "should only be discussed at highest governmental level."[94]

Finally, on 11 April 1946, Washington reached the conclusion (SWNCC 209/1) that a "monarchical form of government in Japan, if so modified as to be a peaceful and responsible constitutional monarchy, would be consistent with American objectives in Japan." Consequently, SCAP "should give aid to Japanese efforts to transform the imperial institution in Japan into a constitutional monarchy" on condition that Japan would make a democratic constitution and "the Emperor is under the Constitution."[95]

COMPLEMENTARY JAPANESE RESPONSES

Japanese responses complemented the US policy, significantly contributing to the sparing of Hirohito from trial. In the Tokyo Trial, the defendants unanimously tried to defend the Emperor's peace-loving character. Inukai Ken, son of a late Prime Minister, testified in reference to the Manchurian Incident: "When my father visited Prince Saionji, he told my father that it was the emperor's wish that Japanese politics should not be controlled solely by the Army." He later continued, "The Emperor frequently said that he hoped that the Manchurian Incident would be stopped as quickly as possible, and before it spread any further." Then, Inukai stated that the Emperor preferred a peaceful settlement, "[paraphrasing the Emperor's words] in order to find some basis of eternal and fundamental peace between the two countries."[96]

Asked during the Tokyo Trial about Japan's withdrawal from the League of Nations, Kido Koichi, Lord Keeper, testified that the Emperor had to yield to the government's demands. "I advised the Emperor that there was nothing else to do but to let the government carry out its decision."[97] Asked by prosecutors about the nature of the Emperor's power, Kido explained the "restricted" meaning of his powers. "His Majesty the Emperor administers the affairs of government with the assistance and on the advice of ministers of state." The prosecutor persisted: "But in any event, the act or the law . . . cannot become effective without his consent if he [the Emperor] decides not to give his consent, is that true?" Kido maintained that the government had the real power: "The wishes or the will of the state becomes complete only with the advice and assistance of the ministers of state." Finally, the prosecutor queried, "Are you intending to say that if the cabinet agreed upon war the Emperor of Japan would have no actual power to prevent it?" Without hesitation, Kido replied, "Yes, the Emperor had no power to prevent it."[98]

Tojo Hideki, wartime Prime Minister, agreed with Kido that the emperor had no real power, testifying: "The Emperor studiously refrained from placing a veto upon any final decision made by the cabinet and the supreme command on their responsibility." He further explained that even the Emperor's own wishes and suggestions "were issued on the recommendation of the Lord Keeper of the Privy Seal." He concluded that "the Emperor had no free choice . . . . He was not in a position to reject the recommendations and advice of the Cabinet and High Command." Consequently, Tojo insisted that it should not be the Emperor but the government that was responsible for the war decision.[99]

The *Asahi Newspaper*, a leading Japanese daily , also segregated the responsibility of the militarists from that of the Emperor. The *Asahi*'s representations of war memory showed that militarists were responsible for the war while the Emperor was the symbol of peace and a new democratic Japan. On 29 September 1945, it reported the Emperor's peace-minded statement that an "eternal peace will not be established by sword or other weapons. Neither the victor nor the vanquished can solve a peace issue with weapons. A true peace will be achieved only through cooperation and accord among free people."[100]

MacArthur's political adviser offered this summation of public opinion in Japan: "It is worthy to note that there has been observed as yet no adverse criticism of the Emperor or the Imperial Institution except by the communists."[101] According to a Japanese public opinion poll, 92 percent of Japanese supported the retention of the Emperor.[102] On 11 February 1946, Max Bishop of the Office of Political Adviser sent a report to the Secretary of State stating, "An estimated 90 to 95 percent of the general population support retention of the Imperial institution in some form, and all except a very small proportion of the educated and ruling classes are of the same view."[103]

On 27 September 1945, Hirohito, the living god for ordinary Japanese, paid a courtesy visit to MacArthur. The *Asahi* published a picture of the short, stern-faced Emperor with a formal tie standing still beside the tall, relaxed MacArthur.[104] MacArthur provided an image of a powerful Shogun. At the same time, he knew that a Shogun could exert his power most efficiently if he utilizes the Emperor's influence.

Hirohito did his best to establish himself as a symbol of the new democratic Japan. He made an announcement that he was not a living god, but just a man. He also stated that Japan should commit itself to peace and to the improvement of living standards.[105] This declaration indicated to SCAP that Hirohito was willing to cooperate with SCAP to establish a democracy in Japan, and MacArthur expressed his satisfaction with Hirohito's declaration.[106] Washington took a punitive approach while MacArthur adopted more flexible, pragmatic means to deal with Emperor Hirohito and the future of the Imperial system. Japan strongly sided with MacArthur, and its view prevailed.

THE EMPEROR AND WAR-RENOUNCING-CLAUSES OF THE CONSTITUTION

General MacArthur expected Japan to enact a democratic constitution voluntarily. In October 1945, MacArthur advised Prime Minister Shidehara Kijuro to create a new constitution. The Shidehara Cabinet established a constitutional committee under the leadership of Matsumoto Joji (Matsumoto Committee) to draft a new constitution.[107]

In February 1946, The *Mainichi Newspaper* published a part of a secret draft of the new constitution. It was not a final draft but just one of many drafts devised during the process. GS, however, assumed that the "published draft apparently was Matsumoto's own draft" and regarded it as "extremely conservative in character and leaves substantially unchanged the status of the Emperor with all rights of sovereignty vested in him."[108] When the Allied Powers established the FEC in late February 1946, it would deprive

MacArthur of his discretionary power over making a new constitution. In February 1946, GS reminded General MacArthur that his "authority to make policy decisions on constitutional reform continues substantially unimpaired until the Far Eastern Commission promulgates its own policy decisions on this subject."[109] Pressured by time, General MacArthur ordered Brigadier General Courtney Whitney, Chief of GS and MacArthur's protégé, to redraft a model constitution containing an image so novel and drastic that world opinion would accept it. He demanded that it include a clause: "War as a sovereign right of the nation is abolished. Japan renounces it as an instrumentality for settling its disputes and even for preserving its own security." He also insisted on putting the Emperor "at the head of the state."[110] In other words, he guaranteed the survival of the Imperial institution.

The origin of the war-renouncing Article Nine lay in the MacArthur-Emperor conversation of 27 September 1945 and the MacArthur-Shidehara meeting of 11 October 1945. General MacArthur explained to the monarch that the progress of war technology, especially the rise of an air force and an atomic bomb meant that the next war would destroy human beings. Wise people, he said, recognized the necessity of directing the world by peace philosophy.[111] Both General MacArthur and Prime Minister Shidehara agreed with the importance of presenting an image of a peace-loving and democratic Japan to the world and of retaining the Imperial institution.[112] Matsumoto explained to the Shidehara cabinet that a new constitution retained clauses on military forces, since any independent nation should have armed forces, even though there was some opposition in the committee. Prime Minister Shidehara, however, countered that "the Allied Powers would surely complain about these clauses on armed forces." He continued to argue that international conditions might force Japan to have military forces in the future, but the retention of these clauses at present seemed too arrogant to be accepted by the Allied Powers.[113]

In just nine days, GS created a draft constitution and submitted it to the Japanese government on 13 February 1946. Chapter I designated the Emperor "the symbol of the State." As for the war-renouncing clause, Colonel Charles L. Kades, Deputy Chief of GS, deleted "even for preserving its own security" from the MacArthur Note because it seemed too idealistic: "War as a sovereign right of the nation is abolished. The threat or use of force is forever renounced as a means for settling disputes with any other nation."[114] It was still an unprecedented clause, despite the clear reality that the raison d'etre of any nation state was preservation of its national security, and waging wars for that purpose was prerequisite to survival as an independent state. MacArthur's intention was to enhance the image of a completely demilitarized, peace-loving Japan by presenting this epoch-making clause to the world. SCAP tried to conciliate anti-Japanese forces abroad that held deep distrust against Japan, channeling their attention to this clause.

Whitney endeavored to make the Japanese leaders accept the new constitution. First, Whitney needed to make a great compromise on the issue of the Emperor in order to have both the Allies and the Japanese accept the new Constitution. On the one hand, the new constitution turned the Emperor into a mere figurehead of the Japanese state, stripping him of any political power. This was necessary to ensure the consent of the Allies. On the other hand, it retained the Imperial Institution itself, which was required to ensure acceptance by the Japanese. He argued, "Acceptance of . . . this new Constitution would render the Emperor practically unassailable. . . . [and] it would bring much closer the day of your freedom from control by the Allied Powers . . . ." He also stimulated their power-lust, claiming, "This is the last opportunity for the conservative group, considered by many to be reactionary, to remain in power; that this can only be done by a sharp swing to the left; and that if you accept this Constitution you can be sure that the Supreme Commander will support your position." Whitney spoke plainly that he could not "emphasize too strongly that the acceptance of the draft Constitution is your only hope of survival."[115]

In his three-hour meeting with Prime Minister Shidehara in February 1946, General MacArthur claimed that Chapters I (the Emperor clause) and II (the war-renouncing clause) were the most important clauses in the new constitution, emphasizing that Japan had to be extremely careful about the reactions of the Allied Powers. Consequently, he argued, Japan had to take a moral leadership, even without followers, in international relations by making a bold announcement of abolishing war as a sovereign right.[116]

Dr. Matsumoto met General Whitney on 22 February 1946. Matsumoto did not fully appreciate the political meaning of Article Nine and asked Whitney if it could "be inserted some place in the Preamble. . . ." Rejecting this request outright, Whitney explained that the General Headquarters (GHQ) placed the clause "deliberately in a separate chapter in order to give all the emphasis possible to this important Article. . . . it must be stated boldly in order to serve its full purpose." The real purpose of Article Nine was "to attract the favorable attention of the world . . . [and] this is a time in which Japan needs the favorable attention of the world" in order to save the Imperial system and to terminate the occupation as soon as possible. He added that the "enunciation of this principle should be unusual and dramatic" in order to create an image of peace-loving and fundamentally altered Japan.[117]

These chapters I and II constituted the two sides of the same coin with which, as a pair, MacArthur forced the Japanese government and induced the world to accept a new constitution. GHQ presented it to Japan as the only way to save the Imperial institution and, at the same time, presented it to the Allied powers as a completely demilitarized constitution.[118] General MacArthur regarded these two clauses as the culmination of Japanese demilitarization and democratization.[119] Japanese "liberals" were shocked when they saw the draft, but they were convinced that this would be the only way to retain the Imperial system; consequently, they accepted the draft and pushed hard to get it ratified.[120] The new constitution was ratified in October 1946. The swift decision by the Japanese to accept a SCAP-made constitution had a complementary effect on MacArthur's program of Japanese occupation. In this sense, the process of Japanese constitution making contributed to sparing the Emperor. Both Washington and SCAP had resolute attitudes toward this issue, and Japanese civilian leaders also promoted thorough demilitarization, culminated in enacting Article Nine.

SIGNIFICANCE OF ARTICLE NINE

Article Nine was a startling clause. The *New York Times* of 6 March 1946 described Article Nine as unrealistic, and worried about weakening Japanese loyalty to this constitution.[121] Ishibashi Tanzan, former Finance Minister, criticized adoption of the war-renouncing clause as "the bold unprecedented decision for any independent nation ever existed."[122] In June 1946, Hara Fujiro of the Progressive Party raised the issue of Japan's right of self-defense.[123] Nosaka Sanzo of the Communist Party asserted that aggressive wars were evil but that self-defense against foreign invasions should be acceptable.[124] In August 1946, Nambara Shigeru, Chancellor of Tokyo University, also spoke out for Japan's right of self-defense.[125] JMFA officials had a realistic outlook concerning Japan's future security from the early stages of the US occupation. In January 1946, they felt it essential to equip Japan with at least the minimum amount of armed forces necessary for self-defense in order to exist as an independent country.[126] In April 1946, the ministry claimed that even if Japan declared that it would not resort to force, there would be no guarantee that other nations would refrain from resorting to unjust wars.[127] W. W. Butterworth of the American Embassy in Nanking claimed that even the Americans "who have traditional distaste for things military, are not prepared to subscribe to so revolutionary a principle as a general renunciation of even the means of self-protection." He understood that "there is in Japan at present a strong feeling of disillusionment with militarism and military leadership. This attitude promises much toward the emergence of a true liberal spirit." Nevertheless, in Butterworth's view, the war-renouncing clause was too absurd and impractical, and would "fall of its own weight as soon as our pressure is removed."[128]

On the other hand, Japan also needed political considerations to represent pacifist sentiment and to conciliate foreign antagonism and distrust toward Japan. Iriye Toshiro, the President of the Legislative Bureau, explained at the House of Peers in May 1946, "Section I and Section II [of Article Nine of the draft constitution] were separate.[129] Section I does not theoretically deny the self-defense rights, but Section II will make it impossible to wage war for self-defense." He continued, "It is natural, as a nation, to possess the minimum self-defense rights, but taking a position of never waging war or resorting to armed forces for this purpose is one possible way."[130] Some JMFA officials supported the opinion: "Japan should become a moral champion in the world in order to maintain and promote the idea of international peace and to avoid a Third World War."[131]

Reflecting the widespread popular sentiment of pacifism, Prime Minister Yoshida claimed in the House of Representatives Committee in June 1946 that Section II of Article Nine "renounced war as an exercise of self-defense rights as well as renounced rights to wage wars."[132] Kanamori Tokujiro, a national minister, explained to the House of Representatives in July 1946 that Japan had to play for high stakes by declaring a great ideal to lead all peace-loving nations in the world.[133] In July 1946, during a plenary session of the Diet, the Prime Minister reaffirmed his conviction not to use the right of self-defense as pretext for wars because "wars in recent history have been waged in the name of self-defense such as the Manchurian War, World War II, and others."[134]

Yoshida recognized that because "Article Nine is born out of Allied Powers' anxiety about Japan's rearmament, it would be difficult to amend it."[135] In July 1946, Hara insisted in the closed-door Constitutional Amendment Committee, "We should discuss Chapter II [Article Nine] whether or not it is appropriate as a law, but also what kind of international impact it would have."[136] Yoshida had already stated repeatedly that since foreign countries felt considerable distrust toward Japan, which they perceived as a war-loving country that might implement rearmament for revenge, "Japan's primary task was to correct this wrong image."[137] He then argued in the House of Peers in September 1946 that it was indispensable to insert Article Nine "in consideration of international affairs."[138] In August 1946, the Prime Minister argued, "As a result of reckless war under wrong leadership, we are now isolated from the international community. We have to end this situation quickly and to be accepted as an member of the international society which would contribute to world peace and culture."[139]

Yoshida tried to demonstrate an image of a reborn peace-loving Japan to the world by adopting a war-renouncing clause in order to obtain independence as soon as possible. He continued to sell this image. In July 1950, even after the outbreak of the Korean War, he addressed the House of Councilors: "I am convinced that Japan should not take initiative to pursue rearmament."[140]

If Japanese self-defense forces were necessary, reluctant rearmament forced by US formidable pressure was the only way that the world community would acquiesce and permit Japan to acquire independence. The Japanese pacifist sentiment maintained Article Nine despite pressure for revision from the United States and the right wing at home. Its very existence helped prevent the re-emergence of the Japanese militarists. Survival of the Imperial system and the enactment of Article Nine were the result of SCAP's political expediency and Washington's punitive sentiment against the Japanese immediately after the end of the Asia-Pacific War.

ECONOMIC RESTRUCTURING

Not only demilitarization but also economic restructuring comprised an important step for Japan to return to the Anglo-American bloc because the Allied Powers assumed that the prewar Japanese economic structure partly caused its military expansionism. At the start of the occupation period, SCAP had gone straight to work distributing staple foods and procuring everyday resources such as household fuels and agricultural fertilizer. Beyond the basics, the occupiers linked economic reform with democratization, evidenced in the promotion of labor unionization, land reform and agricultural cooperatives, and in the dissolution of the Zaibatsu, the family-controlled big business oligopolies. Zaibatsu had existed long before the war, but their anti-democratic practices and close connection with the military made them a target of the initial "deconcentration" efforts to generate a climate of fair market entry.

Even though Yoshida and other civilian leaders anticipated that the United States would implement economic democratization, they expected that moderates such as Joseph Grew and those who had close economic ties with Japan would have a moderating influence on Japanese economic restructuring.[141] The JMFA proposed three major reforms to establish a new economic structure: the decentralization of capital through Zaibatsu dissolution; the modernization of employment relationships through labor unionization; and the destruction of agricultural production relationships through land reform. The Ministry assumed that Japan needed an organized capitalism in which business, labor, and agriculture would constitute three major components, each of which would have a large stake in the market economy.[142] Implementation would not be easy because Zaibatsu dissolution damaged big business, labor legislation threatened managers, and land reform subverted landowners who generally supported conservative politicians. Such voluntary reforms, however, were necessary to contain radicalism and to soften Allied demand for reform.

Since the MCI and the Ministry of Ammunition had been empowered to control and regulate the economy, Japanese bureaucrats had gained experience in managing the economy through directives, regulations, adjustment of currency circulation, and other means during the Asia-Pacific War.[143] They remained in power during the occupation and continued to coordinate the Japanese economy to realize the envisioned, organized capitalism. As long as agriculture, labor, and business extracted profits from this capitalism, they would be supportive. In order to prevent the three sectors from struggling for a bigger share of the economic pie, the state had to ensure continuous economic growth.[144]

SCAP was thinking along the same lines, to implement a "revolution" from above in order to contain a revolution from below. Courtney Whitney advised Japanese officials: "The only thing that will save your country is a sharp swing to the left."[145] Often lurking behind Japan's reforms were the prejudices of General MacArthur and others who thought that Japan had not transcended its past as a pre-modern, feudal nation.[146] General MacArthur was convinced that both militarism and communism were remnants of Japan's feudal social structure, and democracy must be implemented to eliminate such a past.[147] The American leaders often assumed that the Japanese, with their traditions of power, prestige, and authority, would not be able to understand or implement democracy, market principles or rational reasoning. Ken R. Dyke, Chief of the occupation force's Civil Information and Education section, believed, "[The Japanese person] does not understand the new freedoms nor does he have any constructive ideas as to how to use them. . . . He is still confused and would be willing to follow almost any leadership that offered itself to him."[148] Thus, the occupation authorities destroyed the authoritarian social system in Japan by exerting authority; in a historically famous ironic gesture, the Japanese were forced to be democratic.

General MacArthur foresaw a postwar democratic Japan, buttressed by a liberal capitalist economy, seeking to maintain a balance among the major economic components of business, labor, and agriculture. The United States expected that destruction of the pre-war political regime and economy would lead to the creation of a broad middle class with a stake in the market economy. The United States Initial Post-Defeat Policy directed: "Encouragement shall be given and favor shown to the development of organizations in labor, industry, and agriculture, organized on a democratic basis. Policies shall be favored which permit a wide distribution of income and of the ownership of the means of production and trade."[149] In this sense, what the United States struggled to establish in postwar Japan simulated what the Japanese civilian leaders envisioned.

The United States Initial Post-Defeat Policy provided only general guidance about the economic deconcentration in that SCAP should "favor a program for the dissolution of the large industrial and banking combinations which have exercised control of a great part of Japan's trade and industry." Consequently, it gave SCAP wide discretionary authority to implement the program.[150] Colonel Raymond Kramer, Chief of the Economic and Scientific Section (ESS) in 1945, encouraged the Zaibatsu themselves to undertake their own dissolution programs because he assumed the process would require voluntary cooperation.[151] Agreeing with Kramer, General MacArthur sent a telegram to the JCS in October 1945 stating that the "purpose has been to have Zaibatsu take initiative in dissolution so that desired objectives can be achieved as rapidly as possible. . . . If such [voluntary] action is taken it will greatly expedite action by others who may be unwilling to initiate such action today."[152] On 6 October 1945, Watanabe Takeshi, a Finance Ministry officer, strongly advised representatives of Mitsui, Mitsubishi, Sumitomo, and Yasuda to make a concrete dissolution scheme promptly; otherwise, GHQ would issue a directive for a punitive program.[153] In response, Yasuda Zaibatsu swiftly proposed a voluntary reorganization plan. Accepting the Yasuda Plan, MacArthur urged Washington's approval: "Because of obvious advantages of voluntary action and influence of such action in this problem on securing voluntary action in other fields request approval at earliest practicable time." Two days later, he sent another telegram to the JCS reporting that Mitsui and Sumitomo also had adopted voluntary dissolution plans.[154]

These voluntary dissolution plans targeted only the top holding companies, without breaking solid and complicated interlocking and linkages in the Zaibatsu organization.[155] The State Department complained that none of the voluntary dissolution programs was far-reaching enough and that it was not advisable for Zaibatsu to cooperate with SCAP to devise these plans. It clearly explained its view: "Dissolution of Zaibatsu should not be effected on a contractual basis but should be by direction of the military government without commitment to Zaibatsu in any particular. Control Commission should not be staffed by Japanese but should be part your staff."[156]

Assistant Secretary of War John McCloy and Assistant Secretary of State for Economic Affairs Will Clayton recommended sending a fact-finding Zaibatsu mission to Japan.[157] With State Department consent, a mission headed by Corwin Edwards, a Northwestern University economist, arrived in Japan in January 1946 (Edwards mission). Two months later, Edwards submitted a report in which he defined Zaibatsu in a broad way, arguing that "any private enterprise or combination operated for profit belongs to the Zaibatsu if it is very large in total assets; if, though somewhat smaller in assets, it is engaged in business in various unrelated fields; if it controls substantial financial institutions as well as substantial industrial or commercial ones; if it controls a substantial number of other corporate enterprises; or if it produces or sells a large proportion of the total supply of the products of a major industry."[158] Finding the Zaibatsu "among the groups principally responsible for the war and as a principal factor in the Japanese war potential," it regarded the Yasuda Plan too modest and superficial, and recommended far-reaching and widespread economic deconcentration.[159] Edward C. Welsh, Chief of the Antitrust and Cartels Division, considered the Edwards program beneficial because it permitted "parent companies to jettison unproductive but costly subsidiaries which had been retained under the Japanese clan system." He regarded the existence of big business itself as undemocratic and inefficient with a firm opinion that "reorganization would result in more efficient operation of industry in Japan and a consequent increase in production."[160]

In disagreement, Major Ben Locke, Chief of the Industrial and Financial Division, warned: "Destroy the Zaibatsu, and you must have chaos for the next ten years, or have a socialist economy."[161] In April 1946, Robert Fearey of the State Department voiced his concern that the economic deconcentration program might alter Japanese pro-US orientation and swing that country to the Soviet bloc.[162] Secretary of Army Kenneth Royall worried about "the danger of breaking up concentrations into units so small as to be unworkable."[163] William Marquat, Chief of the ESS, agreed in principle with the Edwards report as "fundamentally sound, particularly in connection with the objectives to be attained," but disagreed on implementation because it was "quite possible to dissolve monopolistic controls and to prevent their recurrence without penalizing industry or stifling big business operations offering both producer and consumer benefits."[164]

General MacArthur dismissed the Edwards report because it was "quite beyond the size and organization of the Occupation Forces [to impose]."[165] He recognized the necessity of dismantling Zaibatsu in order to contain possible domestic turmoil, claiming, "If this concentration of economic power is not torn down and redistributed peacefully and in order under the Occupation, there is no slightest doubt that its cleansing will eventually occur through a blood bath of revolutionary violence." The general, however, opposed the Edwards mission's radical proposal because economic deconcentration was just a means to create a more democratic and balanced capitalist society in Japan. SCAP contended that the creation of a broad middle class "which, having a stake in the economic well-being of the country, will support the ideal of democracy as their way of life" would bring stability to Japan.[166]

In August 1946, Tokyo established a Holding Company Liquidation Commission (HCLC) to implement the Zaibatsu dissolution program. The HCLC designated only 5 companies to be dissolved at first, but the number reached 83 by July 1947. In November 1945, GHQ froze the assets of 15 Zaibatsu, and accepted spontaneous dissolution programs of Mitsui, Mitsubishi, Sumitomo, and Yasuda. In September 1946, the headquarters of four major Zaibatsu dissolved themselves. The restructuring of Japanese business community had just begun.

The Zaibatsu dissolution caused a major change in the Japanese economic structure, and there were various opinions as to its impact. Edo Hideo, a former executive of Mitsui, was convinced that the dissolution led to a rapid postwar economic growth in Japan, whereas Okano Hojiro, one-time president of Mitsubishi Heavy Industry, believed that it weakened the Japanese economy.[167] While the program caused short-term confusion in the Japanese economy, in the long run, it reduced the degree of industrial concentration and led to intra-industry competition and rapid economic growth after the 1950s.[168] The economic decentralization released managers from all Zaibatsu-related companies from the control of the Zaibatsu headquarters, which facilitated the rise of young and energetic managers, though they had less experience in corporate management. They progressively introduced modern scientific management and advanced technology into Japanese business.[169] The program also gradually helped create a more balanced economic structure in which a broad middle class had a stake in a market economy and from which the working class benefited.

SCAP was confident that the "working classes are the strongest single bulwark of the new democratic regime," regarding them as politically conscious, open to new ideas, and numerically larger and therefore of "greater potential political strength than the middle class of business and professional men." Consequently, SCAP encouraged their unionization. Unionized workers jumped from 5 million in 1946 to 6.7 million by the end of 1948.[170] In March 1947, MacArthur stated in his grandiose fashion: "I do not think the history of labor throughout the last two thousand years has shown such an extraordinary, magnificent development in such a short space of time."[171] A healthy labor movement would balance business and help create a moderated economic structure, giving workers an important stake in market economy.

SCAP labor policy, however, became problematic because organized workers proved uncooperative with the new system. In 1946, there occurred a series of strikes primarily controlled by the Communists because, at the time, labor had not yet benefited from the newly evolving economy. Matsushima, the Vice Foreign Minister, explained to the FEC that ordinary Japanese people mistakenly regarded radical egoism and class struggle as democracy and liberalism.[172] In May 1946, Prime Minister Yoshida criticized radical labor movements for their misuse of democracy, insisting that both managers and workers cooperate for the same purpose of increasing production.[173] In October 1946, Emperor Hirohito told MacArthur that when the Japanese worked for economic recovery, labor strikes spoiled their efforts. He added that the Japanese tended to accept rights but to neglect duties. The Emperor indicated that since they were less cultivated, they mistakenly believed that resorting to strikes would lead to a democracy. This situation made him despair of the future of Japan's economic recovery. General MacArthur agreed that labor movements per se were quite healthy, but if they aimed at political objectives, they would become dangerous.[174]

The unrest culminated in a call for general strikes in February 1947. SCAP reluctantly banned them since they might paralyze the weak Japanese economy and prevent Congress from appropriating more funds for the relief program in Japan.[175] MacArthur commented that "professional agitators, political elements" exploited workers "for their own purposes."[176] Atcheson indicated negative consequences of the rapid progress of Japanese unionization arguing, "the unions in Japan are somewhat lacking in discipline, fail to appreciate the full obligations which unionization entails and appear to be concerned too unilaterally with the rights which are granted to union organizations."[177] SCAP recognized that "failure to demonstrate to the laboring class the concrete advantages of democracy could result in sections of them being again led astray by anti-democratic propaganda. . . . Raising standards of Japanese labor is desirable. . . ."[178] Yoshida argued that labor might better endeavor to enlarge its compensation by producing more efficiently instead of demanding a greater share of a weak economy.[179] Japanese labor problems indicated that there would be no stability without continuous economic expansion.

Meanwhile, the rural sector also faced serious problems. The Ministry of Agriculture and Forestry had considered an agricultural reform plan even during the war in order to increase food production. The ministry devised a rather progressive bill but conservative Representatives shot it down. In December 1945, Tokyo finally enacted a moderate land reform program which allowed landowners to retain substantial holdings, and the government encouraged the owners to sell to tenant farmers; it was a sure prescription against land redistribution.[180] The Soviet Union and Great Britain criticized this plan as being too conservative and favoring landowners, inducing MacArthur to intervene in order to introduce "comprehensive [land] reform."[181] He expected that appropriate land reform would "emerge in Japan, from a field heretofore fertile to the spread of communism, a new class of small capitalistic landowners which itself will stand firm against efforts to destroy the system of capitalistic economy of which it will then form an integral part."[182] Since SCAP and the Allied Council for Japan (ACJ)[183] shared similar views on the need for more drastic land reform, they jointly pressured Japan to accept a more radical land reform program. SCAP's new program limited the amount of land that landowners could possess, virtually prohibited absentee landowners, and mandated state-mediated land purchase transactions. Due to spiraling inflation, a large number of tenants were able to buy land with ease.[184]

The land reform achieved a more egalitarian income distribution, increased the farmers' level of consumption, and accomplished a wide redistribution of land ownership.[185] Yoshida recognized that land reform would raise rural living standards and that the agrarian population would turn out to be customers with large purchasing power.[186] W. MacMahon Ball, a British representative in Japan, observed that the agrarian reform was "the first and most important step . . . No democracy can be built on a foundation of agricultural serfdom."[187] MacArthur was "convinced that these [land reform] measures . . . will finally and surely tear from the soil of the Japanese countryside the blight of feudal landlordism. . . ."[188] In the long run, the land reform provided farmers with incentives to produce cash crops for the market. Bringing farmers into the cash economy helped eradicate poverty and stifled the spread of communism in rural areas.

The immediate economic effect, however, was not as positive as expected.[189] It did not significantly improve production per man-year since it kept the same production structure where farmers' land was too small to make production efficient. [190] Japan had to continue importing foodstuffs, which partly caused its trade deficit. Despite the revolutionary redistribution of land, farmers did not support any specific conservative party until the 1950s when the Korean War boom provided them with economic prosperity. It was only then that the farmers became solid supporters of the conservative party, which indicated that economic expansion was indispensable to creating farmer support for democratic capitalism.[191]

Demilitarization and the major economic restructuring were successful since the Japanese themselves supported these reforms. The SWNCC had recognized that it was "axiomatic that the only effective political reform must stem from the people themselves. Political reforms imposed solely by the fiat of a military occupant will either be resisted by the people, or will be ignored by them."[192] "Like the bamboo of folklore, the Japanese people bent with the storm," adjusting themselves to the Westernization process.[193] The United States was satisfied with this process and with the adaptability of the Japanese. Blakeslee concluded in February 1946, that "the broad foundations of democracy have already been laid and appear to be acceptable to the Japanese."[194] Atcheson praised the Japanese adaptability that the "occupation authorities already have Jap cooperation. More and more as time goes on, the Japs have come to realize with increasing force and clarity that our ultimate aims are in the best interests of the Japs as well as in the interests of the world at large."[195] W. W. Butterworth, Minister-Counselor of Embassy in China, was impressed with Japan's intention of returning to "normalcy," observing," the war has left a remarkably small aftermath of animosity toward the United States among the Japanese . . . their traditional admiration for American achievements has not been diminished by the beating they have received at our hands."[196] The combination of Japan's intention of returning to the Anglo-American bloc and the powerful and determined US social experiments swiftly completed the first two objectives of the occupation, demilitarization and democratization. There is much truth in MacArthur's hyperbole: "Japan's war-making power and potential is destroyed, the framework to democratic government has been erected, reforms essential to the reshaping of Japanese lives and institutions to conform to democratic ideals have been instituted, and the people have been accorded the fundamentals of human liberty."[197]

The development of democratic capitalism transformed the Japanese semi-feudal and oligarchic economic structure by providing a more egalitarian, competitive infrastructure, which had long-term positive effects on Japanese productivity.[198] Indeed, destruction of the prewar economic structure constituted a necessary condition to create organized capitalism. SCAP implemented almost all the democratic reform plans by mid-1947, when it was time to consolidate what it had executed.[199] This consolidation required economic recovery. Washington had a more punitive approach while SCAP had a more benevolent attitude concerning economic deconcentration issues. Japan's voluntary economic reform resonated in harmony with MacArthur's moderate policy to contain radicalism and softened the punitive, excessive demand for reform from the Allied Powers.

CHAPTER TWO

SHIFT IN AMERICAN OCCUPATION POLICIES

George Kennan, then Acting Ambassador of the United States to the Soviet Union, sent a long telegram to the State Department on 22 February 1946 and published his famous "X" article in July 1947, in which he defined the Soviet threat as essentially ideological and political.[1] Advocating a long-term, ideological, and political containment against Soviet expansionism, the effect of his writing in Washington was "nothing less than sensational." Kennan later explained that it was "one of those moments when official Washington, whose states of receptivity or the opposite are determined by subjective emotional currents . . . was ready to receive a given message." Kennan's long telegram provided Washington with a persuasive analysis and an authoritative referent to explain Soviet conduct. Kennan recalled, "Six months earlier this message would probably have been received in the Department of State with raised eyebrows and lips pursed in disapproval. Six months later, it would probably have sounded redundant."[2]

The United States began to regard the Soviet Union not as an alienated ally but as a potential enemy.[3] In June 1946, Clark Clifford, Special Advisor to the President, strongly influenced by Kennan's long telegram, recommended a tough policy toward the Soviet Union.[4] The Joint Staff Planners (JSP) believed that "the basic objective of the USSR appears to be a limitless expansion of Soviet communism accompanied by a considerable territorial expansion of Russian imperialism." The West, therefore, had to "mobilize their political and military resources to support . . . the preservation . . . of democratic economic and political processes, emphasizing individual and national freedom."[5] The Central Intelligence Agency (CIA) reviewed the world situation in September

1947, suggesting that even though the Soviet Union was "incapable of direct attack upon the United States," it was capable of threatening "continental Europe, the Near East, northern China, and Korea."[6] Since US officials began to believe that the Soviet Union had a grand strategy to spread communism around the world, they perceived even indigenous problems in other countries as acts of Soviet plots. They mistakenly regarded civil war in Korea as a Soviet challenge to the West.[7] They felt that the United States and the Soviet Union were playing a zero-sum game in which a Soviet gain automatically became an American loss. It is questionable if the Soviet Union, which was busy with internal reconstruction, was capable of dominating the world, but the US paranoia created an image of limitless expansion of communism, regardless of world realities. This anti-communism mind-frame (cold-war mentality) gradually became established among US officials.

The historical development of American society may partly account for this psychic crisis that prevailed in the United States. America began with the modern age. Since Americans have experienced only liberal society, they tend to consider it an absolute truth, not a stage of historical development. Consequently, they fail to comprehend, deny, or despise other forms of society, such as feudal, authoritarian, and socialist societies. After Americans experimented and failed with republicanism based on citizens' virtue in the late 18th century, they recognized that only market values and opportunity for economic expansion could tighten the intricate fabric of liberal society. Liberalism and market economy based on individualism constitute the core values of American society. Because Soviet communism rejected a market economy and promoted authoritarian state control of society, it seemed to be the direct antithesis of the American value system. Anti-communism was a self-justification for Americans of their own society.[8]

By the end of 1946, the cold-war mentality caused Washington to perceive communist expansionism as a threat to America's security.[9] In March 1947, the White House issued the Truman Doctrine that represented US recognition of global hegemony, and its Cold War sentiment set the tone of global commitment for future US foreign policy.[10] In March 1948, the NSC made a geopolitical analysis of the power struggle between the United States and the Soviet Union: "Between the United States and the USSR, there are in Europe and Asia areas of great potential power which if added to the existing strength of the Soviet world would enable the latter to become so superior in manpower, resources and territory that the prospect for the survival of the United States as a free nation would be slight." These circumstances convinced the NSC, "Our national security is at stake and from which we cannot withdraw short of eventual national suicide." The NSC officials could see that the "Soviet-directed world communism has achieved alarming success." This sense of alarm motivated them to organize "a world-wide counter-offensive aimed at mobilizing and strengthening our own and anti-communist forces in the non-Soviet world, and at undermining the strength of the communist forces in the Soviet world."[11]

Washington at this time regarded communism as virus likely to spread to the weakest part of the world-system.[12] Since Asia presented one of the most unstable and weakest areas in the world, American officials believed that communism could easily penetrate it. They could not then comprehend that Asia was as intricate as other areas, requiring sophisticated expertise and analyses to form and implement appropriate policies. Americans, who had experienced only modernity, were likely to consider the pre-modern societies of most Asian countries as less developed. The relative Asian backwardness provided the United States with a superiority complex by which Americans reaffirmed the validity of their own liberal-capitalist society. Convinced that Asian traditions would not facilitate the development of liberal democracy, the Americans assumed that Asians with pre-modern traditions of power, prestige, and authority did not think according to market principles or rational reasoning. At the end of the war in the Pacific region, Americans held only primitive and often biased images of Asians, which led Washington officials to believe that the Japanese would not stick to their principles but would shift their allegiance from one leadership to another without much hesitation. Furthermore, because of their long history of despotism, they would respect and follow powerful leaders. Colonel C. Stanton Babcock asserted: "Communism, with its positive policy and organized pressure, would take enormous strides unless a strong new [political] movement . . . could emerge and capture the imagination of that great mass of people."[13] The conviction, moreover, that Asians respected power led the United States gradually to employ more militant policy measures in Asia.

Ken R. Dyke, Chief of the Civil Information and Education section, doubted if the Japanese could truly appreciate the meaning of freedom: "He [a Japanese] does not understand the new freedoms nor does he have any constructive ideas as to how to use them." Dyke was concerned with possible negative consequences of the confusion caused by the newly acquired freedom among the Japanese people. "He is still confused, and would be willing to follow almost any leadership that offered itself to him."[14] In concurrence with this line of thinking, Senator Elbert D. Thomas argued in August 1947, "Japan is a nation that definitely wants to be led in world affairs. She needs the association of an honest mind and teacher. . . . every act of Japan since the arrival of Admiral Perry . . . has been an act of following and not of leadership."[15]

The United States sought to create and maintain the image that it would exert the most powerful leadership in Asian affairs and that siding with it would be the most beneficial to the Japanese people in order to keep Japan within the fold of advanced nations. Washington had to provide Asian countries with psychological as well as material satisfaction and a sense of security. Ironically, in order to bring freedom, liberty, and democracy to Japan, the United States had to show its muscle and to teach the Japanese, sometimes forcefully, how to acquire these principles.

Japanese officials also helped raise anti-communist sentiment among the American officials. In March 1948, after meeting with Kurusu Takeo, Director-General of the Economic Stabilization Board (ESB)[16] and Watanabe Yoshio, Chief of Liaison of Ministry of Finance, William Sebald reported that the "Japanese contend that Japan, together with the Philippines, can more easily be a bulwark against communism than China."[17] In April 1948, Japanese leaders including Mizutani Chozaburo, Minister of Commerce and Industry; Wada Hiroo, Director General of ESB; Kurusu Takeo, Finance Minister; Matsuoka Komakichi, Speaker of the House of Representative; and Matsudaira Tsuneo, President of the House of Councilors, asked for US economic assistance to Japan in order to prevent the spread of communism in the Far East. The Cold War meant a danger to Asia while it gave an opportunity to Japan to exercise "intimidation by the weak": Japanese officials tried to exploit the American Cold War mentality in order to induce more generous aid to Japan.[18]

DECONCENTRATION AND SCAP'S ADJUSTMENT

The Edwards Mission concluded its final report in March 1946. Despite SCAP's strong reservations, the SWNCC adopted its recommendation (SWNCC 302/2), and submitted the secret proposal of "Policy on Excessive Concentration of Economic Power in Japan" to the FEC in May 1947 (FEC-230). FEC-230, a long policy document with over 8,000 words, was the product of Washington's punitive attitudes immediately after the Asia-Pacific War. It was an unprecedented directive to SCAP because it contained elaborate and detailed measures. It aimed at not only economic deconcentration but also at the prevention of a future revival of big business. Based on this directive, the Japanese government submitted an economic deconcentration bill to the House of Representatives in October 1947.[19]

While the Cold War mindset gradually prevailed in Washington, the Japan Lobby[20] questioned the US economic policies in Japan. Since they expected Japan to be a profitable economic partner in the Asia-Pacific region, they opposed the economic deconcentration policy. In August, this group sent James Lee Kauffman, a prominent attorney, to Tokyo to prepare a recommendation "for use in determining what course they should pursue in connection with their Japanese investment." He somehow acquired the FEC-230, and in September 1947, sent a shocking report: "So long as present conditions continue in Japan, I believe it inadvisable to make any investment in that country." Believing that SCAP, rather than the State Department, promoted FEC-230, he characterized SCAP economic policies as radical, criticizing the scheme which would "distribute the wealth of Japan to the workers, farmers and small traders through the medium of taxes, sales of valuable properties at nominal values, financial assistance and regulation." He was especially hostile to MacArthur's Zaibatsu destruction policy, claiming that all "business is to come under the knife of the economic quack . . . split into as many small units as some gentleman sitting in Tokyo [MacArthur] may deem appropriate." He made two specific recommendations: "First, put an end to the economic experiment being conducted in Japan, and second, replace the theorists now there with men of ability and experience."[21]

Kauffman's report made significant impact on those who read it, including Secretary of Defense James Forrestal, Secretary of the Army Kenneth Royall, Undersecretary of State Robert Lovett, Secretary of Commerce W. Averill Harriman, and Executive Secretary of the NSC Admiral Sidney Souers among others. In October 1947, the War Department advised MacArthur to postpone the economic deconcentration program.[22]

General MacArthur sensed changes of attitudes in Washington to which he gradually adapted. Although junior officers such as Edward C. Welsh, Chief of Anti-Trust & Cartels Division, and Colonel Charles Kades, Deputy Chief of Government Section, were vocal advocates of destroying big business in Japan, Colonel L. E. Bunker of SCAP advised Watanabe Takeshi, a Finance Ministry official, that since the economic deconcentration was a high-level political issue, the Japanese government did not have to worry too much about agitation by these junior officers. He added that only William Marquat, Chief of the ESS, had authority to speak on this matter. In November 1947, Marquat informed Kurusu that Washington modified the economic deconcentration program to dissolve only "excessive" concentration. In addition, he implicitly indicated that the strict policy advocated by Welsh was not a SCAP official policy. Feeling Washington's intention to ease the Zaibatsu program, MacArthur informed high-ranking officials that SCAP would modify the economic deconcentration policy in the near future. Without MacArthur's prior support, neither Bunker nor Marquat could have made such statements.[23]

Pressured by these criticisms of the deconcentration policy, Acting Secretary of State Robert Lovett informed the Secretary of the Army in November 1947 that even though "it is not necessary or desirable at this time to undertake a complete revision of the basic policy involved in the [deconcentration] Program . . . the State Department is in fact currently preparing a new draft of the paper (FEC 230) for the purpose of removing or changing

any passages which may go beyond the real intent of the policy."[24] In
November 1947, Marquat advised Watanabe that Japan should pass an economic deconcentration bill, but SCAP would ensure its flexible operation. In
December, Marquat again informed Watanabe that SCAP would eliminate
only excessive concentration and that SCAP would establish a committee to
make a moderate interpretation of this legislation. The Japanese government
enacted the Elimination of Excessive Concentration of Economic Power Act
on 18 December 1947.[25] General MacArthur protected his integrity by
enacting this legislation while it allowed SCAP to interpret "Excessive
Concentration" in a flexible way to suit its needs.

Kauffman explained that MacArthur's deconcentration policy would ironically "lead to socialism in Japan, despite the fact that General MacArthur feels
it will save Japan from socialism by promoting free competitive enterprise." He
warned that "a crisis is approaching which, if not averted, will destroy all the
achievements of the occupation. Furthermore, the policy is leading Japan to
Communism."[26] In December 1947, Senator William Knowland criticized the
FEC-230 in the Senate: "I was so shocked by what I read . . . it was unbeliev-
able that such a document could be put forward as representing the policy of
the Government of which I am a part."[27] A month later, he argued, "The military phase of the occupation was completed months ago and was succeeded
by the necessity of restoring the Japanese economy to the point where it can
be self-supporting and not a continual drain upon the United States
Treasury."[28]

The National Foreign Trade Council, consisting of major trade corporations in the United States, warned that the economic deconcentration policies
would discourage US private investment in Japan.[29] Royall anticipated, "The
dissolution of the zaibatsu may present in itself no serious economic problem,
but at some stage extreme deconcentration of industry, while further impairing
the ability to make war, may at the same time impair manufacturing efficiency
of Japanese industry."[30] Aware of all these opinions, Frank R. McCoy, in
January 1948, made a carefully worded announcement at the FEC that the
Allied Powers "should take all possible and necessary steps consistent with the
basic policies of the occupation, to bring about the early revival of the Japanese
economy on a peaceful, self-supporting basis."[31]

Washington's tide gradually turned against economic deconcentration and
its decision to dissolve 325 companies. After discussing FEC-230 with
Butterworth, William Draper,[32] and General Schuyler, George Kennan, in
February 1948, found out that they were "in agreement that this paper should
be withdrawn from the Far Eastern Commission."[33] In March 1948 the War
Department directed SCAP not to support FEC-230.[34] In April 1948, Secretary
of the Army, Royall asked SCAP to reduce the number of companies to be

dissolved. While admitting to Kennan that left-wing academic theories had influenced some of his reform policies, General MacArthur replied, "It has always been my firm intention to implement the deconcentration program in such manner as will preclude any disruption of Japan's going economy and will insure rigorous limitation of the number of companies required to be subject to reorganization."[35]

Resonating with Washington's changed attitude, MacArthur relaxed the economic deconcentration policy, asking Marquat to lower the number of designated companies. In April 1948, Welsh proposed that he could drop 33 companies from the deconcentration list whereas Marquat suggested that 300 companies be taken off the list, leaving only 20 to 25 companies designated as excessively concentrated. In the end, General MacArthur dismantled only 11 companies.[36] In September 1948, Butterworth recommended, "The U.S. representative of the Economic Committee [of the FEC] simply announce that this Government does not consider a policy decision on deconcentration necessary." Following Butterworth's recommendation, Paul Nitze, Deputy to the Assistant Secretary of State for Economic Affairs, also agreed to the "formal withdrawal of FEC 230."[37] In December 1948, McCoy announced in the FEC that the United States would no longer support FEC-230.

TOWARD A PEACE TREATY: FIRST ROUND

Despite MacArthur's opposition, initiatives of occupation policies, not only in economic but also in political fields, gradually shifted from SCAP to Washington. Nothing illustrates this better than the peace treaty issue. General MacArthur took strong initiatives in bringing the occupation to an early end, making a sudden public announcement, in March 1947, that the Allied Powers should conclude a peace treaty with Japan as soon as possible. He claimed, "Japan's warmaking power and potential is destroyed, the framework to democratic government has been erected, reforms essential to the reshaping of Japanese lives and institutions to conform to democratic ideals have been instituted, and the people have been accorded the fundamentals of human liberty."[38] He maintained that the United States should withdraw its forces from Japan immediately after the conclusion of a peace treaty, and that the United Nations would take responsibility for Japan's security since he presumed that the Allied Powers (including the Soviet Union) would respect the war-renouncing clause of the Japanese constitution and accept a disarmed and neutral Japan.[39] His way of thinking was apparently based on his experience of wartime cooperation between the United States and the Soviet Union. His views were contrary to the basic Cold War confrontational assumption of the Truman Doctrine declared in March 1947. MacArthur did not have any imminent fear of the Soviet Union, partly because his vigorous commitment to social reforms in Japan prevented him from keeping updated information on international affairs and partly because he regarded the US bases in Okinawa as sufficient to protect Japan from communist threat.

In September 1947, MacArthur made another surprise announcement that within "six months the occupational force, unless unforeseen factors arise, will probably number not more than 200,000 men." This statement so outraged Acting Secretary of State Dean Acheson as to complain to President Truman that MacArthur's statement "would do a great deal of damage and was wholly uncalled for. . . ." On the following day, Acheson denied the reduction by claiming that nobody "can see at this time the number of forces that will be necessary in Japan."[40]

MacArthur's sudden public announcements coincided with the US failure in mediating the Chinese civil war, forcing Washington to pay more attention to Asian affairs in general and to the Japanese occupation policy in particular. MacArthur's prestige in Japan had prevented Washington from intervening with his activities directly, but Washington gradually sought to restrict his authority after 1947.[41] Reorganization in the Truman administration established a coalition able to shift the initiatives of occupation policies from SCAP to Washington. They disdained MacArthur's impudent behavior. Those who challenged MacArthur's authority in Japan were such prominent officials as Secretary of State George C. Marshall, Undersecretary of State Dean Acheson, Director of the Policy Planning Staff (PPS) George Kennan, Secretary of Defense James Forrestal, Secretary of the Army Kenneth Royall, and Undersecretary of the Army William Draper.[42] Peace treaty issues became focal points in the dispute.

MacArthur's statement of March 1947 was not the first announcement of a peace treaty. In February 1946, Secretary of State James Byrnes stated that the occupation would end within 18 months.[43] In June 1946, he revealed a punitive plan to keep post-occupation demilitarized Japan under military surveillance for twenty-five years.[44] In October 1946, a group headed by Hugh Borton, Chief of the Office of Northeast Asian Affairs, (Borton group) began to consider a peace treaty that basically followed Byrnes's severe scheme.[45] General MacArthur was critical of Borton's draft peace treaty in March 1947 because it was punitive and "imperialistic in concept, in purpose, and in form."[46] The Borton group, however, considered it necessary to conclude an early peace treaty.[47] After MacArthur's public statement on the possible peace treaty, similar requests emerged from various people. George Atcheson agreed, "We are coming to a turning point in the Occupation." The Allied occupation, he believed, "no longer serves its purpose and becomes a deterrent to its own objectives."[48] Max Bishop of the Division of Northeast Asian

Affairs claimed that it was "impractical to attempt measures to revive the economies of the Far East until the existence of a state of war has been resolved. . . . Any delay in proceeding to a settlement with Japan would have serious psychological repercussions, highly detrimental to United States interest." He concluded, "The Occupation has accomplished its purpose and the point of diminishing returns has now been reached."[49]

Those who advocated an early peace treaty, however, met fierce resistance. W. W. Butterworth, Director of the Office of Far Eastern Affairs, worried that there were "doubts as to the advisability of hastening negotiations until our basic position is firm, until we can better estimate the amount of support we can count on for this position."[50] The PPS contended that there were "great risks in an early relinquishment of Allied control over Japan. . . . [because] it has no satisfactory evidence that Japanese society would be politically or economically stable if turned loose and left to its own devices at this stage."[51] Since a politically and economically unstable Japan was likely to invite communist penetration, the PPS recommended that the United States "keep the [peace treaty] talks exploratory and non-binding and hold open some possibility of further postponement of final decision, until we can arrive at a firm judgment on certain of the basic issues involved." Washington half- heartedly proposed an early peace treaty, which would require a two-thirds vote by the FEC countries, "assuming that there is no agreement on a two-thirds rule, we should permit the whole question to carry over to next spring before proceeding with the talks at all."[52] As expected, the Soviet Union claimed that the Four-Power Foreign Ministerial Conference had authority to deal with this issue, with each participant having veto power.

In October 1947, Dr. Wang Shih Chieh, the Chinese Foreign Minister told Secretary of State George Marshall that his country wished to avoid any action that might provoke the Soviet Union.[53] He later asserted strongly that any peace treaty without Soviet participation would be a failure.[54] In February 1948, John Stuart, the Ambassador in China, informed Marshall, "They [the Chinese] are deathly afraid of the Soviets and are unwilling to take any position which might aggravate [the] situation."[55] However, A. R. Hussey Jr., Chief Government Powers Division of SCAP, insisted, "A peace treaty with Japan without Russian and Chinese adherence is out of the question."[56] Nonetheless, in December 1947, the Office of Intelligence Research (OIR) of the Department of State recommended "substantial concessions to the Soviet Union or to China for the sole purpose of attaining an early peace conference would appear unnecessary."[57]

Kennan, however, recognized, "The occupation is in many ways entering on a period of diminishing returns . . . ."[58] He feared that "if a peace treaty were to be concluded now, and the protecting and helping hand of the United

States withdrawn, Japan would be really totally incapable of coping with the problem of making its way economically in the postwar world." He pessimistically concluded, "We will not be able to afford to cut her [Japan] loose without provoking conditions which would be a direct invitation to unrest and to the despair and confusion in which communism breeds."[59] In June 1948, the NSC stated, "This Government should not press for a treaty of peace at this time."[60]

Since Washington had paid little attention to Asian affairs and had given MacArthur a relatively free hand in Japan, it had little information about the local situation. Since SCAP reported Japanese situation selectively to Washington, Kennan recommended that some high-ranking officials undertake a fact-finding mission.[61] In March 1948, the State Department sent him to Japan to collect necessary information and to coordinate opinions between SCAP and Washington. A series of Kennan-MacArthur talks in March 1948 revealed both points of commonality as well as wide differences between SCAP and Washington concerning the peace treaty issue. Both agreed that "economic recovery should be made the prime objective of United States policy in Japan. . . . " They also concurred that the occupation was entering a period of assimilation, and, except for a few more programs, SCAP would soon be able to relax some of its measures.[62] They, however, also differed on a variety of important points.

MacArthur insisted on an early peace treaty even without Soviet participation, while Kennan maintained his view that the United States "should not press for a treaty of peace at this time."[63] The divergence stemmed from their differing assessments of the occupation. MacArthur was confident that the occupation had been a success and that Japan was a healthy and democratic country: "Peoples who once learned what freedom and democracy meant would never willingly return to slavery. . . . they [the Japanese] would never willingly accept Communist domination." He also optimistically observed that "the Communists [in Japan] were no menace."[64] In contrast, Kennan argued that he did "not think that Japan's powers of resistance to Communism can be taken for granted." He clung to his notion that Japanese society was weak and unstable. "It is a problem of penetrating Japanese society and seizing its key positions. At present, it looks to me as though Japanese society were decidedly vulnerable to such attacks."[65] In terms of Japan's security, MacArthur claimed that the United States would not need any base in Japan. He also vehemently opposed any Japanese rearmament, citing Japan's economic difficulties, Japanese unwillingness, Japanese constitutional restraint, and international factors. He advocated that as long as the United States preserved military bases in Okinawa, which would be able to defend Japan from any enemy, a complete demilitarization under an international guarantee would maintain Japan's security.⁶⁶ Kennan stubbornly maintained, "Either we must not have the treaty at all and retain allied troops in Japan or we must permit Japan to re-arm to the extent that it would no longer constitute an open invitation to military aggression."⁶⁷

PPS 28 of March 1948 recommended the assimilation of previous reforms so as to transfer policy-making initiatives from SCAP to Washington. "While SCAP should not stand in the way of reform measures initiated by the Japanese if it finds them consistent with the overall objectives of the occupation, it should be authorized not to press upon the Japanese Government any further reform legislation."⁶⁸ Kennan argued, "The greatest danger to the security of Japan lay, as I saw it, in the possibilities for intrigue, subversion, and seizure of power by the Japanese Communists . . . [W]hat Japan most needed, therefore, was . . . the bolstering of her capabilities for assuring internal security."⁶⁹ Consequently, economic recovery was able to solidify political stability and make the country strong enough to fend off communism. Kennan strongly advocated that the economic recovery "should be made the prime objective of United States policy in Japan for the coming period. . . ."⁷⁰

The CIA made a similar analysis that one of "the probable basic intentions of the Kremlin for the next decade [is] . . . to wage political, economic, and psychological warfare . . . in particular, to prevent or retard . . . the stabilization of the situation in . . . [the] Far East." It considered that the Japanese Communist Party (JCP) gave "no promise in the immediate future of altering its minor party status at the polls. . . . The JCP advantages in Japan are largely economic." The CIA, however, feared, "Until the public is shown tangible evidence of economic recovery, it will be susceptible to the Party's antigovernment and anti-Occupation propaganda, and without relatively stable living standards labor especially will find militant tactics attractive."⁷¹ Kennan's argument and the CIA's analysis were not baseless. In fact, in the general election held in January 1949, the JCP increased its members in the Diet over eightfold from four to thirty-five seats. Kennan and the CIA demonstrated that economic recovery was vital to repel communist internal subversion that was a prerequisite to peace treaty negotiations.

Japan also had serious interest in peace treaty issues. As early as November 1945, the JMFA unofficially established an informal Peace Treaty Committee (PTC), predicting peace treaty negotiations before the US election in 1948.⁷² In June 1947, Hagiwara Toru, Director of the Treaty Bureau, expected that when the Allied Powers finished with reparations problems, it would be relatively easy to conclude a peace treaty. He believed that if Japan began negotiations at the end of the year or at the beginning of the following year, Japan might conclude the treaty by the following summer.⁷³ The basic principal of the PTC was to "do our best to meet the Allied Powers' demands such as establishing a domestic democratic system. We believe that our efforts will eventually soothe the sentiment of their abomination, hatred, and revenge."[74] Japan, however, did not wish to be readmitted into the world-system until it had digested the experiments under isolated conditions.[75] Even though the JMFA proposed, in January 1946, that Japan should make active efforts to conclude a favorable peace treaty, it did not recommend pursuing an early treaty. The JMFA argued that a favorable peace treaty would require a cooling-off period. During this period, it advocated that voluntary, thorough, quick democratization and rationalization should preempt the Allies punitive intervention.[76] In July 1947, Japan established a formal committee within the JMFA to investigate a peace treaty, and shortly after provided the United States with relevant materials. In June 1948, however, the Treaty Bureau of the JMFA concluded that American presidential politics and the onset of the Cold War would delay progress toward a peace treaty.[77]

THE REPARATIONS ISSUE

SCAP was not explicitly responsible for Japan's economic rehabilitation. In November 1945, Washington sent a directive to MacArthur: "You will not assume any responsibility for the economic rehabilitation of Japan or the strengthening of the Japanese economy. You will make it clear to the Japanese people that . . . you assume no obligation to maintain or have maintained, any particular standard of living in Japan."[78] Postwar Japan's hyper-inflation caused the United States to fear that the country would depend on Washington to relieve it from the economic mess. According to the directive, "The Japanese shall be given to understand that the reconstruction of their country is their responsibility," although it was "not to be construed to mean that G.H.Q. will not assist in the rehabilitation of the economy." GHQ tried to use the economic assistance as an incentive to make Japan cooperate with the United States, suggesting that the "speed with which it [reconstruction] is achieved will be conditioned by the degree with which they [the Japanese] sincerely and actively cooperate in the achievement of the objectives of the occupation."[79]

As soon as the occupation began, however, the Truman administration had to deal with a reparations issue that was directly connected with the level of Japanese industry, which in turn would decide what kind of economic role Japan would play in the Asia-Pacific region in the future. In the summer of 1945, Truman sent Edwin Pauley[80] to Moscow, as the US representative, in order to negotiate German reparations matters with Great Britain and the Soviet Union. The president also directed Pauley to handle Japanese reparations issues and sent him to Tokyo in November 1945. The US reparations policy in Japan replicated that in Germany, with the crucial difference that in Japan the United States alone possessed overwhelming influence to shape the policy. At the Yalta Conference in February 1945, the United States agreed to set a substantial sum (20 billion dollars) as a reparations level. As in the German case, Pauley made a commitment to a considerable amount of reparations. He also insisted, as he did in Germany, on the physical removal of machinery and plants rather than reparations from current production. Pauley devised a punitive scheme, weakening Japanese economic power, preventing Japanese economic domination in Asia, and creating a new industrial structure based on equilibrium among Asian nations.[81] In his Preliminary Statement in October 1945, Pauley insisted that Japan not "be allowed to rehabilitate her economic life in a form which will allow her to gain control, or to secure an advantage, over her neighbors." He advised, "Japan will not be left with any plant which represents a key phase in the processing of the raw materials of any of her neighbors," believing that the reduction of Japanese power would be the surest way for "the rehabilitation of East Asia."[82] F.D. Maxwell, Chief of Staff, recommended to Pauley in December 1945 that the "allocation of surplus Japanese industrial potential to . . . neighboring Asiatic countries, should improve the economic balance . . . [and] even up the level of industrialization."[83] Pauley's plan was based on the redistribution of Japanese wealth and equalization among Asian nations at a lower economic level. He sought the de-industrialization of Japan while trying to increase the industrial power of other Asian countries through distributing Japan's reparations. In other words, his plan, if implemented, would have established a new economic and industrial structure in Asia, consisting of nations with roughly equal economic power.[84]

When Pauley visited the Philippines in December 1945, he claimed, "Japan will be reduced to the level of a small power and her people will not be permitted to have in the future a living standard higher than those nations which she has overrun, such as the Philippines."[85] He recommended taking "no action to assist Japan in maintaining a standard of living higher than that of neighboring Asiatic countries injured by Japanese aggression."[86] In a final report of April 1946 to the President, he concluded that it would be critical to reverse the prewar Asian economic relations between Japan (commodity supplier) and other Asian nations (raw material suppliers): "To encourage the circulation of commodities in an economically sound relationship, this [prewar] situation should be reversed, making Japan dependent on Asia for pig iron rather than for ore."[87] Based on Pauley's report, the SFE recommended in May 1946 that the "removal of Japanese industrial facilities and their distribution . . . should contribute . . . to the general security and economic development of Pacific countries. . . . [We need] a more balanced and economic development of the Far East as a whole."[88] President Truman approved Pauley's punitive reparations plan in principle.

The Japanese government opposed the plan, reminding the United States that, besides the demilitarization of economy, the Potsdam Declaration also contained the assurance of peaceful economic development in Japan. Since the Asian regional economies were supplementary, the JMFA warned that the destruction of the Japanese economy would hinder East Asian economic development; instead, it proposed that the United States should reintegrate Japan into the East Asian economy in order to maximize the benefits to the whole region. In other words, rather than establishing equilibrium relations in Asia, Tokyo claimed that it would be mutually beneficial for Japan and other Asian nations to build an efficient economic linkage based on the regional economic division of labor. The JMFA stressed complementary economic relationships in Asia in which Japan was the natural workshop.[89]

SCAP warned that Pauley's dream of balancing Asian industry would destroy an intra-Asian trade in which Japan was to provide consumer goods and would create a chaotic vacuum in Asia.[90] MacArthur believed that experts had to make a careful survey regarding the most efficient removal.[91] In February 1946, SCAP asked Washington to "leave to this Headquarters discretion in the matter of which reparations are to be chosen and when they are to be removed. . . . it is necessary that the reparations removal program be characterized by the greatest flexibility."[92] When the JCS authorized MacArthur to exclude industries if their removal would harm occupation policies, he delayed reparations decisions.

The FEC determined the Japanese industrial capacity for reparations in 1946, but recipient countries could not agree among themselves what amount of reparations each should receive. At last, in April 1947, the United States issued an interim directive to transfer 30% of the industrial capacity determined by the FEC to four countries: China, the Philippines, the Netherlands, and the United Kingdom.[93] Since it was not a simple procedure to select a factory and to move machinery abroad, SCAP invited delegates from reparations claimants to establish a selection procedure. This tactic led to further delay because each nation demanded as much of a share of reparations goods as possible.[94] In October 1947 when the delegates finally designated the machinery to be removed, it took another three months for inspection and packing. It was not until January 1948 when SCAP finally shipped the first war reparations, the value of which amounted to only $18.4 million.[95]

Pauley's plan had assumed that the Japanese economy would become self-sufficient with its recovery of foreign trade. He predicted, "There is . . . in 1948, a probable visible trade surplus of 123 million yen (of 1936 value)."[96] As Assistant Secretary of War for Occupied Areas Howard C. Peterson correctly pointed out, however, Pauley's assumption was wrong because Japan failed to recover the dollar market in silks and textiles.[97] Things were more serious than Pauley had expected. The trade deficit ran $360 million and $420 million in 1947 and 1948 respectively.[98] According to Robert Barnett, a member of the Pauley mission, Pauley also presumed, "China would become the chief industrial force in Asia, using Japanese equipment as the nucleus of her industrial development." As it turned out, "the situation in Asia did not develop as envisioned."[99]

Pauley's punitive program stimulated those who supported moderate economic policies toward Japan, precipitating a backlash both in Washington and SCAP. In addition, the unexpectedly rapid success of demilitarization and democratization, as well as economic deterioration, made it imperative to implement Japanese economic recovery. The moderates advocated a dramatic reduction or elimination of war reparations. In January 1947, the War Department established a Special Committee on Japanese Reparations, headed by Clifford Strike, president of McGraw Engineering, which made a 31-day-trip to Japan to examine the whole reparations program (the Strike Committee). When MacArthur met with the Committee, he insisted on the urgent necessity of an economic recovery in Japan. In February 1947, R. M. Cheseldine of the War Department, who accompanied the Strike mission, reported that MacArthur "impressed upon the group the importance and gravity of the economic situation and the value to the United States of prompt decisions regarding reparations removals and consequent removal of restrictions upon the industry to remain in Japan." The Strike committee concluded that since "the present reparations program . . . would have a disastrous effect on the Japanese economy . . . reparations of industrial equipment should not affect Japan's ability to produce sufficient goods."[100] Cheseldine criticized Pauley's plan because it would prolong US aid to Japan and become a heavy burden on American taxpayers. SCAP also feared that Pauley's scheme would reduce the Japanese trade balance.[101]

Cheseldine insisted that the "paramount issue should not be to provide any country with reparations, but rather to reactivate a reasonable economy to make Japan self supporting . . . cement friendly relations with the Japanese through proof of the efficacy and strength of our capitalistic democracy." He believed that the present reparations policy, based on a punitive sentiment, was "in error" because of wrong assumption that "a nation to wage war must of necessity have expanded its industrial plant far beyond peacetime requirements and, therefore, must have quantities of excess equipment." He pointed out that Japan had to deal with the issues of "obsolescence, war damage, 'wear and tear', and need of replacement . . . and places an undue burden on an internal economy, thereby creating a continuing burden upon the nation which has the responsibility for the occupation."[102] In October 1947, the PPS recommended, "Minimum reparations, consistent with existing commitments, should be exacted, and none out of current production."[103]

In order to collect more first hand information, Washington sent a series of economic missions to Japan in 1948. It asked the Overseas Consultants Incorporated (OCI) to send the delegates to Japan headed by Clifford Strike. In February 1948, the OCI submitted a report, recommending retaining Japanese plants because "Japan should be able to turn out industrial products, including new capital equipment, and exchange them for the food and raw materials." Since the OCI believed that "this can be achieved most surely by leaving Japan free to reconstruct and use as quickly as possible the bulk of her industrial capacity . . . [it recommended against] the removal of productive facilities (except primary war facilities) which can be effectively used in Japan."[104]

When George Kennan, Director of PPS, visited Japan in March 1948, he claimed, "It was incomprehensible how people could have seriously believed that . . . [the current reparations program] could ever have had a satisfactory practical application." General MacArthur agreed that it would be costly to implement the program and that none of the recipients could make use of the reparations effectively.[105] On his return to Washington, Kennan recommended, "We should announce that our Government is not prepared to permit the removal of reparations items from Japan in excess of the existing 30% project . . . the United States will oppose the exaction of reparations from Japan under any future peace treaty."[106]

In March 1948, the Army sent a special economic mission, headed by Percey Johnston (the Johnston mission), to study Japanese economic conditions, especially reparations issues.[107] In April 1948, this mission reported that severe reparations would halt Japanese economic recovery when "other Far Eastern countries are in need of industrial equipment." Consequently, "the ultimate decision with respect to reparations should be based on a balancing of needs to obtain optimum benefits for the region as a whole." The Johnston mission articulated that removal of productive facilities from Japan, even if fully implemented, was irrational because "the costs involved in moving plants and equipment from a conquered nation and reestablishing them in a victorious nation are high and that the ultimate usefulness and value of such plants are small, being poorly adapted to needs of the new owners."[108]

Pauley's punitive approach could not achieve a consensus agreement among Washington officials. An indefinite reparations policy prevented Japanese industries from resuming full operation or making new investments for fear of confiscation to pay reparations. George Atcheson agreed, "The revival and reconversion of industry continues to be obstructed by non-settlement of the reparations question."[109] He warned the Secretary of State, "Whether we like it or not, this country has become an economic responsibility of the United States. . . . We are hoping very much for the earliest possible settlement of the reparations question because that is one of the necessary factors for revival of industry" and because the Japanese "must manufacture exports with which to pay for necessary imports of food and other products."[110]

General MacArthur agreed to the critical necessity of making a solid and prompt decision on the reparations issues.[111] The Strike Committee believed that the "uncertainty . . . of the reparations program has had a retarding effect on reconversion to peace-time production." It indicated that economic self-sufficiency could not "be achieved until the Japanese can be told what plants and facilities are to be removed." Hence, it advocated an "imperative need for prompt action on reparations."[112] SWNCC 236/43 concurred with the report that the "prompt handling of the Japanese reparations problem is essential in the attainment of US occupational objectives and in alleviating Japanese economic and industrial inertia, thereby reducing US costs, it is believed that prompt unilateral US action will be necessary."[113] In October 1947, PPS 10 also agreed that the "reparations program should be wound up at the earliest possible date."[114] Frank Hussey, SCAP political adviser, argued that Japan would definitely need early settlement of the reparations issue.[115] The OCI anticipated in February 1948, "There has been little incentive to rehabilitate industry as the Japanese are not informed as to which plants or parts of plants they will be permitted to retain." Time was crucial. "The longer this uncertainty continues, the more difficult the problem of rehabilitation will become."[116] In April 1948, the Johnston Mission warned, "The threat of removal for reparations hangs over much of Japan's industry, especially heavy industry." It was, therefore, "imperative that [a] decision be reached promptly as to which excess Japanese plants and equipment are to be subject to removal as reparations and that the rest be given assurance that they will remain untouched."[117] In October 1948, R. E. Reid, a member of the Office of Undersecretary of the Army, complained, "Current uncertainties over reparations represent one of the greatest single drags on the Japanese recovery program," recommending that the United States "announce its intention of enforcing them unilaterally if no FEC approval is forthcoming."[118]

There existed doubts, though, about the relaxation of reparations. Having read OCI's interim report, Charles Saltzman, Assistant Secretary of State for Occupied Areas, objected to it because "if these recommendations are accepted, there will undoubtedly be many questions raised by the governments claiming reparations."[119] Willard Thorp, Assistant Secretary of State for Economic Affairs, warned that the reparations issue was "essentially a political problem, the form which they are to take is an economic one. A decision to reduce reparations will have major political repercussions." He also added that the Asian countries "associated intimately in their minds the reparations and security problems."[120] In May the Secretary of the Army advised to rely on the recommendations by the OCI and the Johnston Committee to determine the level of Japanese industry. Charles Saltzman, however, maintained that "the Department of State should reject the Army's view on the level of industry issue" because the OCI's economic analysis was incorrect, and the "Army's position would be so unacceptable and antagonizing to FEC member nations as to result in long-term disadvantages to the United States."[121] Potential recipients of reparations transfers were sensitive to American lenient attitudes toward Japan. Ely, Chief of the Division of Philippine Affairs, told General McCoy that the Philippine Government was seriously concerned about the recent moderation in US policy toward Japan. Thorp anticipated that a "decision to reduce reparations will have major political repercussions. All Far Eastern countries feel deeply that simple justice requires that Japan make reparation in some form." He warned that the US unilateral decision would cause "deepest resentment and inviting the antagonism of the FEC countries."[122] Frank McCoy had already expressed his disagreement with the lenient recommendation because it would dismiss the dominant opinion of the FEC.[123]

The State Department anticipated that easing the war reparations policy "will meet with extremely strong opposition from friendly FEC countries." If the United States met formidable antagonism in the FEC, the State Department argued, "This Government will withdraw its proposal [of reducing reparations]."[124] Fiercely disagreeing with this suggestion, Secretary of the Army Kenneth Royall countered that he could not "see how I could agree . . . to withhold our proposals from the FEC if the preliminary conversations indicate that the essentials of our present proposals are not acceptable." He insisted on forcing the way if necessary. "If no agreement is reached [in the FEC] after a reasonable period of considerations . . . I believe it essential that this interim directive [revoking the previous reparations programs] be issued."[125]

Even though Thorp recognized that a unilateral US decision would precipitate political repercussions in Asia, he urged "some definite and final settlement of the reparations problem" promptly in one way or another because "further delay, review, or restudy of details would reflect a type of vacillation which is more damaging to Japan than almost any kind of concrete program."[126] By October, NSC 13/2 still could not articulate the American reparations policy.[127]

Paul Nitze, Deputy Director of the Office of International Trade, continued opposing a lenient policy because he considered reparations a political, not economic, issue which would sooth ill feelings among Asian victims. He feared that the termination of the reparations transfer would "provoke international reactions so hostile as to embarrass Japan's trade prospects in the Far East."[128] Edwin M. Martin, Director of Japanese and Korean Economic Affairs, agreed with Nitze that good feelings among Asian countries would be indispensable for stimulating regional trade. Nevertheless, other State Department officials such as Max Bishop and W. W. Butterworth, Director of Far Eastern Affairs, held out for a soft policy.[129] By early 1949, however, Washington still could not reach a consensus on the reparations issue.

The Departments of State and the Army nonetheless shared the recognition that the war reparations issue was a primary obstacle to Japanese economic recovery. In December 1948, Bishop argued, "If our position on reparations is skilfully presented in the context of our overall policies toward Japan for the coming period," the State Department could compromise with the Department of the Army.[130] Recognizing that it would be undesirable to "repudiate the agreements previously made in FEC," Secretary of State Dean Acheson, in February 1949, claimed that the United States could "properly insist that both SCAP's duty and the interests of the United States as the nation which makes up the deficit, as well as of all the nations party to FEC, call for the speedy recovery of Japan and the placing of that country on a self-supporting basis." He advised, "We are warranted in ceasing deliveries [of the reparations]."[131] Pressures stemming from the need to make a firm reparations policy induced the Departments of State and the Army finally to agree in May 1949, "Current transfers of reparations . . . should be terminated and every effort made to secure acceptance by the other reparations claimant countries of the principle that the reparations question as a whole should be reduced to the status of a dead letter." On 12 May 1949, the United States announced, "The existing Far Eastern Commission policy decisions regarding reparations are incapable of implementation."[132]

CHAPTER THREE

THE ROAD TO ECONOMIC STABILITY

THE SEARCH FOR ECONOMIC STABILITY

As early as April 1946, Robert Fearey, of the Office of the Political Adviser in Japan, warned that Japanese economic conditions would influence "the tendency of the Japanese in future to align themselves . . . with the United States or with a potential enemy. . . ."[1] The unexpectedly swift success in demilitarization and democratization made it imperative for the United States to accelerate the Japanese economic recovery in order to consolidate earlier accomplishments. Moreover, because the Cold War mentality had supplanted punitive sentiment, Washington felt it necessary to strengthen Japan and to keep it in the Western bloc. Thus, Washington gradually turned its attention to Japanese economic recovery.

From the beginning of the occupation, US officials recognized a close linkage between demilitarization and democratization on the one hand and economic recovery on the other. The SWNCC indicated, "A process of [democratic] reorientation will only be as effective as it goes hand in hand with some gradual improvement in the economic condition of the ordinary Japanese toward whom it is directed."[2] George E. Blakeslee, a member of the FEC's mission to Japan, also recognized that "the immediate problem is economic. A sane democracy cannot rest on an empty stomach." He warned that a malfunctioning economy might ruin the early accomplishment of the United States. "Economic distress normally leads to an attempt to change the existing government to one which promises relief–either an extreme right wing or an extreme left wing government."[3] Robert Fearey warned that failure in the economic recovery would make success in the first two objectives meaningless. He contended that Japan's "current pro-American, pro-democratic and anti-Soviet, anti-communist tendencies could be completely reversed. . . . if impelled by acute economic distress or national insecurity, possibly combined with Soviet pressure."[4] SCAP proclaimed that the occupation policy should convince the Japanese people that democracy would pay off: "Nothing will serve better to win the Japanese people over to a peaceful, democratic way of life than the discovery that it brings rewards in the way of better living and increasing economic security."[5] Colonel R. M. Cheseldine of the War Department warned, "Our failure to assist in the recovery of her economy will cause her to lose confidence in our form of democracy." [6] In April 1947, the American Institute of Pacific Relations held a round table discussion dealing with American policy toward Japan. Participants generally held the opinion that the Japanese industrial recovery, with appropriate guidance, would accelerate the spread of democracy in Japan.[7] George Atcheson, Political Adviser in Japan, believed, "The ultimate success of the Occupation will depend to a great extent upon economic factors."[8] Senator Elbert D. Thomas agreed that in the long run, "the final test of our policies will take place in the economic field. If we fail there, democracy will not stand in Japan."[9] R. W. Barnett of the State Department also regarded it imperative to adopt positive policies for economic recovery: "U.S. policy statement should be formulated in such terms as make clear the desirability for a 'shift in emphasis' from a passive, restrictive, or negative attitude toward a positive attitude so far as increasing trade and industrial productivity are concerned. . . ."[10] State Department officials advised Frank Hussey, SCAP political adviser, "Sentiment was gradually building up in the United States to concentrate full attention to the economic recovery of occupied areas so that American tax payer may be relieved of the burden of supporting them."[11]

As late as 1948, production was still only a third of what it was before the war,[12] but leaders increasingly regarded inflation as the leading villain in the drama to bring about economic stabilization. Inflation was the most serious economic problem in Japan.[13] From September 1945 to August 1948, prices rose more than 700% and continuous inflation created social unrest in Japan.[14] The Japanese government established the ESB in August 1946, to manage the Japanese economy and the Reconstruction Finance Bank (RFB) in January 1947 to allocate funds to important industries.[15] Indeed Japanese economic planning in the early occupation policy increased production of targeted industries, but it also caused hyperinflation because of large quantities of funds from the RFB whose major resources came from the Bank of Japan. There were two major groups in the ESS: One fiscal conservative group regarded it quite inflationary while the other liberal group supported the policy because they considered the revival of production more important.[16] In the early stages of occupation, the latter group was prevalent because increasing production had top priority.

MacArthur circulated some of the anti-inflation ideas. He drafted a letter to Prime Minister Katayama Tetsu on 22 March 1947 to protest Japan's complacency in the face of economic precariousness. The General threatened to terminate American aid if the Japanese government failed to take action to halt inflation. According to Dick Nanto, the letter was "cordially acknowledged" but "politely ignored." In response, the General issued an outline of 15 economic points, but they barely received attention. The ESB imposed limits on new currency issues, creating a minor decline in consumer prices (about four percent).[17]

The ESS warned that if "this [inflationary] situation continues, the consequent social unrest among the lowest real income groups is likely to endanger the basic aims of the Occupation." It recommended that economic stabilization was "the indispensable prerequisite to Japan's economic recovery which must be attained if faith in democratic ways is to be affirmed and totalitarian alternatives rejected by the Japanese people."[18] According to SWNCC, "the first phase of the occupation has been completed. . . . [but] the establishment of a self-supporting economy in Japan, without which the achievements of the occupation cannot be consolidated, has not yet been accomplished."[19] William Draper of the Army Department insisted, "Further progress toward the reestablishment of Japan as a productive and respected member of the community of nations will be difficult, if not impossible, without the creation of a self-sustained Japanese economy."[20] In January 1948, Secretary of Army Kenneth Royall claimed, "Both Departments [of the Army and the State] realize that for political stability to continue and for free government to succeed in the future, there must be a sound and self-supporting economy. . . ."[21] In January 1948, the ESB averred that the grave conditions of the Japanese economy were like "a ball rolling down on a steep downgrade to a bottomless pit."[22] Nelson Spinks of SCAP told Hugh Borton, Chief of the Office of Northeast Asian Affairs in the State Department, that inflation was the biggest problem in Japan.[23] Both Japan and the United States recognized that economic stabilization was a pressing need for Japan.

In February 1948, the ESB proposed a "middle-of-the-road stabilization program" to allocate resources primarily into strategically important industries such as coal and steel, to increase consumption goods through foreign aid, to stabilize wages, and to restore gradually the fiscal balance without immediately halting inflation.[24] When Prime Minister Ashida Hitoshi asked Under Secretary of the Army William Draper, Jr. for a one-billion-dollar loan in the spring of 1948, Draper presented three conditions: an increase in the produc-

tion of important materials, a recovery of foreign trade, and the realization of
a balanced budget.[25] Draper especially requested that Ashida balance the
budget because otherwise Congress would likely reduce direct aid to Japan in
the near future.[26]

THE ROAD TO A NINE-POINT PROGRAM

Some Americans began to question the funneling of their funds into the
Japanese economy, especially since the United States was experiencing its own
recession in the spring of 1948. The National Advisory Council on
International Monetary Affairs (NAC) insisted that the US effective aid to
Japan should be dependent on Japanese economic stabilization.[27] Secretary of
Treasury John Snyder, a St. Louis investment banker, chaired the NAC whose
tight money and austerity policy characterized the US economic measures
toward Japan.[28] When Draper returned to Washington from Japan in April
1948, the NAC warned that assistance for Japan's economic recovery "should
be accompanied by measures to achieve internal economic stability and effectively to enforce the economic controls necessary thereto." In the same month,
the Army Department claimed, "Drastic and continuing efforts by the
Japanese themselves are necessary to balance the national budget. Self-help
and self-sacrifice in clarifying and controlling internal price and wage relationships . . . are essential to proper use of any American assistance and, of course,
to economic recovery itself."[29] Recession, which began in the United States in
May 1948, induced the reduction of US aid to Japan.[30]

As a coordinating measure to reconcile the NAC, Draper decided to send
a Special Mission on Yen Foreign Exchange Policy to Japan headed by Ralph
Young, Associate Director of the Research Division of the Federal Reserve
Board.[31] The Japanese government used thousands of different exchange rates
in order to subsidize trading companies: Importers used lower rates and
exporters higher ones. On 12 June 1948, he submitted a report (the Young
Report) in which he advocated that a single exchange rate was necessary for
Japan's economic recovery, especially in order to provide monetary stability at
a time when Japan began to end its isolation from the world economy. Young
recommended that "SCAP be authorized to fix a level [of a single exchange
rate] within a range of 270 yen to 330 yen per dollar . . . not later than 1
October 1948." The Young mission recommended "supplementary measures
to accompany the operation of such a rate," including a credit control program, deficit reduction, effective tax collection, the introduction of a new tax,
effective allocation of raw materials, wage stabilization, foreign trade control,
foreign exchange control, and efficient food collection. Even though the mission's main concern was to find an appropriate foreign exchange rate, the

major contribution of the Young mission was that it articulated the urgent necessity of economic stabilization in Japan.[32]

The speed at which to implement recovery, however, was an area of contention, especially as SCAP leaders were beginning to feel their power base erode. MacArthur, along with the Department of the Army, believed that the Young mission's recommendations would have drastic repercussions if implemented too quickly, and that it was too early to initiate a general exchange rate. Others in Washington wanted the entire reform package and the exchange rate to be implemented as soon as possible. Most importantly, SCAP argued that severe economic measures would jeopardize the harmonious relations between occupation leaders and the Japanese people.[33]

In June 1948, the NAC advised both State and Army Departments that an "energetic program for financial stabilization in Japan is essential to the promotion of exchange stability under any yen exchange rate arrangement: the various component measures in such a program should be initiated or strengthened without delay." According to the NAC meeting minutes, "MacArthur had strong views . . . to the effect that a substantial change in the exchange rate might cause unemployment, dissatisfaction and uncertainty and affect the political as well as the economic situation."[34] The Treasury Department supported the Young report. "Washington does not fully accept SCAP's view that the Japanese people have submitted to a severe degree of austerity and have accepted *drastic* economic deprivations." Heavier taxes were not "beyond realization under the existing conditions of poverty in Japan"[35] (emphasis original). With SCAP's strong opposition supported by the Army, the NAC could not reach any consensus but only advised to set the rate "as soon as administratively possible" without any specific deadline.[36]

Charles Saltzman, Assistant Secretary of State, claimed that there was a consensus in Washington: "Stabilization efforts must be greatly intensified to be successful. . . ."[37] In accordance with these movements in Washington, SCAP also propelled a stabilization scheme in Japan. In June 1948, William Marquat, Chief of the ESS, informed Tokyo that rigid domestic economic conditions, such as the elimination of black markets, effective tax collection, and a balanced budget, would be essential to set a single exchange rate and to reenter the international economy.[38] In July 1948, he sent the Japanese government a memorandum called "Essentials of Economic Stabilization Program," the so-called ten-point program, which largely followed the Young recommendations.[39] For SCAP, it was nothing new, but just a new name for the same continuing policy. Watanabe Takeshi, a Finance Ministry officer, asked the Finance Division of SCAP for more details about this program, but nobody in the Division had been consulted and they had nothing concrete to provide with regard to this program.[40] SCAP officials did not fully discuss the program nor did they accept Young's core recommendation to set up the single exchange rate immediately.[41] The Japanese business community and government did not take this program seriously because it was just a SCAP recommendation, not a directive.[42] They continued the gradual stabilization policy led by the ESB and the RFB.

Japan's slow progress toward economic recovery irritated both SCAP and Washington. Between 1945 and 1949, US aid to Japan amounted to 1.53 billion dollars: approximately 60-70 percent of total Japan's imports.[43] NSC 13 of June 1948 declared that economic recovery was "the prime objective of United States policy in Japan for the coming period."[44] In September 1948, the CIA reported to President Truman, "[The] future political stability and orientation of Japan depend largely on the attainment of a viable economy."[45] NSC 13/1 upgraded Japanese economic recovery to "second only to U.S. security interests."[46] Washington understood that America's generous aid to Japan would become a waste without economic stabilization and the NAC would no longer tolerate benevolent aid to the country. In December 1948, the NAC Staff Committee rejected the aid for the Economic Recovery for Occupied Area (EROA)[47] to Japan for 1950 due to Japan's lack of stabilization.

The NAC questioned SCAP's economic management in Japan, insisting that unless the United States took powerful economic stabilization measures, it would not provide aid for Japanese economic recovery. The NAC only accepted the aid request on condition that the Army would take immediate measures with which Draper agreed. The NAC strongly recommended to President Truman that Washington give top priority to Japan's economic stabilization.[48] Accepting the NAC's advice, Truman finally sent to SCAP a nine-point economic stabilization program, arguing that since the NAC and the NSC "have come to the conclusion that the situation is sufficiently serious . . . it must be directed to carry out this necessary program of stabilization."[49] The nine-point directive ordered Japan to: (1) balance the consolidated budgets; (2) increase tax collection efficiency; (3) restrict the increase of credit extension; (4) control wages; (5) control prices; (6) control foreign trade; (7) maximize exports by improving allocation and rationing systems; (8) increase industrial and mining production; and (9) increase efficiency of food collection program.[50]

Delivering the nine-point program, General MacArthur explained to Yoshida, "The prompt economic stabilization of Japan is a primary objective common both to the Allied Powers and the Japanese people. . . ." In addition, SCAP declared that this plan had "a series of objectives designed to achieve fiscal, monetary, price and wage stability in Japan as rapidly as possible . . . [this plan] will call for increased austerity in every phase of Japanese life."[51] He claimed that there would be no "place for ideological opposition as the purpose to be served is common to all of the people, and any attempt to delay or frustrate its accomplishment must be curbed as menacing the general welfare."[52]

SCAP, however, had ambivalent feelings toward the nine-point program. On the one hand, some effective measures to accomplish economic stability in Japan were necessary, while on the other hand, the program was a kind of blow to MacArthur because it implied that SCAP was incompetent to control inflation.[53] MacArthur also regarded it undesirable to set the single exchange rate immediately, because it would bring confusion to the Japanese economy. Consequently, even though the original directive from Washington demanded that the Japanese government set the rate within three months, MacArthur eliminated this concrete time limit.[54]

JAPANESE POLITICAL DEVELOPMENT

Meanwhile, Japanese political development involved the preparation of conditions to accept a powerful stabilizing program. The weak Katayama Administration (coalition government) collapsed in February 1948 primarily because its internal conflict prevented the passage of the budget in the Diet. One month later, Ashida Hitoshi of the Democratic Party established another coalition government, but, as indicated by the fact that the Socialist Party acquired more cabinet posts than the Democratic Party, this coalition government was also weak and unstable. This administration fell in only seven months primarily because of the Showa Denko Scandal. This scandal was one of the worst bribery scandals during the occupation. Showa Denko, a chemical company producing fertilizer, provided bribes for high-ranking officials and politicians in the Ashida Cabinet, including those in the ESB and the RFB, in return for their influence and cooperation in channelling about 3 billion yen of the RFB's loans to Showa Denko. Showa Denko was believed to have spent some 350 million yen on bribery. In June 1948, the president of Showa Denko was arrested. The prosecutor indicted 64 people including Kurusu Takeo, the Director General of the ESB who had been Finance Minister in June when the scandal broke, Nishio Suehiro, former Deputy Premier, and forced the resignation of Prime Minister Ashida, who was later arrested. The State Department complained that Japan's postwar politics had been styled by "a series of coalition governments characterized by divided policies, ineffective administration, and public scandal."[55] A strong government was necessary to implement unpopular austerity programs.

In the election of January 1949, the Democratic-Liberal Party (DLP) led by Yoshida won the majority of seats (264 seats out of 466). This was the beginning of stable postwar conservative rule. Japan, for the first time since the end of the Asia-Pacific War, had a majority single-party government. General MacArthur argued that this result clearly showed the Japanese willingness to choose political conservatism.[56] This political shift from a left and middle-of-the-road coalition government to a single conservative administration created the proper climate for the lean and mean nine-point program. It also presaged the postwar conservative rule that would last for thirty-eight years, with the formation of the Liberal Democratic Party (LDP) in 1955.

The DLP had rectified the party organization when it was out of power. The party enrolled former bureaucrats including Ikeda Hayato, former Finance Vice-Minister, Satoh Eisaku, former Transportation Vice-Minister, Okazaki Katsuo, former Foreign Vice-Minister, Kotake Keiichi, former Labor Vice-Minister, and others.[57] The DLP also consolidated its local organizations.[58] In 1949, a large number of former bureaucrats of the DLP won the election. They played the key linkage role between the party and bureaucracy, substantially increasing its policy-making ability and administrative tactics.[59] Yoshida primarily relied on those former bureaucrats to consolidate his power base within the DLP.[60] The DLP absorbed over 20 Diet members from the Democratic Party in March 1950. Yoshida designated former Prime Minister Shidehara Kijuro, and after him Vice Prime Minister Hayashi Joji, as Speaker of the House of Representatives, seeking to maneuver it by using his most reliable senior politicians. He also allocated Chairmanship of the House of Councilors to Satoh Naotake, a member of the *Ryokufukai* [The Green Wind Party] which held the largest number of seats, in order to obtain the majority votes there. The third Yoshida Cabinet steadily brought stability to Japanese politics.[61] Some scholars, such as Shiratori Rei and John Dower, argue that the Yoshida Cabinet established in 1949 was probably the most powerful cabinet since the Meiji Restoration. The Yoshida Era had truly begun.[62] This political development created the basis to implement the nine-point program.

Japan, however, contained potential seeds of destruction. According to State Department research of February 1949, "unless the economic recovery program gives early promise of success, and does so without patently inequitable distribution of burdens on major economic group, there is no guarantee of continuing political stability under Democratic-Liberal leadership. . . ."[63] This election also witnessed remarkable progress for the Japan Communist Party; it won 35 seats in the Diet. Fearing the increase of Communists' influence, Harry Kern, Foreign Editor of *Newsweek*, warned that Japan was facing "the ever-increasing Communist infiltration into every rank of the communities. . . . they [the Communists] will more than double the present force in the Diet in the next election. Students, farmers, small businessmen are going Communist in alarming numbers."[64] The CIA regarded the Communist success "as a protest against the ineffectiveness of the middle-of-the-road coalition government, or against the Occupation. . . ." It, however, predicted that "in the event that Japanese economic conditions were to improve measurably in the near future, the Party's support could easily be halved."[65] Economic stability and prosperity were necessary to strengthen conservative elements in Japan.

APPOINTMENT OF JOSEPH DODGE

Choosing the appropriate person to authorize and implement more drastic measures to stabilize the Japanese economy would be crucial. MacArthur's authority and popularity, at least among the Japanese people, were not to be dismissed. For their own politics, Washington leaders typecast MacArthur as inept with economics—but by denying him an assertive economic role they also preserved his quasi-deified authority to be "above" economics in Japan. SCAP was full of military experts, but it lacked competent economists. In April 1947 Dean Acheson, Acting Secretary of State, realized "the necessity for making available to General MacArthur civilian personnel of outstanding skill and experience to deal with the economic and financial aspects of the occupation."[66] Tsuru Shigeto, Deputy Director of the ESB, candidly complained to the State Department officials that there were few high-ranking advisers to SCAP on economic matters.[67] According to George Kennan, General MacArthur agreed, "This [economic recovery] should be made a primary objective of occupational policy but did not know what he could do today that he was not already doing to achieve it."[68] In May 1948, MacArthur requested Washington to "find me somebody who knows something about running the economy of Japan, because I don't. And my military officers who are responsible for it don't either."[69] In order to meet these demands, and especially to implement the nine-point program, President Truman in December 1948 requested Joseph M. Dodge, President of the Detroit Bank, to visit Japan as an economic adviser to SCAP.[70] He had to stabilize the Japanese economy because Congress would not continue providing a large amount of aid to Japan unless that country brought stability to its economy. In December 1948, Dodge wrote, "Mr. Truman stated that the Japanese economic problem had moved to the highest level of consideration, that he had taken a personal interest in it, and was completely informed about it."[71] By chance or by choice, the perception of MacArthur as an economically challenged pacifist sustained his good reputation in Japan while at the same time earning him the right to a financial advisor from America. And that advisor, Joseph Dodge, in turn protected the General's aura by spearheading reforms that an image-conscious leader would want no part of.

On 17 January 1949, barely two weeks after Dodge's telegram of refusal, the President of the United States officially appointed the President of the Detroit Bank as "Financial Adviser to the Supreme Commander for Allied Powers with the personal rank of Minister."[72] "As I understand it," General Clay wrote to Dodge from Berlin, "there was never developed in Japan a definite fiscal and economic objective. If that is true and conditions fail to improve, it will cast a shadow over General MacArthur's [sic] other magnificent achievements in occupation and ultimately on the Army's part in the show."[73] Clay wrote those words in a congratulatory letter to Dodge upon hearing of his former advisor's Tokyo appointment, conceding polite envy that MacArthur would now obtain the wise banker's services. Dodge arrived in Tokyo on 1 February 1949 with his team of two scholars, Paul O'Leary of Cornell University and Audley Stephan of Rutgers University; two officials, William W. Diehl of the Treasury Department and Orville J. McDiarmid of the State Department, and Ralph Reid of the Department of the Army.[74]

INITIAL IMPLEMENTATION OF THE DODGE LINE

The Dodge Line, based on the nine-point directive, was one of the most important deflationary fiscal and monetary policies in modern Japanese history. There exist various assessments of the Dodge program (Dodge Line). Some scholars regard it as simply one of the many programs to limit inflation.[75] Other scholars downgrade its significance.[76] Still others believe that the Dodge Line played an important part in curbing the Japanese inflation.[77] These previous studies underestimated the importance of the Dodge Line. The Dodge Line constituted one of the most significant turning points in the occupation: It not only stopped inflation and brought stability to the Japanese economy but also carried out the groundwork toward establishing a liberal economic system managed primarily by the financial community.[78] Dodge shifted the US focus from a "production-first" strategy to an "export-first" program. Moreover, although previous studies have paid little attention to the Dodge Line's impact on US policy, the Dodge Line indeed led Washington to commit itself more deeply in Asian affairs.

Truman reminded Dodge: "Recovery rather than relief must be our aim."[79] Dodge was the only man stoic and unsentimental enough to carry out the mission. Dodge kept a low profile, perhaps not always by choice, and left few suggestions of personality in his record other than strict professionalism, tactful decorum, and always, "just the facts." In February 1949, Dodge advocated a tight money, anti-inflation policy, and therefore politically unfavorable measures, as an absolute imperative in Japan to balance the budget. The Dodge Line consisted of the following measures: (1) balancing the consolidated budget; (2) more efficient tax collection; (3) tight credit; (4) reducing wage and price increases; (5) controlling trade; (6) allocating supplies to exporters; (7) replacing the RFB with yen counterpart funds; (8) establishing a single exchange rate; and (9) decreasing the amount of currency circulation.[80] On 23 February 1949, the Japanese government submitted its budget proposal to Dodge. It maintained balance in a general account by reducing a price-adjustment budget while introducing income tax reduction and increasing a public works budget. A special account, however, was to have deficit because of issuing national bonds for railroad and communication.[81] After scrutinizing the Japanese budget, Dodge, in March 1949, gave the Japanese government a revised proposal based on rigid balance in the consolidated budget, including those of general, special, other government related institutions, and local governments, which would result in a 156.7 billion yen surplus to repay the RFB's debt. Utilizing various statistics, the New Dealers in SCAP advised Dodge that if he cut the subsidies, the price level would rise while production would decline. On 1 March, Dodge asked Ikeda about the possible effect of cutting the subsidies on the general price level. Ikeda believed that the government should reduce the subsidies in order for private companies to regain autonomy: "As long as the government provide private companies with subsidies, the government has to intervene in their internal affairs." Ikeda replied to Dodge, "Since the current statistics are unreliable, there is no way but to have the guts to cut the subsidies." Ikeda later recalled, "The best way to teach a person how to swim is to throw him into water, and if he is about to get drowned, we should do something to help him. Let's throw him into water! We made a big decision. It was indeed a wild thought." Prime Minister Yoshida understood that because Washington was firmly behind Dodge, it would be profitable for Japan to follow the Dodge Line. He felt that when Japan arrived at a critical juncture, Washington would do something. In other words, none of Dodge, Ikeda, or Yoshida implemented the Dodge Line with firm confidence but just as a venture to carry out the tight-money policy.[82] Instead of eliminating all the subsidies, Dodge left around 200 billion yen of price-adjustment in the 1949 budget (approximately three times that of 1948). He intended to use this fund for a temporary adjustment measure to promote industrial rationalization and to make Japanese companies competitive in the world market. Dodge allowed the Finance Ministry to decrease the amount according to economic conditions. In the end, the Ministry reduced the amount by about 20 billion yen.[83] Finance Minister Ikeda submitted the Dodge proposal with little modification to the Diet which passed it on 20 April 1949. This proposed budget could not be used to implement the DLP's election pledge of reducing income tax, eliminating turnover tax, and increasing public works.[84] Ikeda recalled, "The DLP criticized me harshly because of the extremely tight budget. . . . We managed to submit the budget proposal, but I believed that I would have to resign."[85]

Indeed, the Japanese economy had already begun to control inflation at a moderate pace prior to the Dodge Line.[86] In March 1949, the ESB reported, "The Japanese economy in 1948 is showing sings [sic] of economic stabilization in (1) the steady increase in production, (2) the slowing down of inflation, and (3) the rise in real wages."[87] It was, however, only American officials who would be able to push through the drastic austerity measures to control inflation with one stroke.[88] Inflation spiraled downward almost immediately after the Line was cast (although economic scholars have debated the extent to which the Dodge Line itself deserves credit): The inflation rate dropped from 80% per year in 1948 to 24% in 1949.[89] The price of production goods on the black market dropped 35 percent between January 1949 and May 1950 and the price of consumer goods on the black market decreased by 38 percent during the same period. Although Japan suffered from the budget deficit of 160 billion yen in 1948, it enjoyed a surplus of 260 billion yen in 1949. Currency circulation increased by only 20 billion yen in 1949, while the figure was 100 billion in 1948.[90] Working closely with Dodge in coordinating economic plans and implementing policies, Major General Marquat was satisfied with Dodge's performance. In September 1949, Marquat wrote to Dodge that he had "no doubt that your group accomplished more during the time it was here for the actual advancement of Japan than any other group. . . . Prices, wages and living costs have leveled off and note issues has declined."[91]

The ESS did not support Dodge's stabilization-first policy. SCAP economist Sherwood Fine complained to Ikeda, while Dodge was with them, that the recent Japanese economic measures decreased production and exports in order to achieve balanced budget.[92] The Labor Division protested that the fiscal 1949 budget proposal neglected its critical impact of social, political, and economic consequences. Dodge, however, criticized SCAP's soft labor policy and rejected expenditure for unemployment.[93]

Although the ESB had no "basic difference of views regarding the point that currency stabilization is a preliminary condition of economic recovery," it differed from Dodge on "whether the domestic value of currency should be stabilized at a single stroke or whether the domestic and foreign value of currency should be stabilized gradually over a period of about two years."[94] In March 1949, it warned that trying to "restore a normal and sound economy with one stroke even in connection with the establishment of a single exchange rate, for such an attempt would cause serious disturbance and confusion in the domestic economy."[95] The ESB insisted that paying too much attention to stabilization and neglecting capital accumulation would slow down economic recovery in the long run and would face a crisis of deflation in short run.[96] It anticipated that the Dodge Line would "precipitate a financial crisis and force widespread business bankruptcy."[97] Even Finance Minister Ikeda requested Dodge to ease his severe austerity program because "it was too drastic and there would be too much siphoning off of yen currency, which might result in deflation rather than disinflation."[98]

Strongly refuting the ESB's assumption that "credit thus far provided has been both necessary and productive," Dodge argued, "The record reveals that careless and large scale credit extension has encouraged speculative activity, black market transactions, rapidly rising wages and prices, ineffective management and unsound business practice."[99] He articulated, "The strictest emphasis should be on investment in capital outlay which contributes quickly and directly to increased output and productivity. Housing, education, welfare and similar programs contribute to this only indirectly."[100] He reaffirmed that what Japan needed was "productive projects. A completely realistic approach would suggest that public works should be eliminated entirely until productive capacity had been replenished."[101] Dodge concluded, "The primary purpose of this [Fiscal Year 1949] budget is to attain economic stability and that other objectives of the Occupation, worthy though they may be, may have to be deferred or modified until such stability is achieved."[102] In March 1949, he self-appraised his budget as worthy because all the people involved complained equally.[103]

The Dodge Line encouraged, in a sense facilitated, personnel reduction both in public and private sectors. The Japanese National Personnel Authority announced in April 1949 the prospective elimination of approximately 500,000 jobs in the public sector. The National Railroad laid off about 126,000 workers (about 20% of the total number of railroad workforce) in July 1949. The total number of those discharged amounted to approximately 419,000 in the public sector, including those employees in public industries and local governments (between February 1949 and June 1950), and about 505,000 in the private sector (between February 1949 and April 1950). The number of labor organizations declined from the peak of 34,700 in 1949 down to 29,100 in 1950, and the number of organized workers also dropped from the peak of 6.7 million in 1948 to 5.8 million in 1950. Those who participated in strikes drastically decreased in number from the peak of 6.7 million in 1948 to 3.3 million in 1949, and to 2.4 million in 1950.[104] When Finance Minister Ikeda Hayato requested that Dodge consider appropriate unemployment measures in March 1949, Dodge replied that they would create even higher unemployment, saying, "Increase in unemployment will in turn lead to increased efficiency of labor and a greater production . . ."[105] Although unemployment had skyrocketed by April 1950, Dodge optimistically argued, "[The] actual rise in unemployment has been greatly exaggerated. Unemployment is reported at a surprisingly small figure, when the tremendous postwar increase in the Japanese labor forces through overseas repatriation is taken into consideration."[106] The Yoshida administration successfully controlled radical labor movements, while rhetorically shifting the focal point of labor discontent from the privations brought about by the Dodge Line to the long-extended occupation in general. General Marquat praised Dodge, "[The] labor front has settled down greatly with the anti-communist factions gaining ground in spite of the use of the 'austerity' bugaboo used by the Commie propagandists."[107]

LIBERALIZATION OF THE JAPANESE ECONOMIC SYSTEM AND DODGE-IKEDA-ICHIMADA NEXUS

The Dodge Line also liberalized the Japanese economic system. The Showa Denko Scandal demonstrated the danger of direct state intervention in the economy, which precipitated the demise of the planned economic development led by the ESB and the RFB, setting the stage for the rise of a liberal and market-oriented mechanism.[108] According to Yoshida, "It was necessary to discard the idea to manage economy through control and subsidies, and to channel Japanese economy to autonomous route. We needed to change economic policies conducted by the New Dealers in GHQ."[109] In March 1949, Finance Minister Ikeda contended that the Japanese economy "was a greenhouse economy and there was a need to break some of the windows in it or make business swim by throwing them in the water."[110] In his meeting with Dodge in March 1949, Ikeda criticized a weak Japanese economy supported by subsidies, claiming that the Japanese government should push forward to reduce them.[111] On 5 April 1949, he addressed in the 5th session of the House of Representatives, "As a result of focusing only on short-term production increase and neglecting capital accumulation and the basis for healthy production, our industries have become weakened and they will not be able to compete with foreign industries in the future in a free competition, which constituted one of the most important issues in our history." He implicitly criticised the ESB's policy, suggesting it was based on "ineffective and reckless production-first theory." He also expressed his determination to slash administrative personnel thoroughly in order to reduce expenditure. As for exports and subsidies, Ikeda claimed that the government "is going to abolish all export subsidies, to do away with 'green-house' protection, and to promote rationalization and reshuffling of enterprise to enable export industries to withstand from competition in the world market in the future instead of depending upon government support."[112] He was determined to implement "the enforcement of the economic stabilization plan" because he shared Dodge's philosophy that "it is deemed necessary to limit government intervention in the economic sphere to the utmost minimum and return the economy as soon as possible to its natural, rational course based on competitive principles."[113] Ikeda defended the Dodge Line in the Diet, regarding it as the first step to end

Japan's isolation from the world economy. In May 1949, the Economic Recovery Planning Committee in the Japanese government (ERPC) indicated, "Japanese companies have been in a green house. . . . Some companies get used to state subsidies and protection of official set prices so much that they neglect to recover healthy management." Japanese exporting industries had to "get out of the greenhouse of closed economy and face severe international competition."[114] Ichimada Naoto, Governor of the Bank of Japan, observed that Japanese industries had neglected rationalization since 1931.[115] The Dodge Line promoted the rise of those who supported the process of Japanese economic liberalization.[116] In July 1949, the Finance Ministry indicated that since 1938 "the Japanese economy has been distinguished by the absence of competition. . . ."[117]

The Finance Ministry headed by Ikeda became closely connected with the Dodge Line. Yoshida's appointment of Ikeda as Finance Minister was politically extraordinary and elder politicians in his party criticized Yoshida's decision. According to Ikeda's secretary, neither the Ministry of Finance nor his own party welcomed him, and both worked to eliminate his influence. Ikeda was not well-known in the business community either.[118] Surrounded by political enemies both within and outside his party, Ikeda had been looking for his own political power base, and Dodge provided exactly what Ikeda was searching for.[119] On the other hand, Dodge also needed powerful collaborators in economic stabilization within the Japanese government because SCAP was not particularly enthusiastic about, if not hostile to, the Dodge Line and the ESB opposed the nine-point program.[120]

Within the Japanese government, there existed a fierce power struggle between the ESB and the Finance Ministry. The large amount of military expenditure ruined the Japanese economy before and during the Asia-Pacific War. Because of this experience, the Finance Ministry constantly advocated a strictly balanced budget after the war, which was contrary to the ESB's inflationary economic policies. Since the Finance Ministry feared that the ESB might intrude upon the budget decision-making process, Ikeda endeavored to eliminate its influence and to establish a balanced budget with Dodge's assistance.[121]

Because Ichimada had also been making every effort to achieve a balanced budget, he considered the Dodge Line quite valuable. Comparing the Dodge Line to a cancer operation, he indicated, "[The] patient's heart might be a little weakened in order to remove cancer. The patient may suffer from internal disease. It, however, cannot be helped. The Japanese economy is now in a critical situation and we have to try everything we have."[122] Ichimada used Dodge's authority to implement the tight-money policies he had long wished for, claiming in October 1949, "The grand policy for Japanese economic rehabilitation which you so clearly put into effect was a policy which I had always earnestly desired to put into practice myself but had not succeeded in doing so due to my lack of power."[123]

The occupation reforms covered almost all aspects of Japanese society, but they did not make a drastic change in the financial structure led by the Bank of Japan. This was primarily because the Finance Section and the Anti-Trust & Cartel Section within the ESS could not agree which was responsible for financial reform, and because SCAP believed that dissolution of financial institutions might cause credit unrest.[124] The Dodge Line helped the rise of a finance-led economic structure in Japan that had several distinct characteristics.[125] Because the Japanese economy suffered from a serious shortage of money between April and June 1949, the Yoshida Cabinet tried to use monetary policy to stimulate production. After June 1949, the Bank of Japan injected funds into the market by expanding loans to private banks, implementing a purchase operation of bonds and securities from private banks, and reducing the interest rate. Because of the termination of RFB's new loans and decrease of stock prices begun in October 1949, private industries had to change their financial sources drastically from government-backed institutions to private banks.[126]

Zaibatsu dissolution and economic purges, which eliminated between 1,500 and 2,000 managers, helped the rise of new professional managers, and a large company usually had at least one executive who had spent his earlier career in a bank which facilitated a smoother relationship between the lender bank and the borrower.[127] In addition, banks normally sent their executive members to borrower companies to accumulate information and to monitor their management activities. When inappropriate management caused substantial loss of profits, banks intervened and requested a change of managers. On the other hand, the monitoring banks' loans signalled that the management of the borrower industries was healthy, which induced other banks to lend.[128] When the controlled economy gradually became a market economy after the Dodge Line, major banks became industrial monitors and supported inexperienced industrial management.[129] The financial community acquired the power to manage the Japanese economy and the Bank of Japan's controlling power over the finance community grew stronger.[130]

The consolidated government budget deficit amounted to 62 billion yen, 149 billion yen, and 348 billion yen in 1946, 1947, and 1948 respectively, consisting of 10-15 percent of the national income. Prior to the Dodge Line in 1949, the RFB's loan consisted of approximately three fourths of the total investment of all the industries combined.[131] Since these RFB's loans contributed to Japanese hyperinflation, Dodge terminated the RFB's new lending operation.[132] In April 1949, Dodge established a counterpart fund in order to redeem the deficits and to allocate industrial funds more effectively.[133] He also established the stipulation that SCAP (in practice, Dodge himself) approve all funds.[134] Dodge intended to use this fund primarily to write off the outstanding debts, while Ikeda sought to invest it in major targeted industries. Dodge explained that the redemption of the RFB's bond would reinforce the financial basis of the Bank of Japan and private banks, which would in turn provide industrial funds based on more rational lending criteria. He expected industrial monitoring by the financial community. In the 1949 fiscal year, the counterpart fund reached 129 billion yen, approximately 20 percent of the total budget for fiscal 1949, out of which the Japanese government was able to allocate only 50 billion yen towards long-term, low interest rate loans to core industries such as coal mining, ship building, and electric power production.[135] In October 1950, the Japanese business community voiced its request for easing the Dodge Line, which Dodge partly accepted. The supplementary budget of 1950 and the 1951 budget allowed Tokyo to use the counterpart fund for strengthening private investment, establishing the Japan Development Bank, providing long-term, low-interest loans to industry, assisting the Japan Export Bank to increase exports, and for easing restrictions on the Finance Ministry's utilization of its fund for facilitating the activities of long-term loan institutions.[136]

During the early occupation period, the Japanese government continued its control over the economy. "Never has the Japanese bureaucracy exercised greater authority than it did during the Occupation," wrote Hata Ikuhiko.[137] It was the golden age for the MCI that accelerated the planned economy in conjunction with SCAP's New Dealers.[138] Yoshida did not like the MCI's approach and, in cooperation with his close aide, Shirasu Jiro, sought to reduce its influence and to make the Japanese economy more liberal. As the first step to implement their scheme, Yoshida appointed Shirasu head of the Board of Trade in December 1948. Then, in February 1949, the Yoshida Administration suddenly announced the combination of the MCI and the Board of Trade to establish a new Ministry of International Trade and Industry (MITI).[139] Shirasu explained to the Press that this new ministry would primarily stress the promotion of exports instead of the present priority production system. Since the JMFA had a strong influence in the Board of Trade, Yoshida tried to make it the most important section so as to subordinate the MITI to the JMFA.[140]

Because the MITI resulted from the amalgamation of two different organizations, it suffered from an internal division between "domestic industries" and "international trade" factions. The former emphasized industrial rationalization and protection while the latter put priority on the promotion of exports. Their conflict, however, was not a fundamental one but just a matter of priorities.[141] With the existence of different but mutually related factions within the same Ministry, Inagaki Heitaro, the first MITI Minister, made an inaugural speech in May 1949 that the MITI would employ the trade-first principles, but it was also indispensable to expand production, rationalize industries, and improve the level of technology.[142] Moreover, since American backup was the strongest power base for the Japanese officials under the occupation, the Dodge-Ikeda-Ichimada Nexus pushed the Dodge Line in tandem with Yoshida's strong support. In December 1949, Prime Minister Yoshida articulated his determination to realize the nine-point program. "It is not too much to ask the people to bear a life of austerity for a while in order to acquire an exporting market and restructure domestic industries."[143] Ikeda agreed without doubt, "Japan must stick to the principle of 'Export First' and pay her utmost efforts to increase exports in spite of various obstacles."[144] Consequently, the MITI could not stand up to the Dodge Line which destroyed a substantial number of small- and medium-sized inefficient industries.

The essence of the Dodge Line was to establish a liberal economic system so as to return Japan back to the world-system, that is, the replacement of the "production-first" strategy for internal recovery by an "export-first" strategy for regional consumption. Robert Fearey recalled that the Dodge Line had a "fundamental purpose–the expansion of Japanese foreign trade to permit the attainment of a self-supporting economy."[145] For this purpose, setting a single exchange rate was the pressing need, which Dodge regarded "as a *sine qua non* for the reestablishment of Japan's foreign trade."[146] In March 1949, he insisted on the necessity of restraining domestic consumption in order to increase exports.[147] In August 1949, Dodge reaffirmed his belief that Japan's "problem is to prepare itself now to engage in this intense world competition on an effective and self-sustaining basis. . . . Fundamentally the Stabilization Program is aimed at ensuring Japan an opportunity to meet this world trade problem."[148] Other requirements surrounded this imperative, including the consolidated balanced budget, austerity measures, stability in Southeast Asia as a reliable supplier of raw materials as well as an export market, and assuring foreign exchange earnings in one way or another.

EXCHANGE RATE, TRADE, AND REGIONALISM

In June 1948, the Young mission recommended, "SCAP be authorized to fix a level at the appropriate time within a range of 270 yen to 330 yen per dollar."[149] Facing the American order to observe the nine-point program, Tokyo recognized the need for a single exchange rate and established the Council for Setting a Single Exchange Rate, in December 1948, chaired by Prime Minister Yoshida. In this Council, different ministries and agencies suggested various rates between 300 and 400 yen to the dollar. After examination and consultation with SCAP, it advised the setting of the rate as soon as possible at 350 yen to the dollar.[150] In February 1949, Ichimada petitioned, "The establishment of a single exchange rate will be the first actual step toward the realization of the objective [of promoting Japanese trade]" because foreign trade would normalize Japanese economic activities.[151] Ichimada asked himself, "Why could we not set a single foreign exchange rate until now?" He replied, "Because, in a word, it is the result of our current price system that is extremely unbalanced from the international economic perspective . . . in order to set and maintain a single foreign exchange rate, it is indispensable to halt inflation or stabilize economy."[152]

Dodge asserted, "the primary objective must be the accomplishment of a rate which will stimulate exports without unduly penalizing imports, and that an effective economic stabilization is closely related to achieving a sound and satisfactory result."[153] SCAP in the end requested to set the exchange rate at 330 yen to the US dollar with the authority to adjust it within ten percent above or below this rate. The NAC Staff Committee accepted it in principle, but "it strongly recommends that consideration be given to fixing the rate at 360 yen per dollar," ensuring that SCAP would not have any discretionary power to modify the rate and any change required the NAC preapproval.[154] Washington tried to take command of Japanese economic recovery, trying to leave no discretionary power to SCAP. Dodge was reluctant, but he understood that "the pressure for the 360 rate instead of the 330 rate was largely predicated on the need to provide real incentives for maintaining and increasing exports from indigenous resources and in so doing create greater pressure on internal consumption."[155] Under Secretary of the Army Tracy Voorhees conveyed the general consensus in Washington: "State, Federal Reserve and Commerce, with concurrence Martin of Treasury, and with no opposition from any source except Army, strongly favored action approving your establishing an initial rate of 330 but strongly recommending consideration of 360 . . . ."[156] Even if Dodge regarded the rate of 360 yen to the dollar as being lower than justified, he followed the NAC's strong recommendation, finally setting the single foreign exchange rate at 360 yen to the dollar.[157] According to Ikeda, "setting the single exchange rate at 360 yen to the dollar is the first step for Japan's economy to return to normalcy. It was an epoch-making step."[158]

Trade was Japan's lifeblood. The CIA assumed, "Japan's existence as a modern nation depends on its foreign trade. . . . Japan must 'export or die.'"[159] The State Department also recognized "the crucial importance of a revival of Japan's external trade as the key to the attainment of such a self-supporting economy. . . ."[160] Sherwood Fine reported, "Japan, more than any other major nation in the world . . . is dependent upon a healthy and flourishing foreign trade."[161] Dean Acheson articulated, "[The] crux of the Japanese economic recovery problem lies in a revival of its foreign trade. . . . Trade indeed is the life blood of Japan and its rapid revival on a large scale."[162] Although Dodge expected that a significant export increase would compensate for the loss of domestic demand, the failure of export expansion worsened the Japanese economic conditions.[163] The austerity program could not bear fruit because of the unexpected worldwide depression in 1949. Facing the economic deterioration, the ESS considered it imperative to provide concrete economic benefits for getting democracy firmly rooted in Japan. "The Supreme Commander has created in the minds of Japanese people an awareness of the real advantages of democracy. Inability to enjoy such advantages will create the great dissatisfaction which will harbor, indeed foster, communism and fascism."[164] Dodge predicted, "To balance off its trade on a self-sustaining basis, Japan will need to export about six times as much as it did in 1948. . . ."[165] Halting inflation and setting the single exchange rate constituted necessary conditions for Japanese economic recovery, but Washington also had to provide sufficient conditions: a close regional economic linkage in Asia for Japan to obtain necessary raw materials, food stuff, and market.

In order to incorporate Japan in the Asia-Pacific regional economy, Washington sought to establish the "Great Crescent"–a Japan-led economic and American-led military zone that would stretch from Japan across Asia all the way to the Persian Gulf. The Great Crescent, originally the metaphor of Dean Acheson, would secure a broad geometric logic to sustain America's power. Bruce Cumings articulated that the Crescent "would link together nations threatened by socialist state-controlled economies, make Japan self-supporting, weave sinews of economic interdependence between Japan and the United States, and help draw down from the European colonies by getting a Japanese and U.S. foot in the door of the pound and franc blocs in Asia."[166] As a regional economic zone, it resembled the Greater East Asia Co-Prosperity Sphere, and was in fact larger, but it would be charged by American political might rather than Japanese cultural superiority.

The Research and Statistics Division of the ESS (RSD) argued that there was "natural complementarity between the economies of Japan–exporting chiefly higher fabricated good–and other less industrialized areas which can supply Japan with food and raw materials while themselves developing a manufacturing base in textiles and other light industries."[167] William Sebald, Acting Political Advisor to SCAP, reported to the Secretary of State that SCAP would "focus upon eventual integration of the economy of Japan with the economies of Asia and the Far East. . . ."[168] SCAP officials recognized that Japan's economic rehabilitation needed the cooperation of Asian countries. "For Japan, economic recovery depends primarily on the importation of fifteen or twenty raw materials essential to supply its industrial production. . . . Japan's natural sources of raw materials are principally in the Far East."[169] Charles H. Boehringer, SCAP's chief economic adviser, wrote a memo: "Self-support cannot be attained either in a Far East economic vacuum or by integration of Japan's economy with that of the United States. . . . Japan perforce must look to other nearby Asian areas for foodstuffs and raw materials, for which she is prepared to export capital and consumer goods."[170] The ESS report of November 1948 claimed that since "trade indeed is the life blood of Japan and its rapid revival on a large scale . . . the urgency for the most rapid possible reentrance of Japan into world markets, particularly in the Far East, on a much larger scale cannot be over-emphasized." Because Japanese and other Asian economies were complementary, "Japan must re-establish close relations with the natural market areas in Asia, providing them with the capital equipment and consumer goods which they actively demand and drawing from them to the limits of available supplies the industrial raw materials and foodstuffs which they can offer."[171]

The State Department also underscored the importance of the Asian regional linkage. Emphasizing the regional economic linkage, R. W. Barnett of the State Department added that one of "the keys to most effective revival of Japanese productivity . . . [is] intelligent and responsible cooperation with other Far Eastern countries with which Japan's trade inter-relationships must develop."[172] John Davies of the PPS claimed that the "central American objective in this respect is taken to be a stable Japan, integrated into the Pacific economy, friendly to the U.S. and, in case of need, a ready and dependable Ally of the U.S."[173] In July 1947, SWNCC 381 proposed by the State Department considered it "essential to secure the support of the other Far Eastern countries for U.S. plans designed to promote the economic recovery of Japan." J. H. Hilldring, Assistant Secretary of State, advised the War Department that SWNCC 381 was "of the utmost importance and that it should be treated as a matter of the highest priority within the United States Government."[174] John Allison, the Chief of the Division of Northeast Asian Affairs, argued that Japanese economic revival would require an "all-embracing program looking toward the restoration not on Japan's economy alone, but of the economy of the whole Far Eastern area."[175] Because Dodge believed that Japan's economic dependence on the United States was not "the historical pattern of Japanese foreign trade," it was necessary to shift Japan's major trading partners to countries in non-dollar areas.[176] Close linkage between Japan and Southeast Asia indicated that there should exist a more effective division of labor: Southeast Asia would be a cheap supplier of raw materials and foodstuffs while Japan would be a great workshop in Asia.

Poor quality and high cost of the Japanese products prevented most

Japanese industries from competing in the world market. Japan's future seemed to lie primarily in regional economic development since the Japanese and other Asian economies had complementary relations and their geographical proximity kept the shipping costs lower.[177] The State Department predicted: "Dollar markets for Japanese goods, despite our efforts to expand these markets, are likely to be limited. Therefore it is our policy to encourage the expansion of Japan's trade with the Far East and other non-dollar areas where a reasonable basis for such expansion exists."[178] The CIA claimed that for "social as well as economic reasons it is improbable that an industrial power equivalent to that of Europe could be created in East Asia in the next ten years." Japan was only a regional power. "Japan, indeed, came close to the creation of a power complex which, while not equal to that of Europe, might have maintained regional supremacy by reason of its remoteness from other centers of power."[179] Consequently, it believed that there was "little that Japan can export to countries other than the Far East. . . . "[180]

Edwin Martin, Chief of the Division of Japanese and Korean Economic Affairs, expected "a substantial Japanese contribution to the economic recovery of the Far East."[181] R. W. Barnett of the State Department believed that "a productive Japan contributes to the wealth of Asia in the short run and can, in the long run, contribute to economic stability in the Far East as a whole."[182] The State-Army-Navy-Air Coordinating Committee (SANACC) clearly articulated the regionalism concept in February 1948, "Japanese self-support [was] an important feature of Far Eastern revival. . . . It would also have the advantage of helping to bring about that increased Far Eastern productivity which is so necessary to the achievement and maintenance by Japan of a genuinely self-supporting status."[183]

The Johnston mission claimed, "Japan's industrial products are needed throughout the Far East, whose countries also need Japan as a market for their potential exportable production—their tin, rubber, copra, wool, cotton, iron ore, bauxite, sugar and rice."[184] Sebald argued that the "rehabilitation of the Far East" take place "by accelerating a return to normalcy of an important nation in this area, so that mutually satisfactory and beneficial exchange of goods between all Pacific-area countries can be increased."[185] In October 1948, Joseph Dodge articulated the importance of regionalism: "So indispensably is Japanese recovery linked with the whole problem of Far Eastern recovery, however, that in final analysis success of the recovery program in Japan can find a firm and sound basis only in general recovery throughout the entire Far East."[186] Consequently, he contended, "The development of our future Far Eastern policy will require the use of Japan as a springboard and source of supply for the extension of further aid to the Far Eastern areas."[187] In November 1948, Draper explained, in the simplest terms, the concept of Far Eastern regionalism to the Far Eastern Session of National Foreign Trade Council: "The products which Japan could produce, given the raw materials, are needed throughout the Far East. Furthermore, the Far East needs Japan as a market for its tin, wool, iron ore, copper, copra and rice."[188] Philip Jessup, Ambassador-at-Large, advised Dean Acheson that Japan had to "increase its influence in Asia through the expansion of its trade" and promoted Japanese trade to "enable Japan to contribute effectively to the economic progress of the [Far Eastern] area as a whole."[189] The Army Department regarded Japan as the linchpin of Asian development, persisting, "Any program for economic rehabilitation in the Far East should attempt to ensure most favored nation treatment for Japan and should stress aid to Japan as the most expeditious method of providing the manufactured goods requisite for rehabilitation of the Asiatic economy."[190] SCAP also suggested that because of this "complementary economic relationship," the United States would be able to use Japan "as a major factor in assisting overall Asiatic rehabilitation."[191]

The Japanese government also had substantial interest in expanding trade. Yoshida recalled, "The Japanese economy must return to international economy as swiftly as possible. Unless Japanese economy is tested by the rigors of international competition, it cannot be back on its own feet."[192] The JMFA, analyzing regional economic development in East Asia, indicated that Japan's economic distress would "hamper the economic recovery of other regions in East Asia. . . . It would be most desirable, therefore, not to hold Japanese economic development in check but to promote vigorously the industrialization of Asia as a whole, including Japan."[193] According to the ESB, "Japan and East Asia . . . have the relations with each other of strong interdependences economically."[194] It, however, analyzed: "East Asian countries, our primary export market, have made slow progress in economic recovery; consequently, the purchasing power in East Asia is quite limited."[195] In May 1948, the ESB claimed that unless "export to East Asia increases, we cannot expand the whole export business." Consequently, "it is essential to establish political stability and to increase purchasing power in this region through rapid economic recovery." It predicted that in the "course of the industrialization of Japan, where shortage of natural sources is acute, the emphasis should be gradually shifted to the mechinical [sic] industry and chemical industry." As for its primary export markets, Japan "should target East Asian region as our main target."[196] Ichimada Naoto, Governor of the Bank of Japan, trying to induce US commitment to stabilize Asia and an injection of dollars into that region, recommended, "The political as well as economic situations of most of the Far Eastern countries, the principal customers of Japanese goods both in the prewar and post-war days, have been left unstabilized . . . these countries lack sufficient dollar funds."[197]

In March 1949, the Bank of Japan and the Japanese Ministry of Commerce and Industry strongly requested that the United States establish a large regional economic aid program similar to the Marshall Plan for Europe.[198] Ichimada pleaded to John Foster Dulles, US representative for the Japanese peace treaty, that the United States "extend to the Far East as effective a support as she has been extending to Europe."[199] In May 1949, the ERPC highlighted the fact that "East Asia and Japan have an interdependent relationship . . . In other words, Japan's economic recovery will contribute to East Asian prosperity, and restoration of East Asia will lead to Japan's recovery." The ERPC made an explicit request such as "extension of the Marshall Plan to Asia in order to increase purchasing power in East Asia, promotion of a multilateral business settlement agreement, the right for Japanese companies to do business abroad, early conclusion of a peace treaty, and economic aid until Japan becomes self-supporting."[200] The ESB solicited a Marshall Plan for Asia for the amount of 800 million dollars.[201] In December 1949, Tokyo submitted a secret petition on economic regionalism to Washington, pleading that in order to build a democratic and peace-loving country, it was absolutely indispensable to secure a reasonable standard of living for the Japanese. It requested that America continue its generous aid in the post-occupation era, because "assisting the development of trade between us [Japan and Southeast Asia] will not only facilitate Japanese economic recovery, but also increase the development of the Southeast Asian economy and improve the standard of living of millions of people."[202] The Ministry of Finance officials emphasized economic interdependence between Japan and Southeast Asia, insisting that Southeast Asian markets be indispensable for importing raw materials and for exporting heavy-industrial goods such as machinery and chemical goods.[203]

TOWARD POLITICAL STABILITY IN SOUTHEAST ASIA

Establishing a regional economic linkage, however, was a difficult task. Realizing the regionalism concept required political stability in Asia. In September 1947, Sebald pointed out that the primary problem that Japan faced was "the restriction of economic activities resulting from the unstable political situation in various countries of the Far East which, rich in natural resources but poor in industry, would naturally be expected to complement Japan's economy by mutually beneficial trade."[204] Dr. P. S. Lokanathan, Executive Secretary of the Economic Commission for Asia and the Far East (ECAFE), articulated that political stability in Japan as well as in other Asian countries was of "vital importance to economic recovery."[205] Other SCAP officials were also greatly concerned that the "political unrest and economic disorganization of the Far East is a major obstacle to economic recovery in Japan.

... Production, moreover, will not be of much use unless outside markets exist and these again depend upon restoration of reasonable stability in the Far Eastern countries." They persisted that political stability in Asia was "an urgent prerequisite to recovery in Japan."[206] In December 1947, John Allison argued, "[The] cooperation of these Southeast Asian nations may become absolutely essential if Japan is to be kept from falling into Soviet arms . . . ." Max Bishop, Chief of the Division of Northeast Asian Affairs, warned that: "Faced with an overriding necessity to trade, Japan's international alignment must in the last analysis be determined by economic considerations where the facts are not in our favor."[207] Dodge stated, "The outlook for the expansion of future Japanese trade appears to depend on the end of political disturbances in Asia. . . ." He asserted that Japan's overseas economic expansion would require "political stabilization and recovery of the normal Japanese trading areas in the East."[208]

Each country, in the American scheme, was to play a designated role in order to obtain the most efficient economic linkage. The United States feared that Southeast Asian countries would reject this rational logic but pursue their own nationalistic economic development goals. MacArthur blamed Asian countries for their uncooperative attitudes.[209] Washington had to overcome Asian nationalism in order to realize its regionalism concept because Japan's recovery would not be "reached until more settled conditions permit a resumption of trade with Asiatic areas, and to the extent that such conditions are delayed, recovery in Japan will be postponed." [210]

By 1949, Washington focused its attention on bringing political stability to Southeast Asia, namely Indochina, Burma, Thailand, British Malaya, and Indonesia as a primary target area for Japanese economic recovery.[211] The NSC assumed that powerful leadership would bring stability to Southeast Asia. "If SEA [Southeast Asian] countries are to attain stability, they must for the foreseeable future be governed along authoritarian lines, whether benevolently or otherwise."[212] Emphasizing the capability of the Soviet expansion in Asia, American leaders considered the United States as "the only nation which offers a major check to the influence of the USSR."[213] The NSC tried to use US economic leverage "to promote, where possible, economic conditions that will contribute to political stability in friendly countries of Asia. . . ."[214]

One of the major problems was the expansion of communist influence in Asia. The CIA feared that the Soviet domination of "Japan's industrial machine would be more valuable to the USSR than to the US . . . because the USSR will be in effective control of the area (chiefly northern China, Manchuria and Korea) whose natural resources Japanese industry can utilize more effectively." Since Japan was "the key to the development of a self-sufficient war-making complex in the Far East . . . long-range US security interests dictate the denial of Japan's capacity, both economic and military, to USSR exploitation."[215] Under Secretary of the Army Tracy Voorhees insisted that Japan's economic recovery "depends upon keeping communism out of Southeast Asia, promoting economic recovery there . . . as the principal trading areas for Japan."[216] Both Departments of State and Defense endorsed Voorhees recommendation on Japan-Southeast Asian relations: "Continuing, or even maintaining, Japan's economic recovery depends upon keeping communism out of Southeast Asia, promoting economic recovery there and in further developing those countries."[217] According to the CIA, the Soviet Union, in cooperation with the People's Republic of China (PRC), regarded Southeast Asia a major target.[218] NSC 64 concluded that since Indochina was "a key area of Southeast Asia and . . . under immediate threat," it advised, "A decision to contain communist expansion at the border of Indochina [which] must be considered as a part of wider study to prevent communist aggression into other parts of Southeast Asia."[219] R. W. E. Reid, Dodge's right-hand man, warned of "the devastating effect on Japan of the loss of South and East Asia to a hostile power." He argued that not only was "Southeast Asia the principal area with which Japan must increase its trade if it is to become self-supporting in the future, but it is also the principal area outside the U.S. with which Japan must trade even to hold its present economic gains."[220] In April 1950, the JCS requested "long-term measures to provide for Japan and the other offshore islands a secure source of food and other strategic materials from the noncommunist areas held in the Far East."[221]

In February 1950, Voorhees argued that without a close economic linkage to other Asian economies, Japan's economy would have to depend on US assistance, which would be "heavy drain on the U.S. taxpayers."[222] He and Reid suggested a plan to give Southeast Asian countries credit to purchase Japanese goods.[223] Asia suffered from a serious dollar-gap problem; that is, Asian countries that had substantial demand for Japanese goods lacked sufficient foreign exchange to pay for them. Despite their large demands, they lacked the necessary capital to satisfy their needs, which was referred to as the "Dollar Gap." Doherty, a State Department officer, explained, "The factor limiting Japan's exports is the inability of countries desiring goods from Japan to pay for them either with dollars, sterling or their own goods."[224] Understanding the significance of the regionalism concept, Harlan Cleveland, a State Department officer, recommended "the coordination of U.S. activity in the Far East." He sought to use Japan as a procurement center in Asia.[225] In April 1950, Reid advised Voorhees "to assist certain of the countries of Southeast Asia by giving them a credit in Japan."[226] Voorhees sent Robert West, his assistant in the War Department, and Stanley Andrews from the Agriculture Department, on an 8-week trip to Southeast Asia in January 1950. They articulated the importance of Asian regionalism in which "Japan would serve as the chief supplier of manufacturers; other recipients as the chief suppliers of foodstuffs and raw materials . . . Thus, the fact that for the time being dollars provided the other countries might naturally flow into Japan. . . ." They also recommended that Southeast Asia had to gain political and military stability in order to increase its primary production.[227]

Meanwhile, Japan became restless. According to ESS analysis, "Japan has entered a deflationary economic crisis threatening Japan's progress toward economic recovery and self-sufficiency." It blamed the Dodge Line. "The crisis has developed as a result of policies formulated entirely in terms of 'balanced' budgets, debt retirement, note issues, and other purely fiscal and monetary concepts."[228] The Japan Association of Corporate Executives (*Keizai Doyukai*) continuously complained about the excessiveness of the Dodge Line and pressured the government to relax the fiscal policy.[229] Marquat warned Dodge, "The Japanese have tried every possible method of revoking their commitment on the 9-point stabilization program and the JFY 1950-51 budget."[230] The OIR found increasing resistance to SCAP "primarily stemming from opposition to the 'Dodge Line' economic stabilization policy . . . [in] such major segments of Japanese society as organized labor, agricultural groups, the white collar class, and the business community as reflected in press criticisms and other expressions and evidences of antagonism."[231] The Dodge Line constituted a critical turning point in the US occupation of Japan. It linked Japan to the world-system and turned the controlled economy into a freer market economy in Japan. The outcome of the Dodge Line, however, depended on the development of regional economic linkage in Asia.

Even though Southeast Asia was of only peripheral significance, the United States, as a hegemonic power, would have to assume responsibility in stabilizing this area because of its importance for the free world. According to the State Department document prepared for the NSC, "SEA [Southeast Asia] possesses in itself no important potential . . . it is at best of secondary strategic significance." This region, however, was "important to the free world as a source of raw materials . . . and as a crossroads in east-west and north-south global communications."[232] It added, "The United States should carefully avoid assuming responsibility for the economic welfare and development of that continent."[233] This was, however, difficult to accomplish. It was a kind of chain reaction: Every step the United States made compelled it to make another step, and this process continued. The United States tried to stabilize the Japanese economy which forced it to establish a close linkage among Asian economies. For this purpose, however, Washington would have to bring political stability to Asia. As the United States became involved in achieving political stability in Asia, it was gradually dragged deeper and deeper into Asian affairs.

CHAPTER FOUR

JAPAN'S SECURITY

JAPAN'S SEARCH FOR SECURITY

In August 1946, John Davies, the First Secretary of the US Embassy in the Soviet Union, claimed, "Current Soviet policy toward Japan is designed to disrupt to the greatest possible degree the development of a healthy Japan oriented toward the United States." He argued, "It is worse than idle, it is a delusion, to assume that Japan can be reconstructed as a neutral, self-sufficient nation, enjoying friendly relations with both the United States and Soviet Union. The American and Soviet frontiers meet in the Japan Sea."[1] John Emmerson, the Assistant Chief of the Division of Japanese Affairs, foresaw that Japan's future course would be "one of two political alternatives: domination by the United States or capture by the Soviet Union."[2] The hawkish War Department regarded Japan as "the battleground on which is being fought the war of capitalistic democracy against Communism." Since the United States was "committed to wage this war to a successful conclusion," its failure would "forever admit her loss of prestige in the East."[3] The CIA argued that "Japan's defeat in World War II has created a vacuum of power in the Far East where the extension of Soviet influence and US strategic interests have been brought into direct conflict."[4] Joseph Dodge considered Japan as an "important border area in the world-wide clash between Communism and Democracy."[5]

The War Department argued that from "the economic and security points of view, Japan's friendship must be maintained."[6] John Stuart, US ambassador to China, expected that Japan could "be counted on to align herself against

Communism in any clash of ideologies in the Far East."[7] Since complete demilitarization and Article Nine made Japan defenseless, Washington had to provide Japan's security even after the termination of the Allied occupation. According to SCAP officials, the basic implicit assumption of Article Nine was that Japan would rely on the United Nations for its security.[8] From Moscow, John Davis warned: "[If] we withdraw from Japan without having assured ourselves of a favored position there, Japan may in all probability sooner or later be captured by the Soviet Union."[9] George Kennan warned, "[If] economic distress and insecurity prevail in Japan, this will provide greatly added incentive and assistance to communist efforts."[10] He also stated, "There can be no question but that a Japan in unfriendly hands would be dangerously detrimental to our own security."[11] The CIA reported, "As an ally of the USSR, or as part of a large anti-US coalition could Japan become once again dangerous" because "Japan . . . is the key to the development of a self-sufficient war-making complex in the Far East." Consequently, the CIA concluded, "Long-range US security interests dictate the denial of Japan's capacity, both economic and military, to USSR exploitation."[12] Because the emergence of the Cold War enhanced Japan's strategic value, Washington had to make a major commitment to increasing the country's strength.

In preserving security, Japan's own rearmament program was one possible measure despite the existence of Article Nine. In fact, there existed pro-rearmament elements in Japan, SCAP, and Washington. When the Japanese House of Representatives modified the war-renouncing Article Nine to allow the use of forces for self-defense, Colonel Charles Kades of the Government Section acquiesced in the amendment because he regarded it more practical.[13] Charles Willoughby, Chief of SCAP intelligence division (G2), and Lieutenant General Robert Eichelberger, Eighth Army commander, were both earnest advocates of Japanese rearmament.[14] Eichelberger began promoting rearmament in early 1949, with this appraisal of the Japanese soldier: "Dollar for dollar there is no cheaper fighting man in the world than the Japanese. He is already a veteran. His food is simple. His uniform can be manufactured in Japan. . . .This man, if armed, could defend his country from internal uprisings or in the last analysis his country from invasion. . . . Japanese soldiers would be a commander's dream."[15]

General Omar Bradley, Chairman of the JCS, claimed that the United States should not reduce its occupation forces unless Japan built either a constabulary or a strong police force, and the War Department encouraged Japan to establish a small defensive force.[16] Kennan asserted, "Either we must not have the [peace] treaty at all and retain allied troops in Japan or we must permit Japan to re-arm to the extent that it would no longer constitute an open invitation to military aggression."[17] The JCS considered it "essential . . .

that Japan be denied to the Soviets and that Japan maintain her orientation toward the Western Powers . . . [Consequently] Japan's capacity for self-defense must be developed."[18] In concurrence with the JCS, the Defense Department argued that Japanese rearmament "would also be consistent with the overall strategy of the United States of concentrating its power in Europe and maintaining minimum strength in the Far East."[19] The Joint Strategic Survey Committee (JSSC) recommended that a peace treaty should not limit "the strength and composition of armed forces" in Japan, calling for "the establishment of a Japanese constabulary and a Coast Guard."[20]

In April 1948, the Army recommended that Japan amend Article Nine and organize small and lightly armed defense forces of around 200,000 to 300,000 men.[21] In September 1948, Eichelberger suggested to Secretary of State George Marshall that the United States should conclude a bilateral security treaty with Japan, allowing 200,000 army troops, a medium-size navy with small aircraft carriers, and air force consisting of at least 100 airplanes.[22] In November 1948, the Defense Department concluded that Japanese rearmament would be necessary to reduce the occupation forces without compromising US security in the Pacific.[23]

On the other hand, there were anti-rearmament forces in the United States. John Emmerson, Assistant Chief of the Division of Japanese Affairs, regarded Japanese rearmament "contradictory to our enunciated policy . . . [which was] the complete destruction of Japan's military potential. . . ." He recommended that the US "acts in Japan should not be conditioned by a fear of communism so strong that we lean toward the very elements we have set out to destroy."[24] Charles Saltzman, the Assistant Secretary of State for Occupied Areas, argued, "Remilitarization of Japan would be contrary to our most solemn international commitments and basic principles of SCAP policy, and would be impractical from the military-economic point of view. . . ."[25] W. W. Butterworth and John Howard, State Department officials, considered the Defense Department argument "diametrically opposite" to the JCS note in NSC 49 that "there should be prior assurance of Japan's economic, psychological, and political stability, and of her democracy and western orientation." They insisted that diverting US aid and resources to Japan's rearmament would deteriorate economic and political stability in Japan, which might, in turn, alter its pro-Western orientation.[26] In March 1948, General MacArthur assumed that there was little chance of the Soviet invasion of Japan and that the US bases in the Ryukyu Islands would be sufficient to protect the country. Because demilitarization was so successful, he claimed, "From a physical and material standpoint, Japan is utterly incapable of rearming herself for modern war within the 25-year period."[27] In December 1948, SCAP recommended to JCS: "Complete and guaranteed neutrality is the ideal post-treaty status for Japan. . . . A peace treaty for Japan cannot possibly be consummated in the foreseeable future upon any basis other than complete disarmament and neutrality."[28] SCAP warned that the Japanese economy could not bear a military burden: "Establishment of any Japanese armed forces for other than police . . . would jeopardize the attainment of economic stability for Japan."[29] In December 1948, Major General Paul J. Mueller, MacArthur's Chief of Staff, warned the JCS that Japanese rearmament would lead Tokyo to conclude a military alliance with Washington, which in turn would deteriorate their relationship with the Soviet Union and general conditions in Asia, and as a result, the United States would have to increase its armed forces in the Far East. Consequently, except in an emergency, Japanese rearmament was undesirable.[30]

The United States also had those who favored Japanese rearmament, but with reservations. Harry F. Kern advocated that the Japanese "should be permitted a well-armed and well-trained constabulary of at least 150,000 men with a system of control and command such that it could be entrusted with guarding tunnels, bridges and similar installations." He had strong reservations, however, about an independent Japanese army: "Only as a last resort should Japan be permitted otherwise to revive its armed forces, even under a most rigid American supervision."[31] The CIA contended, "[The] reluctance of former enemies to permit a Japanese military renascence will probably preclude Japan's complete defensive self-sufficiency for at least the next twenty years."[32] Secretary of the Army Kenneth Royall posited, "Solely from the military viewpoint, the establishment of Japanese armed forces is desirable. . . . [because] . . . The critical shortage of manpower in our own armed forces makes it mandatory that we employ only minimum forces in the Far East." He, however, feared that "the establishment of even limited Japanese armed forces . . . is not practicable and advisable at this time, because . . . Japan's deficient economy cannot now support a program of limited military armament without additional and prolonged outside assistance."[33] Supporting Royall's recommendation, the JCS advised Secretary of Defense James Forrestal in March 1949 that it was questionable to allow limited Japanese rearmament in the near future.[34] It is sometimes confusing whether observers were for or against the revival of Japanese army because of the different concepts of "rearmament" and "threat." For example, Kern did not regard the constabulary of 150,000 men as armed forces, and Royall did not consider the Japanese army of 200,000 to 300,000 as a threat to neighboring countries.[35]

Because Washington officials could not reach a consensus on the necessity of Japanese full rearmament, NSC 13/3 of May 1949 only planned to establish limited Japanese armed forces.[36] In July 1949, Cloyce Huston, SCAP's political adviser, reported MacArthur's view: "It might be possible to exact a pledge from all the nations concerned, including Soviet Russia, to respect the neutrality of an unarmed Japan." Houston doubted if the United States could rely on the Soviet Union to which SCAP replied, "The Soviets might indeed be difficult to deal with, but . . . the Soviet Government always endeavored to keep its plighted word."[37] In November 1949, the Defense Department recommended postponing the decision on the Japanese rearmament issue since Washington officials could not yet reach a consensus.[38]

TOWARD A PEACE TREATY: SECOND ROUND

The United States first called for peace treaty negotiations in July 1947, but it failed because of Washington's half-hearted effort and procedural disagreements among the Allies.[39] The State Department, however, continued to deal with this issue. In 1948, there occurred a series of communist uprisings in Asia including in China, Indonesia, India, and Malaya, which urged the United States to make Japan into a stabilizing force in the Asia-Pacific region to fend off communism.[40] The revival of nationalism and the rise of anti-American movements in Japan because of the long duration of the occupation also inspired Washington to make swift and strenuous efforts to incorporate Japan into the Western bloc.[41] On the other hand, in April 1949, the JCS argued that a peace treaty was premature. General Collins of the Defense Department warned that the withdrawal of the US forces from Japan might precipitate a Soviet entrance into Hokkaido.[42]

In May 1949, President Truman approved NSC 13/3, confirming, "This Government should not press for a treaty of peace at this time."[43] The JCS and the Defense Department on one hand and the State Department on the other had philosophical differences concerning the Japanese peace treaty: The JCS and the Defense Department sought to maintain stability in Asia through force because of their doubts about the Japanese ability to preserve democracy, while the State Department believed that playing on Japanese wishes for independence would be the best way to sustain Japan's post-occupation orientation to the West. General MacArthur asserted, "[The] existing conflict within the United States Government must be bridged to permit early action toward the effectuation of peace." He was rather optimistic as to say that "the relatively small area of disagreement which appears now to exist, providing reason to hope that there is no irreconcilable point of difference."[44] However, the debate still continued.

In June 1949, the JCS contended "from the military point of view, that a peace treaty would, at the present time, be premature since the continuing Soviet policy of aggressive communist expansion makes it essential . . . [to obtain] prior assurance of Japan's economic, psychological, and political stability, and of her democracy and western orientation. . . ."[45] W. W. Butterworth, however, recalled attention to the fact that the occupation "began to approach the point of diminishing returns almost two years ago. . . ." He warned that the Japanese "have become increasingly restive under conditions of indefinitely continued military occupation, and desire for a peace settlement is widespread."[46] The United States had to take initiatives to conclude a peace treaty rather than be pressured to act by Japan or by other friendly nations.[47] In August 1949, Sebald warned Washington that the occupation was "rapidly outliving its political usefulness." Urging Washington to take the initiative for a peace treaty, Sebald argued, "A courageous and strong foreign policy is needed in handling the Japanese situation and that only by grasping the political initiative which is available for the taking, now, can we hope to stabilize a deteriorating and unbalanced situation in Northeast Asia."[48]

Ernest Bevin, the British Foreign Minister, visited Washington in September 1949 to talk with Secretary of State Dean Acheson. The Japanese peace treaty was one of the important topics of discussions. Before this meeting, Acheson announced that he was not sure if the United States would promote peace treaty negotiations without Soviet participation.[49] However, their frank talks encouraged them to conclude a peace treaty even without Soviet consent.[50] John Allison reaffirmed the US intention to proceed with negotiations regardless of Soviet behavior.[51] The State Department persisted, "The only hope for the preservation and advancement of such democracy and western orientation as now exist in Japan lies in the early conclusion of a peace settlement with that country."[52] During the same period of time, there existed a similar thrust from the communist bloc to conclude an immediate treaty with Japan. In October 1949, Butterworth, Director of the Office of Far Eastern Affairs, reported that the US peace treaty proposal to Japan would have to be generous because the Soviet Union and the PRC might appear to offer a better deal for Japan.[53]

Nevertheless, "in view of the long history of Japan as an authoritarian state," the JCS had no intention of terminating the military occupation "at least until such time as the inbred Japanese habit of submission to autocratic authority and the latent frustration of Japanese national ambitions in the last war be completely overcome."[54] In December 1949, Secretary of Defense Louis Johnson believed that it was not desirable to withdraw or to make a drastic reduction of the US armed forces in Japan, and that the Soviet Union and the PRC had to participate in a peace treaty negotiation. In short, he was asking for the impossible.[55] The real intent of the Defense Department and the JCS was to maintain the right to use American bases in Japan as freely as they wished.[56]

Maintenance of US armed forces in Japan after the occupation was a possible measure to bridge the gap between the two Departments. Retention of the US military bases and armed forces, however, was a sensitive issue touching Japan's sovereignty and there were substantial forces opposing this proposal. For the United States, obtaining the base rights after the occupation was a more important issue than the Japanese rearmament program. John Allison, the Director of the Office of Northeast Asian Affairs, asserted: "The possibility and desirability of obtaining American bases in post treaty Japan is extremely questionable and that some other solution to the security problem should be attempted."[57] Butterworth contended, "There was a recent tendency in Japanese opinion away from the granting of military bases to the United States and that this tendency was likely to harden Japanese public opinion."[58] The PPS opposed the stationing of US army after concluding a peace treaty in Japan because it would be a somewhat psychologically damaging event that might invite political instability in Japan.[59]

Japan's voluntary request for the retention of US bases would mute the anti-base factions. Philip C. Jessup, Ambassador-at-Large, argued that if Japan asked the United States to retain US security forces, it would be politically acceptable.[60] Opposing Japan's rearmament, the State Department sought security "through the presence of US forces in Japan on behalf of the signatory powers and at Japan's request. . . ."[61] The JSSC advised obtaining "by an agreement, a free agreement, outside of the Treaty" the right to acquire "bases in Japan." The US armed forces in Japan "should not be materially reduced or changed until there is a marked improvement in the world situation." Of course it would be up to the American subjective judgment to decide whether "there is a marked improvement in the world situation" or not. The retention of the US military bases in Japan was critically important; sharing the State Department's opinion, the JSSC believed that as long as the US forces remained in Japan, "the prohibition against rearmament in the Japanese Constitution may remain in effect."[62] In December 1949, the JCS revealed "the minimum requirements" including exclusive rights to have military forces and bases on any of the Japanese islands.[63] Dean Acheson considered it "essential that there be retained United States forces in Japan." He made it clear that: "No alternative desirable means for Japan's security exists," because the "rearming of Japan for self-defense is not under present circumstances an acceptable alternative."[64] In February 1950, John Howard of the State Department reported to Dean Rusk that "the minimum security requirements . . . [included] U.S. bases and forces on Japan itself" while the maximum demands would be "the rearmament of Japan and the reactivation of Japanese armed forces."[65] Voorhees argued that "almost all Japanese would welcome U.S. forces and that they were concerned first about Japan's security and only secondly about a peace treaty."[66] General Collins of the Department of Defense suggested that the United States should ask the Japanese leaders whether they were willing to grant the right to use military bases and to station US armed forces in Japan after the occupation.[67] Johnson agreed "to find a way in which to keep United States forces in Japan."[68]

General MacArthur was at first opposed to maintaining military bases in Japan after the occupation, but he gradually compromised with the military opinion in Washington. In November 1949, the general thought a US-Japan treaty based on free will would provide the United States with military bases in Japan, but he could not make a firm decision.[69] Even though he believed that "unarmed neutrality, guaranteed by the great Powers, is from every point of view Japan's most desirable course," he recognized, under the intensified Cold War situation, that "a Soviet guarantee of Japanese neutrality could not now be relied upon, and that this will remain the case until the Soviets undergo a basic change of heart." MacArthur's basic idea was "to retain naval and air bases in Japan after a treaty for the primary purpose of making it unmistakably clear to the USSR that aggression against Japan will mean all-out war with the United States."[70] In December 1949, MacArthur suggested that American forces of 30,000 to 35,000 men should be stationed in Japan for five years.[71] In April 1950, SCAP explained to Sebald, "95% of the Japanese people are opposed to American bases in Japan and that unless a wholehearted request for American troops and bases is made by the Japanese, the entire proposition should be abandoned."[72] He had to find a way of giving the United States the right to keep the bases while being careful not to contradict his previous positions.

In June 1950, Secretary of Defense Johnson with Omar Bradley, Chairman of the JCS, and then Dulles visited Japan separately in order to assess Japanese conditions and exchange opinions with General MacArthur. On 23 June 1950, before the outbreak of the Korean War, MacArthur made a drastic proposal: "The entire area of Japan must be regarded as a potential base for defensive maneuver with unrestricted freedom reserved to the United States. . . ." He justified his change of attitude by the economic benefits which the bases would generate, arguing that "the protecting power should maintain security forces on Japanese soil on a fully 'pay as you go' basis . . . [because the Japanese people] would welcome the contribution to their national economy reflected from a 'pay as you go' basis which under present conditions would mean approximately $300,000,000 annually."[73] He changed his opinion probably because he sensed that without an appropriate security arrangement, Washington would not terminate the occupation for the foreseeable future.[74]

On his return to Washington, Dulles made a draft proposal on "International Peace and Security" which was "designed to give, in a form as inoffensive as possible to the Japanese, the broad power in the United States to place military forces wherever in Japan the United States may determine to be desirable from the standpoint of maintenance of international peace and security in the Japan area."[75] One week later, Dulles telephoned Johnson and said, "I felt it essential that we should deal politically with such problems as

Japan and Germany while the war was on or otherwise we would find at the end that we had lost both of these vital areas." Johnson must have misread Dulles's draft because he said that it "did not carry out the views of the Joint Chiefs of Staff or General MacArthur." Dulles responded that the draft was based on MacArthur's revised view of 23 June, which "gave the United States the right to maintain in Japan as much force as we wanted, anywhere we wanted, for as long as we wanted, and I did not see very well how the Defense Establishment could want more than that." Johnson was delighted to hear this and said that they could "get together and go places."[76] Among other things, the Departments of State and Defense agreed: "The Treaty shall not become effective until such time as the interest of the United States dictate and in no event until after favorable resolution of the present United States military situation in Korea . . . ." Their common security requirement included that the treaty "must give the United States the right to maintain armed forces in Japan, wherever, for so long, and to such extent as it deems necessary." They submitted their agreed proposal to President Truman in early September 1950.[77]

Japan also considered its security from an early period. In as early as January 1946, the Political Bureau of the JMFA concluded that Japan needed a small self-defense force in order to exist as an independent country.[78] In July 1946, George Atcheson argued that the United Nations would protect Japan after the occupation, to which Tokyo responded that since the organization was incomplete and unreliable, Japan needed to cooperate with a third country, namely the United States, for its defense.[79] In conjunction with MacArthur's statement on a possible peace treaty, the JMFA, in June 1947, expressed its anxiety that "in the current international circumstances, the Japanese Government cannot but feel great anxiety about Japan's security because it has been completely disarmed. From this point of view, how to assure Japan's future security is the most important national issue." JMFA officials rejected the idea of Japan as an eternally neutral country or under the protection of one or more countries. They respected the importance of the United Nations, but "in consideration of Japan's special circumstances, Japan's participation in the United Nations would not be enough for its security."[80]

In April 1946, the Treaty Bureau of the JMFA emphasized the necessity of Japan's positive participation in a regional security arrangement under the United Nations auspices. In May 1946, the PTC proposed that the FEC nations would establish a regional security system to protect Japan from external threats while Japan would build a force of armed police or a constabulary to maintain internal tranquility. Consequently, Japan was willing to establish a regional security mechanism in accordance with Article 51 of the United Nations' Charter.[81]

Tokyo believed that this regional arrangement would assure Japan's security without the retention of foreign bases in Japan. In February 1946, the JMFA considered obtaining national security through the US military presence in former Japanese territories rather than the forces stationed in Japan.[82] In July 1947, the JMFA had a rather optimistic view on issues of the stationing of Allied armed forces. "Japan is completely demilitarized. The Allied Powers possess armed forces that can shift swiftly at any time. . . . [Consequently] The Allied armed forces do not have to be stationed in Japan."[83] In July 1947, Foreign Minister Ashida suggested to SCAP that the United States should station its troops around Japan while Japan would maintain bases at home in case of emergency when the US forces would be able to use them.[84]

On 6 May 1947, Emperor Hirohito stated to MacArthur that: "Since the United States, the Anglo-Saxon representative, needs to take an initiative in ensuring Japan's security, we expect your assistance." MacArthur replied in the affirmative.[85] In September 1947, a memorandum by Suzuki Tadakatsu, Head of the Yokohama Branch office of the War-end Liaison Department, defined the Japanese position: If American-Soviet relations did not improve in the future, Japan would have to entrust its defense to the United States which would undertake to "maintain sufficient military strength on certain strategic points in areas outside of, but adjacent to, Japan." In case of emergency, "the United States, after consultation with the Japanese Government, [would] send her armed forces into Japan and use military bases there." For this purpose, Suzuki insisted, "Military bases be constructed and maintained in Japan as satisfactorily as possible to the American requirements." He was confident that this arrangement would be beneficial for both countries. "Such an agreement, without compromising Japan's independence in peace time, will permit the United States to make full use of the bases in Japan in cases of emergency."[86] In August 1948, following Suzuki's argument, Prime Minister Ashida passed a private memo to Eichelberger: "Judging from international relations since last September, unfortunately the US-Soviet relations did not get better; consequently, it becomes more realistic to maintain Japan's security through a Japan-US special arrangement."[87] The US protection of Japan was necessary, but Ashida expected the bases to be located outside the territory of Japan.

On the other hand, keenly appreciating the Cold War conditions, Prime Minister Yoshida, as a pragmatist, recognized the importance and the necessity of having US bases at home in order to conclude a peace treaty. In March 1947, had already declared that it would be "better to have US protection rather than that of the United Nations (UN). The United States must stay in Japan even after the conclusion of a peace treaty."[88] He considered it the only practical measure to accept stationing of the US armed forces through a Japan-US arrangement. Yoshida also expected that the spread of communism in Asia would facilitate peace treaty negotiations.[89]

Japan's method of preserving its security in the post-occupation era would make a difference between a peace treaty with all the powers and that with the majority powers (excluding the Soviet Union).[90] In case of a peace treaty with the majority powers, they anticipated, Japan would not be able to join the United Nations nor could it depend on the UN for its post-occupation security due to interference of the Soviet Union that held the veto power. In that case, Japan's only realistic choice would be to become a member of the US bloc and to depend on the US forces for Japan's own national security. According to the JMFA's analysis of international conditions in December 1949, China's fall into communism forced Washington to make a thorough reconsideration of its policy toward Asia, and the United States was willing to conclude a unilateral peace treaty with Japan.[91] Since the JMFA officials still hoped to conclude a peace treaty with all the countries, they could not make any firm decision at the end of 1949 except to study various measures for Japan's security.[92] By December 1949, they had only gotten as far as analyzing the various possibilities on Japan's security arrangements after the peace treaty, without recommending any specific policy.[93] On the other hand, in May 1950, Yoshida clearly understood that because of America's great influence in the occupation and the bipolar Cold War structure, it would be impractical to conclude a peace treaty with all the powers at once; concluding a treaty with the United States first, and then with other friendly nations one by one would be Japan's best choice.[94]

In December 1949, the Director of the Treaty Bureau of the JMFA reported that the most controversial issue was whether Japan was to allow the retention of US armed forces within Japan after the occupation.[95] The JMFA officials judged that continuation of the occupation would be worse than the retention of the US forces, but they still preferred to avoid maintaining the US forces within Japan. If Japan had to accept the US forces in its own territory, it would have to limit the area and duration.[96] In May 1949, Prime Minister Yoshida argued that since Japan could not have an army, it was desirable to retain the American occupation forces in Japan even after the signing of a peace treaty.[97] There was a wide gap concerning a peace treaty between the JMFA and Yoshida, a gap which remained until they finally clashed seven months later.[98]

In April 1950, Yoshida said to Cloyce Huston, an American officer, "Japan must rely upon the United States for protection as it will possess no armaments of its own" even though he carefully avoided stating that he would favor having American military bases in Japan after the treaty.[99] Since Japanese security was the stumbling block to the start of any peace treaty negotiations, Yoshida sent Finance Minister Ikeda to the United States in April 1950. Ikeda passed on Yoshida's confidential message that a peace treaty would probably "require the maintenance of U.S. forces to secure the treaty terms and for other purposes, if the U.S. Government hesitates to make these conditions, the Japanese Government will try to find a way to offer them." In conjunction with Article Nine, Ikeda explained Tokyo's conclusion: "Even volunteering the continuance of these bases would not be a violation of the Japanese Constitution." In order to push Washington to action, Ikeda conveyed a rumor that the Soviet Union was willing to offer a peace treaty in which it was ready to return Sakharin and the Kuril Islands to Japan. Trying to stimulate American efforts to preserve their own prestige and induce its involvement in Asia, Ikeda indicated the recent developments which raised credibility problems for the US in Asia such as Secretary of the Army Royall's statement regarding abandoning Japan in February 1949, the American ambivalent attitude toward China throughout 1949, the US decision to exclude Formosa from the US defense perimeter, the rise of communist forces in Indochina, the possibility of abandoning South Korea, and India's uncertain attitude as a sign of the demise of US power and status in Asia.[100] High-ranking officials, including Dean Acheson, W. W. Butterworth, John Magruder, Jonn Foster Dulles, and Douglas MacArthur read this message and Butterworth wrote "significant" on the copy.[101] According to Yoshida, rearmament was impracticable and ineffective because no country was able to match the military forces of the United States. He tried to induce the United States to commit itself to Asian security, recognizing that the Japan-US security treaty was the only way to defend Japan.[102]

Shirasu Jiro, Yoshida's confidante, who accompanied Ikeda to Washington, clearly rejected neutrality and rearmament. As for the retention of the US forces and bases, he vaguely considered it difficult for Japan as a sovereign nation to maintain the US bases.[103] Talking with Shirasu, Butterworth perceived that there was "growing popular opposition in Japan to the retention of post-treaty U.S. bases."[104] Ikeda said one thing, and Shirasu said another. Using both an official channel (Ikeda) and an unofficial one (Shirasu), Prime Minister Yoshida tried to confuse Washington officials, to keep them guessing about his real intentions, and to raise the price of the base rights.

In order to increase his bargaining power to deal with Dulles and avoid a heated discussion on post-occupation security issues, Yoshida claimed, contrary to his true intention, in July 1950, at the Foreign Affairs Committee of the House of Councilors: "I am against leasing military bases to any foreign country . . . Allied powers do not intend to present such a demand, as it is the desire of the Allied powers to keep Japan out of war." On 1 August, William Sebald met with Ohta Ichiro, the Vice Minister of Foreign Affairs, to find out Yoshida's intention. Ohta replied that Japan would rely upon UN protection as in the case of the Republic of Korea, and Prime Minister Yoshida was opposed to any foreign troops remaining in Japan upon the conclusion of a peace treaty.[105] One week later, Sebald had another meeting with Ohta to scrutinize Japan's position on security. According to Ohta, since this was a politically sensitive issue, "no Japanese statesman could at this time publicly declare that he is in favor of granting bases or maintaining US troops in Japan subsequent to peace treaty." Ohta suggested that Tokyo's attitude was still flexible to adjust itself to future development, arguing, "If [the] treaty failed [to] contain specific and satisfactory provisions regarding Japan's security, there is every possibility that Japanese Government would ask *US and UN* to guarantee Japan's security, a request which might imply maintaining troops in Japan if necessary to carry out such guarantee"[106] (emphasis added). Ohta's explanation reflected JMFA's basic position that the US forces could be stationed in Japan only under the auspices of the United Nations in order to satisfy Japanese national sentiment. Moreover, Ohta believed that Japan's position was faithful to General MacArthur's strategic concept that "the maintenance of bases and troops in Japan proper is unnecessary so long as Okinawa and other islands would remain under the control of the United States." He did not have the slightest idea of MacArthur's volte-face, as demonstrated clearly in his memorandum of 23 June. Sebald advised Ohta, "In the light of the Korean situation, it might be possible that General MacArthur has changed his mind in this regard. . . ."[107] Privately, however, Yoshida informed Sir Alvary Gascoigne, the head of the British Liaison Mission in Japan, that he intended to permit US troops to be stationed in Japan for its security after the occupation.[108]

In his meeting with Dulles on 22 June 1950, Yoshida avoided any definite commitment to implementing rearmament and providing military bases, which irritated Dulles. In the evening, there was an informal meeting which Dulles, Kern, Marquis Matsudaira of the Imperial Household, and other guests attended. Kern suspected that Yoshida opposed the maintenance of US military bases. Dulles expressed his dissatisfaction with Yoshida's vague, idealistic attitude toward Japan's own security. Matsudaira allegedly passed on the contents of this meeting and Dulles's discontent with Yoshida's attitude to the Imperial Household. He wrote a message on behalf of the Emperor and submitted it to Dulles in August 1950, in which the monarch argued, "the recent *wrong debate* concerning the base issue could have been avoided by a voluntary offer from our side" (emphasis added). The "wrong debate" apparently indicated the debate that took place in the Foreign Affairs Committee in July 1950, which supported Ikeda's message in May 1950 to provide Washington with military bases in Japan.[109]

CHINESE FACTORS

China played an important role in Japan's security after the end of the occupation. The Department of State regarded China as an unstable, backward country. "Industrialization requires political stability and a high degree of administrative competence. Neither of these conditions has [been] obtained in China for several generations."[110] In July 1948, although the CIA recognized that the Chinese National Government was "so unstable that its collapse or overthrow could occur at any time," it optimistically expected that the Chinese civil war would eventually end in the formation of a coalition government.[111] In five months, the CIA altered its opinion and predicted that the CCP would win the civil war.[112] Consequently, it concluded, "No solution can be foreseen in China beyond a gradual accommodation with Communist power."[113]

In October 1948, George Kennan did not see any threat from Chinese Communists even if "the Communists controlled it [China] entirely, (and I think [it] is a very dubious possibility that they could) and even if they retained fidelity to Moscow . . . ."[114] His analysis suggested, "What's going on in China is a very deep social change and almost a revolution. . . . I don't think that anybody could possibly stop what's happening in China today."[115] Deploring US idealistic and legalistic policies toward China, Kennan expected that the development in China would help Washington take a more realistic approach. "I would hope that now, as this process completes itself, for the first time we, in this country, will have a realistic and a workable attitude toward things that go on there."[116]

NSC 34/1 of January 1949 recommended a flexible policy toward China: "Make appropriate plans and timely preparations in order to exploit opportunities in China while maintaining flexibility and avoiding irrevocable commitments to any one course of action or to any one faction."[117] Dean Acheson believed that a wait-and-see attitude would be the best policy because "the house appeared to be falling down and there was not much to be done until it had come down."[118] In February 1949, he explained that the United States would "wait until the dust settled."[119] The PPS also pointed out that there was nothing "to gain from political support of any of the remaining anti-communist public figures in China."[120] In February 1949, the NSC clearly showed that the United States "should avoid military and political support of any non-communist regimes in China unless the respective regimes are willing actively to resist communism with or without U.S. aid and, unless further, it is evident that such support would mean the overthrow of, or at least successful resistance to, the Communists."[121] The NSC held a rather watery image of China. "China does not have the industrial potential to make itself in the foreseeable future a major military power. . . . China will be a chaotic and undependable factor on the Far Eastern scene."[122] Consequently, NSC 41 of February 1949 concluded, "China is at such a low level of economic development that it is not likely that a Chinese Communist regime could, within the next generation or more, create an industrial base which, as an adjunct of Soviet power, would represent a security threat to the United States."[123] Because of the chaotic situation in China, Washington had no choice but to employ a flexible posture toward the CCP.

The NSC, however, made it clear that such a flexible policy was not "construed by the Chinese Communists as a soft policy." The Chinese Communists had to make themselves "aware of the potential power of the United States, in collaboration with other western powers and SCAP, to impose severe restrictions on trade if a Chinese Communist regime were to demonstrate its determination to follow policies inimical to United States strategic interests." The NSC was confident of its economic power over Chinese behavior. "The immediate imposition of a system of controls on United States exports to China, although applied initially to effect a minimum of essential security restrictions, would serve to indicate United States ability and intention to deal drastically with China's foreign trade if necessary."[124] Dean Acheson believed that because of economic necessity, the CCP would definitely depend on the West. "The first conflict between communist theory and Chinese environmental realities will probably come concretely to our attention in the economic field–when the Communists, in attempting to carry out their avowed intent to develop China economically, seek trade with the West."[125] Since the Chinese Communists "are certainly going to require economic assistance from the non-Communist world," Kennan considered it "idiotic if it gave the Chinese Communists anything without a completely adequate quid pro quo in abandonment of the Iron Curtain psychology, in abandonment of the attitude of arrogance, contempt toward the West, which those Communists now have."[126] Stewart Alsop, a well-known journalist, agreed, "The Chinese Communists' absolute need for economic relations with the western trading nations gives the West an instrument of policy in China, which, if intelligently used, might be effective."[127] The China Mission of the Economic Cooperation Administration sought to exploit China's economic weakness "to create the greatest possible dependence of the Chinese upon our markets."[128] The CIA also optimistically predicted, "the Communist movement exhibits a variety of internal weaknesses which, if they can be effectively exploited, might eventually lead to the downfall of the regime, or to a modification in its hostility to the West."[129]

NSC 41 of February 1949 implied the NSC officials' optimistic view that US economic power would be the best weapon to drive a wedge between the PRC and the Soviet Union.[130] In reality, however, the Chinese Communists did not have to depend on US economic assistance because of its vast human resources, its relatively early stage of economic development, and because of economic assistance from the Soviet Union. Even though the CIA found serious economic problems in China, it recognized that "the Communist regime in China is not immediately vulnerable in the sense of being deposed or altered, and that, for the next few years, the CCP's Stalinist leadership will continue to control the Party, while Moscow will continue to control the Party leadership."[131] The United States did not consider Communist China as a threat per se and optimistically believed that it could use its economic leverage to channel China's course of development.

Since the emergence of Communist China had a negative impact on other parts of Asia, the United States tried to consolidate the strength of other areas surrounding Communist China. The CIA anticipated that the US security interests in Asia required "the firm maintenance of positions peripheral to the area of collapse and for the steady development of new sources of influence within the area."[132] Kennan argued that since "communist encroachments in Asia have taken place primarily through the use of the political weapons of ideological propaganda and of the vigorous exploitation of native minority groups," the United States would have to resist it "by similar means."[133] The rise of communism in Asia made Washington assume the grave responsibility of bringing economic and political stability to Asia.

Top US officials held the peculiar belief that "Asiatic Peoples are traditionally submissive to power and habituated to authoritarian government and the suppression of the individual."[134] Consequently, the United States had to preserve its image of toughness, power, determination, and prestige. In August 1949, the NSC staff members supposed that Asians "lack historical experience of liberty and personal experience of individualism. . . . They are peculiarly susceptible to seizure of political power by force or assassination and to the concealed aggression of communism." Since successful establishment of the PRC was a great challenge to the expansion of American influence in Asia, NSC staff advocated in October 1949, a hard policy toward the PRC: "Accommodation by the United States to a communist China would greatly weaken our position in Asia and might make impossible a successful stand against communism in the balance of Asia by means short of war."[135]

Because Washington believed that Asians would respect power and strength, any defeat in the competition in Asia would have negative consequences: "The extension of communist authority in China represents a grievous political defeat for us." As a hegemonic power and a self-appointed policeman in Asia, Washington declared, "The United States is the only nation which offers a major check to the influence of the USSR in Asia." Economic development was the principal means to avoid communist domination, but "political stability and military security are essential to economic recovery." This logic led NSC staff to conclude that active movement to provide stability and security would be a prerequisite to fending off communism and to maintain its power, strength, and prestige in Asia.[136]

Because Southeast Asia was a fragile area, NSC 51 of July 1949 expressed the fear that the "Chinese Communist Party (CCP) appears to have played an unusually large role in the external guidance and support of communist movements in Southeast Asia . . . [because] the CCP was experienced and expert in exploiting the two principal communist issues applicable to East Asia – nationalism in colonial countries and agrarian revolt in independent states."[137] Trying to raise American fears, Wellington Koo, Nationalist China's ambassador to the United States, contended, "Not only are the Communist movements in Indo-China and Malaya directed and carried on by Chinese Communist under orders from the headquarters of international Communism, but the clandestine work of smuggling and supplying arms to the Communist organizations in various Asiatic countries is also conducted and controlled by the Chinese agents of the General Staff of world revolution."[138] Dean Acheson was apprehensive about the deterioration of intra-regional trade in the Asia-Pacific region that would "gradually alienate now friendly disposed Japan and make it easy prey to Commie ideologies."[139] The establishment of the PRC in October 1949 combined with the Soviet success in developing an atomic bomb further heightened Washington's anxiety. Asian instability led Washington to hold a domino theory that the Communist success in China "facilitates communist victory in South China. . . . [and] would support the transformation of Burma and Indo-China into communist regimes . . . [and] open the way for the fall of Thailand and the infiltration of Malaya and Indonesia. . . . [and] increase the pressure on and facilitate eventual control of Japan."[140] Kennan perceived that the most "serious immediate consequence of the victory in China seems to me the possible effect in Southeast Asia. . . . what happened in China could not fail to give a fillip to Chinese activities in Southeast Asia and cause deep anxiety in non-Communist circles already jittery now."[141]

The onset of the Cold War and general instability in Asia added to Japan's importance as the only possible stabilizing force in Asia on which Washington could rely. Kennan's realist's view maintained that the Japanese were the "only truly dynamic and energetic people in the Far East."[142] The CIA was convinced that in the Far East, "the global security position . . . [is] definitely less favorable to the U.S." vis-à-vis the USSR. Consequently, it concluded, "[The] re-establishment of Japan as a viable state becomes essential to the maintenance of a minimum US security position in the region."[143] Joseph Dodge explained to NAC that Japan was currently the "focal point of our established Far Eastern interests. . . . it is the sole Asiatic nation in which we have both a major influence and complete control over all of the factors necessary to achieve our objectives." He then recommended that the United States use "Japan as a springboard and source of supply for the extension of further aid to the Far Eastern areas."[144]

The CIA envisioned, however, that the emergence of the CCP ironically provided Japan with bargaining power vis-à-vis the United States, because "the security situation would enable the Japanese to emphasize the value of Japan as a strategic defense against the expansion of Asiatic communism beyond the mainland." The CIA suspected that Japan would ask for more "financial aid, security guarantees, the reconstruction of an industrial potential, and the reorganization of Japanese manpower for defense purposes."[145] Harry Kern agreed, "the Japanese as a whole realize that because of what is happening in China and because of the Cold War in general, they are regaining some bargaining power in their relations with the United States."[146] The NSC anticipated that Japan might use the 'China card': In order to "restore Japanese influence on the continent of Asia and to regain the advantages of China trade, Japan might conclude that an accommodation with Communist-controlled areas in Asia would serve Japanese interests."[147]

There was a strong voice in the United States that trade with China would be indispensable for Japanese economic recovery. In January 1949, the State Department Intelligence warned, "Japan is not likely to achieve a self-supporting economy unless trade with northeast Asia, particularly China and Manchuria, can be restored. . . . Japan's economy cannot possibly be restored to a self-sustaining basis without a considerable volume of trade with China. . . ." The intelligence report expressed fears that US artificial restrictions on Japan-PRC trade would antagonize the Japanese.[148] Dodge put forward an optimistic argument about this trade that "it should be remembered that the Chinese were a very highly commercialized race and it was doubted that even Communist control would keep their commercial requirements from coming to the front."[149] Since Eugene Dooman, a member of the Council on Foreign Relations (CFR), doubted if Japan could accomplish economic recovery without close economic ties to the mainland of East Asia, he recommended that the United States not impose any restrictions on Japan-PRC trade. Everett Case, another CFR member, argued that from a long-term perspective, it would be better to strengthen China economically through its trade with Japan, which would foster forces in opposition to communism.[150]

On the other hand, there existed influential forces against Sino-Japanese trade. Dulles was inclined to support the opinion "that Japan could achieve a viable economy without undue dependence on the Asiatic mainland." Wallace Donham of the CFR warned of the danger of Japan's economic dependence on the PRC.[151] General Marquat drew attention to the fact that in the 1930s, "the North American continent was a source of greater import volume for Japan than any other single regional area." He was pessimistic about the advantage of Japan-PRC trade persisting, "even if Japan reopened unrestricted trade with Communist China, the Red controlled areas could not furnish

Japan's demands." He concluded, "[The] premise that Japan is completely dependent upon Communist controlled sources for economic survival is a myth."[152]

Prime Minister Yoshida, a self-professed expert on China affairs, possessed a definite view on China. He was confident that communism would not prevail in China and that "the CCP would soon turn as nationalistic and anti-foreign as previous Chinese regimes. . . . [because] [G]eography and economic laws will, I believe prevail in the long run over any ideological differences and artificial trade barriers." He emphasized the importance of China's market to Japan. "I don't care whether China is red or green. China is a national market and it has become necessary for Japan to think about markets."[153] In order to pluck the American anti-communist chord, Yoshida suggested that Japan, if allowed to trade with the PRC freely, would penetrate China economically, which would eventually detach the PRC from the Communist bloc.[154] Ikeda Hayato, Finance Minister, asked for the separation of political considerations from Sino-Japanese trade.[155]

Agreeing with Yoshida, Ichimada Naoto, Governor of the Bank of Japan, claimed in March 1950 that the Chinese would not become completely Sovietized because "the Chinese people, having been deeply affected by Confucianism, never embrace dictatorship but value freedom and they are a nation which rather takes the 'middle of the road' way; at the same time they have marked characteristics as international merchants." He pleaded with Robert West, Deputy to Undersecretary of Army, "Trade between China and Japan and other Far Eastern countries is a factor which cannot be ignored for Far Eastern economic rehabilitation."[156] The ESB also requested that the United States loosen the current trade restrictions on the PRC, since trade with China would contribute to the recovery of Asian economy as a whole.[157]

Divided in their opinions concerning Japan-PRC trade, confused foreign policy establishments in Washington tried to straddle the fence. In February 1949, the NSC recommended, "SCAP should encourage trade with China on a quid-pro-quo basis, but should avoid preponderant dependence on Chinese sources for Japan's critical food and raw material requirements."[158] In March 1949, it permitted SCAP to foster Japan-China trade while at the same time, advising, "Every effort should be made to develop alternate sources on an economic basis, particularly in areas such as Southeast Asia where a need exists for Japanese exports."[159] In December 1949, William Sebald, Political Adviser in SCAP, reported that Japan-PRC trade would be indispensable for Japanese economic recovery while Japan-PRC close political contacts would pose a serious threat to Japanese security.[160]

Even though differences of opinion remained, it was safer and easier for Washington to take a tough position against the PRC, especially after its intervention into the Korean War. In December 1950, SCAP issued a directive to prohibit Japan-China trade.[161] It is questionable whether unrestricted Japan-PRC trade could have been a great benefit to Japan, but, because of trade restrictions, the Japanese government and business community imagined the limitless benefits that they could gain from unrestricted trade. Since this trade was imaginary, the CIA reported that there was "a tendency among the Japanese to overestimate the benefit that Japan . . . would derive from trade with the Communist Bloc."[162] In reality, Japan certainly earned more benefits from its economic ties with the Capitalist world than it would secure from trade with the Communist bloc.[163] The imaginary benefits precipitated Japanese discontent with the US policy and justified demands for more assistance to promote Japanese economic growth.

As for the nature of Sino-Soviet relations, the Truman administration also received mixed and ambivalent messages. NSC 41 of February 1949 indicated that the US leaders were willing to exploit Sino-Soviet differences once they appeared, but there was "little the United States could do initially, beyond adoption of the policy here proposed, to contribute to creation of a conflict."[164] In April 1949, the CIA recognized that even though "the process of consolidation of Soviet control over China will unquestionably encounter considerable difficulty . . . the CCP will remain loyal to Moscow."[165] Wellington Koo stimulated anti-communist sentiment in Washington, insisting, "Chinese Communists are tools of the Soviet Union. They are like Communists everywhere: Russian dominated, supported and led. Their leaders take their orders from Moscow. They are fanatically anti-American."[166]

NSC 34 of October 1948 claimed: "Moscow faces a considerable task in seeking to bring the Chinese Communists under its complete control. . . . It is impossible that the Kremlin could in the space of the next crucial five years mobilize China's resources and manpower to the extent that they would constitute a serious threat to U.S. security."[167] Although George Kennan considered it "dangerous to talk about a Chinese Tito-ism," he recognized that severe "differences of opinion already exist between the Chinese Communists and the Russians, notably over the position of the Russians. . . . These differences can easily become inflamed and others can easily develop, even within the confines of a common ideology."[168] In April 1950, because of Mao's long stay in Moscow, Kennan rightly regarded it "too long a time for it to have been simply a process of dictation by the Kremlin of a set of terms which Mao was asked to sign. Obviously, he was there to negotiate and they [the Russians] had to negotiate with him."[169] President Truman also hoped that "the Russians will turn out to be the 'foreign devils' in China."[170]

Although there were ample signs of Sino-Soviet conflicts, Washington was pessimistic about the possibility of a Sino-Soviet split. An NSC draft of October 1949 claimed, although "'Titoism' may be a possibility in China, its development cannot be expected in time to be of assistance to the United States in solving present security problems in Asia."[171] Even though many Washington officials shared this realistic view, it was easier and safer for them to accept the widespread manufactured view that communism was monolithic because of the prevailing Cold War mentality in Washington.

CHAPTER FIVE

IMPACT OF THE KOREAN WAR ON U.S. POLICY TOWARD ASIA

THE JAPANESE ECONOMIC SITUATION

When the Japanese government implemented the Dodge Line, Japan faced economic deterioration as it suffered from a serious deflationary economic crisis.[1] State Department Intelligence warned that the Dodge Line would precipitate widespread opposition in Japan against the US occupation.[2]

The Korean War came along as a "divine wind." Japan received large orders from the United States to manufacture military supplies and to repair ships, tanks, jeeps, aircraft, and others, which stimulated the Japanese economy, especially the textile, metal, chemical, transportation, machinery, and electricity industries.[3] The war gave a huge boost to the demand for Japanese goods, giving a significant Keynesian lift to the Japanese economy, sufficient to return it to its prewar level of productivity by 1951. The outbreak of the Korean War made Japan not only a military entrepot and large repair base for the US army, but also a key station for the US rearmament program in Asia, which brought an enormous amount of special dollar earnings to Japan.[4] Between June 1950 and June 1951, manufacturing production increased by 50%, manufacturing productivity by 30%, and the wholesale commodity price index by 52%.[5] The manufacturing production index jumped from 68.9 (1934-36 = 100) in 1949 to 189.4 in 1955. The index of manufacturing capacity almost doubled between March 1950 (100) and September 1955 (192.4). Real per capita income increased by six percent annually, from 81 in 1949 (1934-36 = 100) reaching 125 in 1956.[6]

Because the Dodge Line halted inflation, Japan's exports dramatically increased as international prices rose. Between 1949 and 1951, the volume of exports jumped by 270% and production by 70%.[7] Between 1949 and 1950, Japan's ordinary exports increased by 89% and between 1950 and 1951 by another 40%.[8] The Korean War spurred Japanese trade because the United States and European nations were concentrating on arms production. Between 1950 and 1951, the volume of world trade increased by $19 billion or 34%. The war galvanized the world economy, which in turn stimulated Japanese heavy industry. Moreover, because of the American assistance, Japan benefited from easy access to cheap energy and raw material sources.[9] Japan moved from a trade deficit of $300 million at the end of 1949 to a trade surplus of $40 million by December 1950.[10] Since import surpluses amounted to $1.975 billion during the same period, the special procurement paid off the trade deficits and contributed to accumulating capital.[11] American assistance led Japan to import approximately $2 billion annually during the Korean War in comparison with the prewar years when Japan imported around $1 billion.[12] The United States also used Japan as a rest and recreation area where thousands of Americans spent money.

The US "military" assistance program during the war provided both military and civilian goods.[13] Between July 1951 and June 1952, only 3.1% of US military procurement consisted of pure military end-items like rifles. The remainder was dual-use items such as steel and metal manufactures, fuel and lubricants, transportation equipment, processed primary metal products, industrial machinery, and telecommunications equipment.[14] American demand for product specification resulted in product standardization and quality control. The US military contracts trained engineers in many key industries such as automobile, tire, and engine manufacturing.[15] Special offshore procurement precipitated rapid plant investment in heavy-chemical sectors such as the metal, chemical, transportation, machine, and electric power industries.[16]

Even when the Korean War brought a large amount of funds to Asia, the Department of the Army continued to carefully monitor the problem of Asian economic instability and earnestly recommended that the United States continue its aid to Asia, especially Southeast Asia to stabilize the region.[17] In a dollar-gap report on the Far East to the President in October 1950, Gordon Gray, former Secretary of the Army, clearly recognized, "The potential contribution of a stable and democratic Japan is extremely important for economic growth, the improvement of living standards, and the maintenance of peace in the region." The report rightly indicated, "Japan's major problem . . . has been . . . a marketing problem rather than a problem of inadequate economic resources."[18] William F. Marquat argued that the United States should attempt to utilize the tremendous amount of Japan's untapped industrial capacity because the Korean War provided Japan with an opportunity to export capital and consumer goods to Southeast Asia.[19] In July 1951, Charles Wilson, the Defense Mobilization Director, publicly announced that the United States would combine Japan's industrial power with raw materials from other Asian countries.[20] Dean Rusk, the Director of the Far Eastern affairs office, explained before Congress that the need for economic integration, rather than communist threat, propelled the US policy regarding Southeast Asia: "Even without a communist threat . . . it seems to us that we should have to be deeply interested in the strength and stability of these nations and we would want to bind them to us in ties of friendship in whatever ways we could."[21] John Foster Dulles pointed out that trade between "Japan and Southeast Asia and Pacific countries can be mutually advantageous."[22] Joseph Dodge proclaimed that Japan, more than ever, needed "expanding overseas sources of food and the raw materials of production." He understood that it was "not the production capacity of Japan that is the key to survival, but the supply of materials"[23] (emphasis original). The JCS concluded: "United States objectives with respect to Southeast Asia and United States objectives with respect to Japan would appear to be inseparably related. . . . the United States must take into full account Japan's dependence upon Southeast Asia for her economic well-being."[24]

The Korean War increased the importance of establishing solidarity among non-communist Asian countries. Consequently, the war, in conjunction with the instability in Southeast Asia, significantly heightened American anxiety about communist expansion in this region. The United States, however, tried to avoid any military commitment, feeling that the very first step would lead "to a major involvement of the United States in that area similar to that in Korea or even to global war."[25] Nevertheless, conditions in Southeast Asia did not improve and the NSC staff members pessimistically announced in May 1951 that the United States could not "guarantee the denial of Southeast Asia to communism."[26] Southeast Asia, however, was too important to be abandoned: Its fall to communism would prevent the flow of food and strategic raw materials to Japan and Western Europe.[27]

Giving top priority to the rearmament program in Western Europe, Washington could not spare large quantities of resources for Southeast Asia. Russell Fifield of the CFR concluded, "The economic value of Southeast Asia was greater for some of the allies of the United States, like Japan in Asia and certain others in Western Europe, than for itself."[28] Nevertheless, as a hegemonic power, the United States had to commit itself in areas where it had little direct interest in order to assist vital components of the world-system, and Southeast Asia was a good case in point. The CIA correctly pointed out that communism in Southeast Asia would not be a direct threat to US security, but if the region were to fall to the Communist bloc, it would be a huge blow to US prestige and credibility in Asia concerning its ability and will to protect the area against communist expansion.[29] The NSC regarded Indochina as the front line against communist southward expansionism. What Washington feared most was a possible domino effect resulting from communist penetration into Southeast Asia, predicting that the loss of Indochina "would bring about almost immediately a dangerous condition with respect to the internal security of all of the other countries of Southeast Asia . . . and would contribute to their probable eventual fall to communism."[30]

The NSC also warned, "This loss [of Indochina] would have widespread political and psychological repercussions upon other non-communist states throughout the world."[31] Because of the unstable conditions in Southeast Asia, Washington claimed, "The danger of internal Communist subversions are very great – greater in most countries of South and Southeast Asia than those of direct invasion."[32] The anxiety about communist expansion and this domino logic raised serious doubts within the NSC concerning Japan's future political and economic orientation. NSC 124 in February 1952 revealed, "[The] fall of Southeast Asia . . . could result in such economic and political pressures in Japan as to make it extremely difficult to prevent Japan's eventual accommodation to the Soviet bloc."[33] Understanding the vital importance of "Japan's dependence upon Southeast Asia for her economic well-being," the JCS also cautioned that the loss of Southeast Asia would "almost inevitably force Japan into an eventual accommodation with the Communist-controlled areas in Asia."[34]

Admitting that the Korean War provided Japan with substantial economic benefits, Dodge warned that it was "unusual, probably temporary, and subject to obvious limitations."[35] The Japanese business community as well as the government anticipated that the end of the Korean War would terminate the special offshore procurement program and, as a result, cut short the economic boom. Indeed, the worldwide economic expansion precipitated by the Korean War began to recede in April 1951.[36] Dodge advised Ichimada that the end of the Korean War "might bring serious repercussions on business and banking . . . ."[37] He bluntly stated, "Japan can be independent politically but dependent economically."[38]

American officials predicted that the continued special offshore procurement program would be a significant means to establish a solid regional economic linkage and to combat a post-Korea depression. The United States poured aid dollars into Asia, greatly benefiting Japan.[39] For example, Japan received approximately 25% of the purchase orders made by the US special technical and economic mission to Southeast Asian countries as of May 1951. Marquat clearly understood the importance of procurement: "A planned,

properly timed US procurement program can be used to guide the development of Japan and of Southeast Asia so that the ultimate optimum benefit will
be derived by the free world."[40] Kenneth Morrow, Chief of the Programs and
Statistics Division of SCAP, predicted that if Washington made a coherent
plan to implement the triangular US-Japan-Southeast Asia Program, it would
"improve conditions throughout Southeast Asia by raising production, productivity, and the level of trade with Japan." Thus, he recommended, "The U.S.
develop a long-range off-shore procurement program for Japan so that the
Japanese can plan their industrial expansion and the expansion of their raw
materials accordingly."[41] Matthew Ridgway, MacArthur's successor, strongly
urged the Army Department to maintain the same procurement level after the
Korean war.[42]

In conjunction with the continuous procurement, Washington began to
shift its emphasis from Japanese economic self-support to "economic cooperation": economic recovery through the development of defense industries in
Japan.[43] In April 1950, Voorhees regarded the American military forces as
Japan's best customer.[44] The Defense Department believed, "Japan should be a
primary source of MDAP [Mutual Defense Aid Program] supplies for the
democratic nations of the Far East."[45] The Munitions Board in the Department
of Defense concluded, "It would be in the best interests of the U.S. to initiate
industrial mobilization planning in Japan with a view to utilization of Japan as
a supplemental source of supply for U.S. military requirements in another
world conflict."[46] In order to maintain Japanese economic recovery, in late
March 1951, State Department officials reluctantly accepted the Defense
Department position to procure military goods in Japan for the US forces on
the condition that the "existing policy decisions of the Far Eastern
Commission and directives to SCAP continue to govern the production and
export of military equipment in and from Japan."[47]

In the early 1950s, Japan encountered a difficult choice between economic
growth through peace or military industries. This was the period when Japan
was most inclined to rearmament and military production.[48] In January 1951,
eight economic groups including the Federation of Economic Organization
(*Keidanren*) and Japan Federation of Industry (*Nihon Sangyo Kyogikai*) proposed that Japan "establish the minimum defense organization."[49] In February
1951, the *Keidanren* organized the Committee on US-Japan Economic
Cooperation (*Nichibei Keizai Teikei Kondankai*, hereafter CUJEC) to deal with
the defense economic issues. On the assumption that military cooperation
with the United States would be beneficial for Japan's technological development, the CUJEC insisted that through "cooperation with the United States
we will help in strengthening defense production in the Far East and . . . we
will help Japanese industry and technology."[50] The CUJEC also proposed

cooperating with the United States in the development of Southeast Asia.[51] In March 1951, the *Keidanren* recommended that Japan ask the United States to provide economic aid in return for Japanese rearmament.[52] Marquat went to Washington to discuss Japan-US economic cooperation in April 1951. When he returned to Japan, he announced the importance of Japan's participation in an offshore procurement program, of Japan's contribution to the free world by establishing a regional economic linkage with Southeast Asia, and of a healthy development of the Japanese economy.[53] Prime Minister Yoshida stated that Japan would be "glad to do her part in supplying special demand goods needed for the execution of the American defense program and also to cooperate in the economic development of Southeast Asia."[54] In September 1951, Ishikawa Ichiro, President of the *Keidanren*, publicly announced that Japan should develop a domestic military industry. Recognizing the importance of economic cooperation, the MITI actively promoted this program to increase exports and develop technology by soliciting US subsidies for the development of a munitions industry.[55]

On the other hand, the financial community led by the Finance Ministry and the Bank of Japan, opposed the militarization of the Japanese economy because it would take much scarce capital that might otherwise be used for more productive purposes. Moreover, economic cooperation was most likely to contribute to spiraling inflation and distort the Japanese economy.[56] In October 1950, Dodge recommended to Ikeda that Japan should not rearm like the United States; instead, it should restrain domestic consumption and devote itself to increasing exports.[57] Dodge strongly recommended a balanced budget, which in turn contained Japan's rapid remilitarization. The Northeastern Affairs section of the State Department also opposed the remilitarization since it was contrary to the spirit of FEC policies.[58] Charles Boehringer, Economic Counselor in Tokyo criticized Japan-US economic cooperation, arguing that Japan had already become "dependent upon the United States for direction and financial assistance" during the occupation. Citing as evidence the way that Japan, in the name of economic cooperation, requested that the United States provide "paternal assistance to Japan in its national and international problems." He regarded it only as Japan's "wishful thinking" and suggested that the United States should not pursue this cooperation."[59]

Japan's military production in the early 1950s accounted for only 2-3% of Gross National Product and US military procurement consisted primarily of dual-purpose products.[60] The Dodge Line increased the power of the financial community that gradually monitored industrial management and brought stability to the Japanese economy. The Dodge-Ikeda-Ichimada Nexus remained powerful enough to maintain the Dodge program with Yoshida's strong support, which was especially important when the Korean War rekindled inflation. Moreover, even inside the strongly pro-remilitarization Keidanren, there existed some dissenting opinions. For example, Goko Kiyoshi, Chairman of Defense Production Committee of the Keidanren, questioned the validity of Japan-US economic cooperation. He considered it risky to develop defense industries as the core industry of Japan's economy, concluding that Japan's primary industries should be general export and shipping industries.[61] Even though Prime Minister Yoshida welcomed US special offshore procurement, he publicly denied that Japan was rearming, a denial which discouraged investment in the military. Yoshida's reluctant support of rearmament prevented the Japanese economy from depending on military-related production.

The Korean War did not remilitarize the Japanese economy but it provided Japan with US military assistance to promote a dual-purpose economy. Politically, Yoshida's stubborn policy of gradual rearmament channeled Japanese economic development down a civilian course. Economically, the war solidified the Dodge-style, liberal economic system and helped maintain a balanced budget.[62] The MITI and the military industries did not form a solid institutional base within the conservative parties. Not only the left wing of the Socialist Party but also the conservative parties (the Reform Party and the Liberal Party) insisted that the Government should first consider the reduction of defense-related expenditures in order to implement a tight budget.[63] Japan was able to benefit from American military expenditure without remilitarizing its own economy.

JAPAN'S SECURITY ISSUES

The Korean War turned US attention to Asian affairs, forcing the Truman Administration to deal with the growing military threat in Asia, and consolidating the Cold War mentality in Washington. George Kennan advised Secretary of State Dean Acheson to "exhibit a firm determination to see the communist invasion of South Korea repulsed." Otherwise, the inaction of the United States would psychologically encourage communist expansion around Asia.[64] Shocked by the sudden North Korean invasion, the CIA concluded that it was "undoubtedly undertaken at Soviet direction and Soviet material support."[65] Tracy Voorhees reported, "The bald fact is that we, and the Japanese as well, are living in a world which Russian Communism is attempting to conquer by infiltration backed by the threat of ever-increasing military force. Of this the attack on Korea is the most recent proof."[66] On 27 June 1950, President Truman stated, "The attack upon Korea makes it plain beyond all doubt that Communism has passed beyond the use of subversion to conquer independent nations and will now use armed invasion and war." He declared, "I have ordered the Seventh Fleet to prevent any attack upon Formosa."[67] It took only three days after a series of discussions in Washington to make a military commitment to Korea by providing air and naval forces. The State Department hardened its expansionist image of the Communist bloc: "Recent developments in Asia, and particularly in Korea, indicate that the Soviet Union, the Chinese Communist regime and the North Korean regime are moving to dominate Asia."[68] In August 1950, the Joint Secretaries (Secretaries of the Navy, the Army and the Air Force) persisted, "The Soviet movement is monolithic. Satellite troops are just as much Soviet in this sense as if they were members of the Red Army."[69]

Wellington Koo, Chinese Ambassador to the United States, tried his best to deepen US involvement in Asia. He regarded Truman's speech on 27 June as "an epoch-making declaration of common defense of the freedom of Asiatic nations." He conveyed the image of this monolithic Communist bloc: "The important fact to note is that the Communists in Asia, . . . are all members of one great organized body of international communism directly or indirectly under the control and orders of the Kremlin." Koo observed that Truman's speech "furnishes the missing link, so to speak, in the general plan to stop Communist expansionism and uphold the cause of freedom."[70]

In June 1950, the JCS sent a telegram to the Commander in Chief, Far East to dispatch the Seventh Fleet to the Taiwan Strait to prevent both a PRC attack on Taiwan and any Taiwanese advances toward the mainland.[71] In July 1950, MacArthur visited Chiang Kai-shek to discuss Asian affairs. Washington feared that this meeting might send a wrong message both to Taiwan and to the PRC that the United States supported Chiang's intention of returning to the mainland. Truman sent Harriman, Special Assistant to the President, to Japan in order to clarify Washington's policy, and Secretary of Defense Louis Johnson strongly reminded MacArthur that the American policy was to prevent Taiwan from launching an invasion on the mainland.[72] Dulles told Koo that the United States "had decided to freeze it, metaphorically speaking, so that no trouble might develop from that quarter of the world particularly at this time when the Korean campaign was still going on." He reaffirmed the point that what the United States was seeking was to "maintain the status quo in that part of the world, at least for the time being"[73] (emphasis added). Whatever its intention might have been, Washington sowed seeds of further commitment in Asia by sending the Seventh Fleet to the Taiwan Strait. Besides Korea and Formosa, the United States also accelerated its involvement in the Philippines and in Indo-China.

Dulles believed that the Korean War was the beginning of an increase in communist efforts to conquer Japan.[74] The Korean War led him to believe that the Soviet Union increasingly made efforts to secure two workshops in Europe and Asia, Germany and Japan respectively. He predicted, "the future of the world depends largely on whether the Soviet Union will be able to get control over Western Germany and Japan by means short of war."[75] Voorhees warned, "Japanese industry, if captured by the Communists and coupled with the raw materials and other resources on the mainland already under Communist control, could be made a new Frankenstein dominating the Orient."[76] Japan was "a major prize" for the communist aggression in Asia.[77] Kennan abhorred the possibility of these countries under the Soviet control, indicating, "If they [the Soviets] were to extend their power to Japan, the whole fruits of our victory in the Pacific would be lost." Thus, he considered it "essential to us to prevent Soviet seizure of Germany and Japan."[78] The State Department warned, "If [Japan was] added to the resources now possessed by the Soviet Union [it] would greatly alter the balance of power in the world to the disadvantage of the United States and its allies."[79]

The PRC's intervention in the Korean War in October 1950 caused the United Nations' forces to retreat, creating a negative psychological impact on other Asian nations. Hugh Borton anticipated that it had "created doubts as to the wisdom of American policy and the ability of American leadership. . . . [and] many more Asiatic peoples than ever before are becoming convinced that their survival and well being may be enhanced by the acceptance of Communism rather than by alliance with the West." Eugene Dooman apprehended, "[The] prestige of the United States has already suffered severely from the defeat we have incurred in Korea. . . . If now on top of this military beating we should crawl out of Korea, the result would be disastrous." Since Korea was an "excellent base for psychological attack on Japan by the Communists," he insisted, "The United States should not withdraw from Korea if it could be avoided"[80] The Office of Intelligence Research of the State Department warned that a communist expansion into Indo-China, the Near East, Europe, or Korea would damage American credibility, indicating, "The weaker Japanese general confidence in the West and the greater the threat of successful Communist attack on Japan, the more will be the paralytic effect on Japanese cooperation."[81] Since the United States had occupied and trained the Japanese for over five years, Robert Fearey, a member of the Political Adviser's staff in Tokyo, was concerned that failure in incorporating it into the West would have a serious psychological effect on free Asian countries and dissidents in the PRC.[82]

The outbreak of the Korean War seemed to terminate the rearmament controversy among the US officials in favor of the pro-rearmament camp. It induced MacArthur to believe, "Despite Japan's constitutional renunciation of war its right to self defense in case of predatory attack is implicit and inalienable."[83] On 8 July 1950, SCAP issued a directive to the Japanese Government to establish a Police Reserve Force (PRF) of 75,000 men and increased the number of the Maritime Safety Force by 8,500 men.[84] SCAP claimed in July 1950 that the PRF was a separate organization from the regular police. Charles Wiloughby, chief of G2, had already devised a plan to make the PRF into four armed divisions.[85] In September 1950, Sebald admitted the necessity that "Japan must be partially rearmed" in order to protect Japan against possible communist attack.[86] The PPS argued that facing a "new situation radically different from that envisaged in the Potsdam Proclamation . . . we are justified in resorting to extraordinary measures to enable Japan to contribute to its own defense."[87]

Washington officials, however, were not certain how much pressure they could impose on Japan. In July 1950, Dulles reported to Paul Nitze, the Director of the PPS, that Japanese rearmament at this moment "would encounter serious and understandable objections on the part of former victims of Japanese aggression and, indeed, from the Japanese themselves."[88] General MacArthur argued that the Allied Powers still worried more about threat from remilitarized Japan rather than threat of attack against Japan.[89] Foreign policy experts at the CFR agreed that Washington should maintain a delicate balance between "a contribution [to security in the Pacific] by Japan involving limited rearmament . . . [and] the effect of this [rearmament program] on the Japanese economy." They were rather optimistic to say that with proper American aid, "the program need not lead to disastrous consequences."[90]

Sebald expected that the Korean War would induce the Japanese to accept the rearmament program. He reported that Yoshida's repeated remarks about strictly observing Article Nine were only for public consumption and "should not be taken entirely at face value."[91] Talking with Shirasu Jiro, aide to Yoshida, Fearey had the impression that "Yoshida's equivocal position on rearmament has been a matter of public policy rather than of personal opinion." Consequently, he believed that Article Nine "should and can without great difficulty be amended at an early date to permit rearmament."[92] Allison also assumed that the war precipitated "some real thinking about the problem of security" among the Japanese people.[93]

Contrary to these expectations, however, the war did not drastically change Japanese attitudes. The US intelligence reported, "the Korean hostilities increased Japanese hopes that future national security could be guaranteed by the UN. . . . the UN intervention acted as a counterbalance in that it markedly increased the tendency to assume that Japan could depend on the UN rather than its own efforts for security."[94] In July 1950, Prime Minister Yoshida claimed in the Diet that the Korean War proved that arguments of a peace treaty with all nations and of eternal neutrality were completely unrealistic and dangerous because they might be manipulated by communists. The war, however, did not alter Yoshida's conviction that Japan should avoid rearmament.

He argued that the Korean War and the swift UN reaction gave "Japan important indication concerning Japanese security. If we atone for our wrongdoings
in the past and adopt democracy completely, free democratic countries would
assist us once Japan was invaded just like the case of Korea."[95]

Prime Minister Yoshida was ambivalent about the future prospect of Japan's
rearmament: "We Japanese have to defend Japan but it does not necessarily
mean that we will rearm. We do not rearm at the moment, but we cannot
foresee what would happen in the future."[96] He argued that the Japanese had
to be "careful in using the term 'self-defense', but I do not mean to abandon
our self-defense right. When a nation gets independence, it naturally has the
right to protect itself. . . . War is inevitable in order to protect its own country,
but since people often wage wars in the name of self-defense, we have to be
extremely careful in using this term, 'self-defense right.'"[97]

His reluctance of rearmament continued during the Korean War. He
addressed in the House of Councilors on 6 March 1952: "Article 9 prohibits
war potential as a means of settling international disputes, but it does not prohibit it as a means of self-defense." Four days later, however, he said,
"Possessing war power even for self-defense constitutes rearmament, which
requires a constitutional amendment. We do not intend to rearm." Okamoto
of the Ryokufukai, a group of conservative politicians in the House of
Representative, inquired: "I would like to reconfirm that Article 9 prohibits
Japan from having war power even for defense." Yoshida replied in the affirmative.[98] He was a gradualist. "We gradually strengthen our self-defense capabilities in accordance with our national power. The Japan-US security treaty
currently protects Japan, but as Japan's national power gradually increases, we
should consider our own defense in our own ways."[99]

Yoshida's uncertainty was the result of vague and divided opinions among
the Japanese people concerning the rearmament program. Polls conducted by
the major newspapers in Japan revealed: 47.5% were for rearmament and 39%
against (the *Yomiuri Newspaper* of 16 April 1952); 38.3% for and 38% against
(the *Mainichi Newspaper* of 14 April 1952); and 32% for and 26% against (the
Asahi Newspaper of 2-3 March 1952). As for the necessity of amending Article
Nine, the *Asahi Newspaper* poll showed that 31% were for the amendment and
42% against it; 38% for building military forces without amending Article
Nine, 14% for conditional military buildup, and 29% against any rearmament
program (14 February 1953). This indicated that 30-40% of the Japanese
people were willing to support some kind of rearmament program while
approximately the same percentage of the people opposed it. Yoshida told
Ridgway that he would wait for a greater consensus in public opinion before
pushing for rearmament and for the necessary constitutional amendment.[100]
Ikeda Hayato was also flexible about his treatment of Article Nine: "I do not

stick to keep Article Nine unmodified forever nor do I approve of early amendment of the constitution or rearmament program." He believed that Japan would first have to consolidate both on a spiritual and material basis: "Two conditions are prerequisite to amend the constitution: The intention of the Japanese people to defend their own country and economic prosperity to support the cost of self-defense."[101]

Japanese civilian leaders understood that rearmament was likely to strengthen the power of the militarists and extreme nationalists. Washington also doubted that Japanese democracy was strong enough to resist their revival. The PPS "strongly doubts that any Japanese political system, . . . will be recognizable as 'democracy' from the U.S. viewpoint."[102] The CIA's analysis indicated that "democracy in Japan is still a tender plant. . . . much of the philosophy of humanism or individualism that underlies Western democracy does not yet exist in sufficient degree in Japan. . . ."[103]

Pro-rearmament forces, however, did exist in Japan. Charles Wiloughby preserved a handful of Japanese military experts centered around former Colonel Hattori Takushiro (Hattori Group) in order to prepare for a US-Soviet war. Former Lieutenant General Tatsumi Eiichi became Yoshida's private adviser in military affairs and played a liaison role between Yoshida and G2.[104] They advocated establishing Japan's own independent armed forces with a high degree of autonomy.[105] The Democratic Party led by Ashida Hitoshi made the rearmament program its official policy, pleading with SCAP in December 1950 to create 15 divisions of armed forces of 200,000 men.[106] The party publicly confirmed in December 1950 that it would support a Japanese rearmament program.[107] In February 1951, Hatoyama Ichiro of the Liberal Party conveyed to Dulles his support of the rearmament program. He complained about the fact that Americans who were not familiar with Japanese customs and psychology directed the present constabulary, hinting that Japan would need more autonomous armed forces.[108] Criticizing Yoshida's reluctant rearmament policy, Ashida proclaimed that what Yoshida did was to prolong Japan's decision concerning the size and timing of Japan's rearmament. In effect, he regarded Yoshida's policy of intensifying Japan's military, political, and economic dependence on the United States, as stimulating Japanese nationalism at the time of independence.[109]

The pro-rearmament forces were visible nationalists, who used the rearmament issue as the means of eliminating the US influence in Japan. They had little intention of having Japan participate in a collective security arrangement. SCAP regarded Hatoyama as a politician who lacked confidence and leadership and whose arguments were often illogical.[110] Since the argument of the pro-rearmament forces was likely to plant seeds of neutralism, and to signal the pursuit autonomous military power, it made US officials nervous.[111]

American distrust of visible Japanese nationalists limited its pressure for Japanese rearmament. If US officials wanted political stability and pro-US orientation in Japan, they had no choice but to support the conservative forces led by Yoshida. M. Bronfenbrenner of the ESS and Joseph Dodge agreed that from an economic-political point of view the "Yoshida Cabinet is our best asset."[112]

It is important to note that Yoshida was a pragmatic gradualist, not a pacifist, and strove for the very minimum requirement of defense forces that would not imperil US-Japan relations. He was willing to increase military capabilities, but the establishment of a firm economic base was a prerequisite condition. Dulles agreed with Yoshida about the necessity of constructing a healthy economic base.[113] Yoshida also anticipated that Japanese rearmament would not only precipitate a heated controversy domestically but also rekindle Asian antagonism toward Japan.[114] Article Nine gave legitimacy to anti-rearmament forces in Japan. In order to justify Japan's rearmament, Dulles referred to Article 51 of the United Nations Charter, arguing, "There is a solemn recognition that every nation has an inherent right of individual or collective self defense."[115] The JCS presumed that Japan would alter its constitution so as to develop its defense forces legally.[116] Article Nine, however, was a Pandora's box. Since any move to alter it was likely to precipitate heated political ordeal, no right-minded politician in Japan would dare touch it.[117] According to the JMFA, Japan's reluctant acceptance of a rearmament program due to the forceful American pressure was "expedient not only in view of political considerations toward domestic and international conditions but also in order to gain military and economic aid from the United States." By doing so, Japan formed an image of a peaceful and anti-militaristic nation.[118] The Yoshida Cabinet was also clever enough to use the rearmament issue as a trump card to obtain maximum economic assistance from the United States, arguing that a solid economic base was essential to increase military capabilities.[119]

The outbreak of the Korean War proved to be a double-edged sword, complicating peace treaty negotiations for John Foster Dulles. On the one hand, it was indeed an opportunity to persuade Japan to accept the US terms and conditions on the security issue of a peace treaty.[120] Dulles recommended to Acheson, "The Korean attack makes it more important, rather than less important, to act [for peace treaty negotiations]." He felt that defeat in the war and the occupation placed the Japanese "in somewhat of a postwar stupor." He intended to resort to shock therapy: "The Korean attack is awakening them and . . . that their mood for a long time may be determined by whether we take advantage of this awakening to bring them an insight into the possibilities of the free world and their responsibility as a member of it."[121] On the other hand, the Korean War provided Japan with more bargaining power because the United States was using Japan as a primary outpost base in its fight in Korea. Dulles understood that the longer the war went on, the more bargaining power Japan would acquire.[122]

JSSC agreed with Dulles that the United States should take a strong leadership position in concluding the peace treaty. It advised the JCS, "The Western Powers would be seriously embarrassed if the USSR in the near future forced the issue of a peace conference with Japan or negotiated a separate peace. . . ."[123] On 7 September 1950, the Secretaries of State and Defense sent a memorandum to President Truman that the United States "should now proceed with preliminary negotiations for a Japanese Peace Treaty." They argued that the peace treaty "must not contain any prohibition, direct or indirect, now or in the future, of Japan's inalienable right to self-defense. . . ." They also claimed that the treaty "must give the United States the right to maintain armed forces in Japan, wherever, for so long, and to such extent as it deems necessary."[124] These demands indicated that the United States made sure that Japan had an avenue for future rearmament and stopped short of demanding that Japan implement an immediate rearmament program. They also suggested that acquiring bases in Japan was more imperative than the rearmament issue. The agreement between the Departments of State and Defense culminated in NSC 60/1, approved by Truman on 8 September 1950. On 14 September 1950, President Truman made it public that the United States would begin preliminary negotiations on a peace treaty.

THE CHINA SYNDROME

The PRC's intervention in the Korean War obliged Dulles to assume solid USSR-PRC cooperation to implement their grand design for world communism. Weakening this communist alliance was "the primary objective of the U.S."[125] Overestimating the solidarity of the Communist bloc, Dulles believed, "there is a comprehensive program, in which the Soviet and Chinese Communist are cooperating, designed as a present phase to eliminate all Western influence on the Asiatic mainland . . . such a program has been carefully worked out. . . ." He anticipated that any hint of military weakness in Korea "would have grave psychological repercussions upon the Japanese nation and the countries and islands of Southeast Asia."[126] The CIA presumed that the PRC entered the Korean War with "explicit assurance of effective Soviet support."[127] Hugh Borton claimed, "Chinese objectives in Asia are identical with those of the Soviet Union."[128] The NSC senior staff members also assumed that China closely cooperated with the Soviet Union.[129]

After the Korean War, Dean Acheson still insisted that the continuation of hard policy toward the PRC would be the best choice. Dulles agreed, "if your major objective is to get a break [between China and] Moscow, the way to get that is to make the going tough, not easy."[130] Although NSC 48/5 in May 1951 proposed that the United States should continue to find and exploit every possible difference between the Soviet Union and PRC, it confirmed that hard policy toward China would further increase PRC's dependence on the Soviet Union.[131] Later in July 1951, NSC 114 indicated, "The Korean War has increased the dependence of the Chinese Communists on the U.S.S.R."[132] The US generals in the NSC also anticipated that no real split would take place for the foreseeable future between the two communist countries.[133]

Contrary to the expectation that PRC would have great difficulty in managing a new nation state, the CIA reported that it would "retain exclusive governmental control of mainland China."[134] Realizing that the PRC would not be overthrown, the Economic Cooperation Administration advised securing multi-national agreement to take long-term, all-out economic containment measures against the PRC.[135] In March 1951, the NSC senior staff members concluded that the PRC constituted the central problem in Asia. The PRC's impact on other Asians was predominantly psychological. Winning the Chinese civil war against the US-backed Nationalist Regime and demonstrating its ability to fight an even match with the United States in the Korean War gave great prestige to the Chinese communists. The American Consul General in Hong Kong reported, "[The] informed Asian, whatever his attitude toward communism, can hardly have overlooked the fact that Chinese armies fought to a standstill the forces of the most powerful nations of the Western world."[136]

The PRC constituted a major psychological threat to the US scheme of regional economic and military integration and Washington had to recover its prestige in order to maintain its influence in Asia. Since Asians were closely watching the power struggle between the Communist and Capitalist blocs, "any impression that the free world neither can nor will meet the threat of Communist aggression against the countries of Asia" would shake their trust in and dependence on the United States.[137] The State Department articulated that the PRC "poses the most difficult question of all for American foreign policy. . . . we must prevent the spread of Chinese Communist imperialism and contain it within China."[138]

The NSC and the JCS held inflated fears, psychological as well as geopolitical, that the PRC might expand its influence both directly and indirectly to Southeast Asia. Washington feared a domino effect because of the unstable conditions in both Japan and Southeast Asia. The NSC staff members anticipated, "The danger of an overt military attack against Southeast Asia is inherent in the existence of a hostile and aggressive Communist China."[139] They made a critical analysis: "Communist control of both China and

Southeast Asia would place Japan in a dangerously vulnerable position and therefore seriously affect the entire security position of the U.S. in the Pacific."[140] Unless the United States secured regional economic integration, the communist forces would win.

After the PRC's intervention in the Korean War, the United States increased its commitment to Taiwan, sending a military advisory group and over $1.4 billion worth of aid before 1954, and concluding a military agreement in 1954.[141] The China syndrome also induced the United States dramatically to accelerate its involvement in Southeast Asia.[142] NSC 125 of July 1951 predicted that the communist conquest of "Southeast Asia . . . would almost inevitably force Japan into an eventual accommodation with the communists controlled areas in Asia."[143] Dean Rusk testified before Congress in 1951, "[The communist] absorption of additional countries in Asia would bring about a severe dislocation of the economic patterns which are of the greatest importance to the strength and well-being of Western Europe and the Unites States and particularly of course to countries like Japan."[144] If the United States did not stop the PRC's expansion into Southeast Asia and satisfy Japan's increased economic needs, Japan would be likely to cooperate with the PRC and adopt a policy of neutralism.[145] NSC staff articulated the critical importance of Southeast Asia for Japan: "Exclusion of Japan from trade with Southeast Asia would seriously affect the Japanese economy . . . [and] lead to eventual Japanese orientation toward the Soviet orbit."[146] In January 1952, Ohashi, Former Japanese Vice Minister of Foreign Affairs, asked Allison whether the United States would provide Japan with assistance if communists dominated Southeast Asia. Allison replied that the United States was conscious of this threat and would prevent the communist takeover since trade with Southeast Asia would be essential for Japan.[147] On 1 February 1952, the Steering Committee of NSC submitted a draft of its analysis concerning communist aggression in Southeast Asia that emphasized the psychological effect on Asian countries of further communist expansion: "Any successful identifiable Chinese Communist aggression in this area . . . would have psychological and political consequences which might result in the relatively swift accommodation of the rest of Asia . . . to communism." The loss of Southeast Asia could also lead to "Japan's eventual accommodation to communism."[148] NSC 124 of February 1952 reconfirmed the US domino theory: "In the long run the loss of Southeast Asia, . . . could result in such economic and political pressures in Japan as to make it extremely difficult to prevent Japan's eventual accommodation to the Soviet bloc."[149] The China syndrome increased the US concern that the entire Asian region was at risk of becoming communist, and thus of becoming antagonistic to the interests of the United States. This realization spurred Washington to further increase its commitment to Asian affairs.

CHAPTER SIX

THE DULLES-YOSHIDA NEGOTIATIONS

THE ROAD TO JAPAN-UNITED STATES NEGOTIATIONS

In September 1950, the United States publicly announced that it was ready to proceed with Japanese peace treaty negotiations.[1] In the JMFA's preparations for the negotiations, the method of preservation of Japan's security was the most important issue. Nishimura Kumao, the Director of the Treaty Bureau of the JMFA, argued that the United Nations would preserve Japan's general security. Because the UN security system centered on the Security Council did not always function smoothly, he argued, the United States would have to supplement and strengthen this UN security function by stationing its armed forces in Japan. He believed that the US bases in Japan under the auspices of the United Nations would not have a deleterious effect on Japanese sentiment or on Japan's national prestige.[2]

The JMFA predicted, "The United States will dispatch its armed forces to Japan for the purpose of collaborative defense in response to Japan's request; consequently, contents of the agreement concerning the stationing of the US forces . . . are most likely to be substantially flexible. . . . the US armed forces would hold enough freedom of movement."[3] In order to create the image that Japan, as a sovereign nation, voluntarily concluded a security agreement, it strongly requested that Washington separate the security agreement from the peace treaty because "a peace treaty has a coercive nature while we are supposedly willing to invite the US armed forces to Japan."[4] As for Japan's rearmament program, the JMFA "appreciates the fact that the proposed peace treaty has no provision to prohibit or limit Japanese rearmament and respects

Japan's autonomy while at the same time it is necessary for Japan to explain clearly that Japan has no intention of rearming."[5]

In early October 1950, the JMFA devised a general policy on peace treaty matters (Work A) and submitted it to Prime Minister Yoshida. According to Work A, the United States was to station its armed forces in Japan with a resolution from the United Nations General Assembly. Washington had to decide on the specific duration of the bases and had to terminate the agreement when the General Assembly made a resolution to do so. In short, the United Nations would sanction the stationing of US armed forces in Japan.

Yoshida was disappointed with Work A because it did not live up to his expectations of using Japan's strategic importance, increased by the Korean War, to obtain the maximum benefits from the coming negotiations with Dulles. He recognized that it was only realistic to rely on unilateral US protection regardless of UN decisions. He returned Work A with critical comments to the JMFA: "[The] JMFA has simply observed objective developments, but seriously lacked considerations in devising measures to deal with them. Please reconsider. I regret to say that you lacked experience as a pragmatic and tough negotiator." Yoshida tried to obtain US tacit approval of not pushing Japan for rearmament too hard in return for stationing American troops in Japan, which was in accord with Dulles' idea. There existed a basic agreement between Yoshida and Dulles that the US acquisition of base rights was non-negotiable and that Yoshida would accept the necessity of Japan's rearmament, but Dulles would acquiesce to its slow progression. Yoshida also commented: "This proposal is similar to opinions of opposition parties and it is not worth consideration at all. Since this is to be a recommendation for a realistic negotiation [with the United States] it requires more practical wisdom." Yoshida also wrote, "Study hard in terms of increasing our national interests." The divide between the JMFA and Yoshida concerning the peace treaty culminated with Yoshida's severe criticism of Work A. His criticism indicated that Work A was based on the old assumption that Japan would have to conclude a peace treaty with all the powers, an assumption which the JMFA would have to abandon.[6]

Prime Minister Yoshida established his own private advisory group to consider the peace treaty (Group A), which had close contact with the JMFA. This group consisted of a small number of advisers from political, business, academic, and media circles as well as Iguchi Sadao, Vice Minister of Foreign Affairs and Nishimura Kumao, Director of the Treaty Bureau of the JMFA. On 5 October 1950, Arita Hachiro, former Foreign Minister and a member of Group A, objected to rearmament because of the lack of economic resources. On the other hand, Itakura Takuzo, another adviser, insisted that international circumstances would inevitably lead Japan to rearmament. Keeping these suggestions in mind, Yoshida claimed that despite US pressure, he would reject rearmament prior to the conclusion of a peace treaty.[7]

In October 1950, based on the Group A study, the JMFA designed a proposal for a "Japan-US security agreement" (Work B). According to Work B, Japan would oppose rearmament, and the United States would be responsible, on behalf of the United Nations, for maintaining Japan's security. The JMFA officials suggested that because Japan inherently possessed a right to self-defense , but did not have the necessary military forces to resist invasion, Japan should allow the United States to retain its forces in Japan to compensate for Japan's lack of military power. They, however, clearly realized that this was an "extremely grave political decision."[8] The JMFA still requested the obtaining of UN auspices to allow the United States to maintain its bases in Japan after the occupation. Yoshida's critical comments on Work A clearly indicated that he would not accept this line of thinking and the JMFA would later have to revise this proposal.

In October 1950, the JMFA proposed that the peace treaty should enable Japan to realize economic independence and to create the basic grounds to contribute to the stability and prosperity of East Asia. The ministry also requested a security system which would not cause any anxiety about Japan's safety under any circumstances. The JMFA officials added that the "Japanese police force should maintain domestic tranquility while it would be the best measure for Japan to depend on the de facto US protection under the UN auspices for its external security." They predicted that the United States would first assume all military responsibility for assuring Japan's security, but eventually it would concentrate primarily on the Air Force and the Navy, leaving Japan responsible for the land forces. Consequently, the United States would open the door for Japan's rearmament. The officials advocated, "In the case that the rearmament was absolutely necessary in the future, it would have to be requested by the United Nations or by the Allied Powers." They tried to make the best use of the rearmament issue in order to avoid political complications: "Japan should not take initiatives in the rearmament program. This would be beneficial in terms of internal and international political considerations." In addition, Japan's reluctance toward rearmament would "induce the United States to provide more military and economic aid to Japan." They regarded the retention of the US armed forces as the only measure capable of ensuring external security.[9]

Prime Minister Yoshida tried to calm Cold War sentiment and a Japanese fear of communist expansionism. Even after the PRC's intervention in the Korean War, in December 1950, he addressed the press, "We will have a 'nerve war' rather than an actual war. When we say that we are currently in revolutionary conditions, we already suffer from a nerve war, and we have to be very careful. International relations will not change easily. The Japanese must judge the situation from a calm perspective." He also expressed his careful posture on Japan's rearmament: "We should not easily talk about rearmament. . . . Even if we are forced to rearm, we have to consider the fact that because of excessive militarization in the past, we had to suffer greatly both in internal and external affairs. As a result, we fought a reckless war, the Great East Asia War. . . . Talking about rearmament reminds neighboring countries of the past Japanese aggression, which will have a negative effect on a peace treaty."[10] In January 1951, Yoshida reaffirmed his intention of rejecting rearmament because of his assessment that, due to the current international situation, the Communist and Western blocs would not wage an all-out war, the Soviet Union would not invade Japan, and the Cold War would persist for some time. Yoshida asserted that Japan should not be swayed by the pessimistic US warning cry that "the Soviet Union will wage a war."[11]

On 5 October, Yoshida mentioned at the Group A meeting that it might be a good idea to establish a demilitarization zone in the Northwestern Pacific area. In October 1950, he assembled military experts including former imperial generals as his personal advisory group (Group B), which primarily discussed this Asian demilitarization scheme during four meetings between October 1950 and January 1951. Hotta Masaaki, Former Ambassador to Italy and Chairman of Group B, indicated, "Regardless of its practical usefulness, we will prepare this scheme to demonstrate what Japan envisioned as a general security picture." On 28 December 1950, the JMFA submitted a proposal to undergird peace and security in the Northern Pacific region (Work C). This proposal designated Japan, Korea, and border areas with Korea as demilitarized regions. According to Work C, the United States, the USSR, Great Britain, and China would maintain the military status quo in the area to the east of 110 degrees of east longitude, to the north of 20 degrees of north latitude, and to the west of 170 degrees of east longitude. The United Nations would monitor those four powers' observing of this agreement. Yoshida probably did not consider this plan practical, but he intended to present it in case the United States suggested a withdrawal of its military forces from Asia.[12]

In January 1951, Group B held a meeting. When military advisors presented actual figures of armed forces from a purely military point of view not only for internal tranquility but also for external defense, Chairman Hotta explained, "Once a war breaks out, we will let America fight for us." Then Kawabe Koshiro, former Lieutenant General, questioned the assumption of US perpetual defense of Japan. Hotta replied that the Japanese government assumed that the United States would stay there for a long time in order to protect Japan. He was cautious about Japan's rapid rearmament. "Increasing tax for rearmament will strengthen the communists, which will cause anti-American sentiment."[13]

Meanwhile, Yoshida's rejection of Work A and Work B compelled the JMFA to make drastic revisions. Finally, in January 1951, the JMFA formulated a basic policy for the negotiations with John Foster Dulles (Work D). Work D indicated that because of critical developments in international relations, the United States was making every effort to organize a defense system of the Democratic countries against the Communist bloc. Consequently, the United States would surely request a consolidation of Japan-US relations and a strengthening of Japan's defense capabilities. Japan's primary goal was to recover complete independence. For this purpose, Japan would reject communism and demonstrate its willingness to be a firm member of the Western bloc. Japan was ready to conclude a peace treaty with the nations in the Western bloc, and if necessary, even with the United States alone. Work D explicitly articulated that post-occupation security constituted the most important issue. Even though both Work A and Work B relied on UN approval for the stationing of US armed forces, Work D completely abandoned this line of thinking, pursuing a US-Japanese bilateral alliance to preserve Japan's security. Although Work D did not support rearmament at that time, it was quite ambivalent about Japan's military program.[14]

Truman's directive of September 1950 prohibited any definite peace treaty "until after favorable resolution of the present United States military situation in Korea."[15] In October, the PRC intervened in the Korean War and the position of the UN forces deteriorated drastically. Consequently, in late December of 1950, the JSSC changed its opinion and did "urge most strongly that the United States refrain from proceeding now with any negotiations with Japan leading to a peace treaty, and that any such negotiations await a resolution of the situation in Korea" since the United States, at that time, was in an unfavorable position in the Korean War. The JSSC was pessimistic about the prospects of the war, recommending against negotiations "under circumstances of extreme weakness . . . with our inadequate military forces fully committed in Korea and elsewhere." It comprehended that a peace treaty "would deprive United States forces of the use of Japan as the major base of operations in the Korean War." They expected not only to use Japan as the operation base but also to lead Japan to execute a rearmament program "for its own security and defense at the earliest practicable date." In addition, since the United States was responsible for global stability, it could not assume "a formal obligation . . . [to] make the security of that nation a military commitment of the United States."[16] Any security agreement had to consider these factors in order to get approval from the military establishment.

Dulles anticipated, "Since the Chinese Communist intervention in Korea, it has seemed unlikely that there would be any such 'favorable resolution'. . . ." Trying to urge prompt action, Dulles contended, "The delay is causing disquiet in Japan and a feeling that it may well be that . . . we have no firm resolve to try to hold the island chain of which Japan forms part." He warned, "We are already in the dangerous area."[17] Agreeing with Dulles, the President finally sent a new directive to him on 10 January 1951: "The United States should proceed with further steps to bring about a peace settlement with Japan without awaiting a favorable resolution of the military situation in Korea."[18] Before leaving for Japan, Dulles regarded his real purpose was to "find out how dependable a commitment could be obtained from the Japanese Government to align with the nations of the free world against Communist imperialism."[19] Dulles expected even a nominal military commitment, but Shirasu indicated that the United States "should utilize Japanese industrial capacity to the full in the coming period of shortages to help supply the needs of the free world. There can be no more effective way of firmly binding Japan to the free world."[20]

In receiving the news that MacArthur "did not wish to play an active part in the Mission's work," Dulles was quite surprised and said that SCAP's assistance was indispensable. Dulles feared what would happen if he could not rely on the basic assumption of his peace treaty scheme: "Do we get the right to station as many troops in Japan as we want where we want and for as long as we want or do we not? That is the principal question. General MacArthur said last June that Japan would give us the right and we have proceeded blindly on that basis." His anxiety was quite understandable because any nation "which does give us such privileges . . . will be vulnerable to attack as having permitted a derogation of Japan's sovereignty."[21] On 27 January 1951, SCAP confidently informed Dulles that there would be "no difficulty in securing Japan's acceptance" because of Japan's earnest desire to get independence.[22]

THE DULLES-YOSHIDA NEGOTIATIONS

On 29 January 1951, Yoshida and Dulles had their first official meeting. Yoshida expressed the Japanese desire to acquire independence, which gave the Americans the impression that "the Japanese were so eager for a treaty that they would be willing to approve almost anything." Dulles solicited Yoshida's view on Japan's rearmament. Yoshida replied, "It was necessary to go very slowly in connection with any possible rearmament" because of two primary obstacles: possible rise of the Japanese militarists and the deficiency of economic resources. Even if he recognized Japan's unstable economic condition, Dulles persisted, "In the present state of the world it was necessary for all nations that wanted to remain free to make sacrifices." His purpose was to confirm Japan's willingness to commit itself to the free world. "No one would expect the Japanese contribution at present to be large but it was felt that *Japan should be willing to make at least a token contribution and a commitment* to a general cause of collective security" (emphasis added). Dulles asked Yoshida what kind of contribution Japan could make to strengthen the free world. Yoshida argued that Japan was willing to make some contribution, but did not specify what kind. Then, he asked Dulles if the United States could "incorporate" Japan in a larger sense. Yoshida might have intended to confuse Dulles or simply might not have made himself understood clearly in English. Whatever Yoshida's purpose might have been, his responses irritated Dulles who showed his perplexity, if not outright anger, during the meetings. Yoshida promised to submit Japan's view on a peace treaty the following day.[23] On 30 January, Allison wrote a memorandum stating that William Sebald thought that "the Prime Minister came to yesterday's conference totally unprepared to discuss detailed provisions and that his remarks were more in the nature of feelers rather than any effort to come to grips with the real problems."[24] Dulles also regarded the meeting as "a puffball performance."[25] Dulles and Yoshida had a similar ideas for gradual, nominal rearmament; however, their miscommunication made the first meeting rather awkward, but because there existed fundamental agreement on security issues, subsequent meetings proceeded smoothly.

On 30 January 1951, the Japanese Government submitted *Our View* to the United States.[26] The JMFA wrote it in consultation with Yoshida on 29 January. Yoshida had written a marginal note: "I am setting forth below my private views, on which the cabinet is yet to be consulted. They do not, therefore, represent necessarily the official and final opinion of the government.–S .Y."[27] According to *Our View*, "Japan will ensure internal security by herself. But as regards external security, the cooperation of the United Nations and, especially, of the United States is desired through appropriate means such as the stationing of troops." Dulles obtained Yoshida's commitment to provide the United States with bases in Japan, which ensured the basic assumption of his peace treaty scheme. *Our View* reiterated that it was impossible for Japan to implement a rearmament program for some time, indicating that economic stability would be a prerequisite for a military buildup. Japan opposed rearmament because it would also have to consider its neighbors' anxiety that Japan might use its military power for aggression and at the same time watch carefully for the possible rise of militarism in Japan. Within these limitations, however, Japan was willing to discuss what specific contribution it could make to the collaborative defense of the free world.[28]

On 31 January 1951, Yoshida and Dulles had their second official talk. The US delegates said that *Our View* was "helpful." Dulles' responses to *Our View* were largely what the JMFA had expected.[29] He was satisfied to know that Japan was willing to ensure internal security. He then argued that when faced with a small-size military attack from outside, Japan's own defense power would not be enough and the United States was willing to assist. Dulles recognized that giving the United States the base rights would be politically unprecedented. In order to acquire Japan's continuous commitment to the free world, he linked the base issue to Japanese rearmament. "The US armed forces will stay in Japan until Japan can defend itself. We cannot, however, stay here forever. As Japan increases its defensive power, the United States will reduce its bases."[30] While showing his sympathy with Japan's economic difficulties, Dulles, nevertheless, did not accept them as a sufficient excuse to waive Japan's rearmament. Dulles requested that Yoshida overcome the difficulties and make even a nominal military contribution, offering US assistance for Japanese efforts. He also added that when Japan joined the United Nations, it would have to contribute to its peacekeeping efforts. Dulles tried to use the UN admission to induce Japanese rearmament.[31] Dulles argued that strengthening the police force was the first step and that Japan had to consider measures after that. Yoshida stubbornly replied that Japan would contribute to the defense of the free world by its productive power.[32]

The US delegates complained about Yoshida's stubbornness with regard to rearmament, asking if Yoshida understood Dulles's intention. They even wondered if Yoshida fully comprehended Dulles' English. Taking this complaint seriously, the Japanese officials recommended to Yoshida that Japan seek to achieve substantial gains by submitting a concrete national security scheme.[33]

On the morning of 1 February 1951, the JMFA submitted its "Formula Concerning Japanese-American Cooperation for Their Mutual Security" to the US delegates. It stated, "Japan will agree to the stationing of United States forces within the Japanese territory...."[34] On the same day, there was a meeting between Japanese and American bureaucrats. The Americans asked if Japan would not allow free movement of the US armed forces because the draft did not include this clause. The Japanese counterparts responded that Japan would accept such free movement. The US officials repeatedly requested that Japan contribute to the defense of the free world not only by use of its police forces and industrial power but also to a certain extent with its ground forces. They understood that Japan could only increase their forces gradually, but wanted to know the rough size of the first stage because the United States could then appropriately allocate its ground forces to other regions in the world. The US officials assured the JFMA that they would provide enough assistance, both fiscally and materially, to build up Japanese ground forces. The Japanese delegates responded that they would like to know first what amount of assistance they could expect before they began to discuss the size of the Japanese ground forces. In other words, the Japanese Government accepted the US proposal to build up Japanese ground forces in principal and they tried to acquire the best deal. The focus of the negotiation was not whether Japan would implement a rearmament program but rather the terms and conditions of Japan's rearmament. All agreed that only the United States would have the right to station armed forces in Japan. The US delegates also asked whether it would be difficult to amend the Constitution to allow rearmament, to which the Japanese counterparts responded that this was a quite delicate issue at the moment, indicating that they wanted to avoid touching on the issue.[35]

On 2 February 1951, there was another meeting between Japanese and American bureaucrats. The United States made sure that Japan clearly requested the stationing of US troops. The Japanese draft said, "Japan will agree to the stationing of United States forces. . . ." The US draft changed this phrase: "Japan requests and the United States agrees to the stationing of United States forces. . . ."[36] As for rearmament, the Japanese officials affirmed that until the Japanese public sentiment matured enough to accept rearmament, the best measure would be to include "physical force" in the general concept of "police force" and to accomplish, in this manner, the aim of rearmament. They added that the size of the "physical force" would depend on the amount of fiscal and material assistance from the United States.[37] The Americans countered that it was necessary to make efforts to defend their own country by themselves. After the meeting, these officials discussed with the Prime Minister that "any provision which allowed Japan to possess armed forces and to become a belligerent power would be problematic externally and would precipitate critical and complicated problems and would obstruct the peace treaty. It is wise to delete such a clause. This, however, does not mean to prohibit Japan from possessing armed forces or becoming a belligerent power." The JMFA bureaucrats recommended keeping any discussion on Japan's rearmament secret.[38] Later that day, Dulles publicly announced that the United States was willing to station its armed forces in and around Japan if the Japanese people wished.[39]

In the evening of 2 February, Yoshida informed the JMFA, "Since they [the Dulles Mission] strongly want to know our plan of establishing ground force as the first step of rearmament after the peace treaty, it would be helpful to show our intention in order to accelerate the negotiation. You need to devise one concrete program." Yoshida allowed them to include "a security force of 50,000 men." Tokyo finally submitted *A First Step for a Rearmament Scheme* on 3 February 1951 in which Japan proposed the establishment of a defense force of 50,000 men and the consideration of the establishment of a ministry of national security. The Yoshida faction of the Liberal Party (Jiyuto) tried to maintain a delicate balance between meeting the American demand to raise an army of 300,000 and satisfying the lingering anti-rearmament sentiment at home. The Hatoyama faction of the Liberal Party openly supported the US rearmament program to establish a force of 300,000 men and Group B made a plan to build up a 200,000 strong armed force.[40] Yoshida reduced these figures down to 50,000 in his negotiation with Dulles because of their fundamental agreement that what they needed was Japan's commitment to rearmament.[41]

In order to meet the JSSC's request, Dulles argued, "The US would want rights [to station troops] rather than obligation [to guarantee Japan's security]."[42] The United States was not "prepared to commit itself to maintain forces here indefinitely." Because of a lack of manpower in the United States, Dulles expected that Japan "could at least create a land force." He was "inclined to be patient," but would not allow Japan to become a free rider: "We are not prepared to make long-term formal engagements . . . while Japan is not in a position to assume correlative obligations."[43] Dulles publicly reaffirmed this point in his press conference on 19 April 1951: "The United States is not prepared to guarantee Japan's security permanently until it is clear what Japan's own contribution will be."[44] Dulles regarded the security treaty as tentative, expecting Japan's gradual progress toward rearmament.

Washington officials, however, were not monolithic in their opinions of how much pressure should be put on Japan for rearmament. There were fairly large forces that were ambivalent about the possible effects of such strong US pressure. Holland of the CFR argued, "It would be a serious drain on the Japanese economy if Japan were required to raise and sustain any considerable force of its own. . . . The consequences for Japan would be entirely different, however, if its main effort were devoted to the manufacture of military equipment that could be sold for foreign exchange." Hugh Borton agreed, "We should urge that the Japanese rearmament effort be directed into productive channels, such as the shipbuilding and automotive industries."[45] The Psychological Strategy Board advised not to push Japan too hard, warning that Japan's pro-Western orientation "may radically change, . . . if a serious effort to rearm Japan is undertaken in the present psychological climate. There is no doubt that the vast majority of the Japanese people oppose rearmament."[46] NSC 125 of February 1952, in more reserved terms, expected that "the Japanese must be led to understand that the United States-Japanese security arrangements are a common enterprise." The NSC's primary objective was to maintain Japan's voluntary pro-Western orientation.[47] Japan was something of a showcase in Asia because the Japan-US relationship was "an association between peoples of different races, different cultures, and backgrounds."[48] Dulles clearly recognized that the Japanese were "extremely pacifist [*sic*] in their mood. . . ." He was rather cautious because he knew that "you're not going to get the results that you want if you try to be coercive."[49]

On 6 February, in his meeting with MacArthur, Yoshida requested that the peace treaty avoid any indication that the Japanese constabulary would become a military force or that Japan would implement a rearmament program—a request with which MacArthur concurred.[50] Yoshida succeeded in creating an image of a pacifist Japan, which was necessary to contain anti-rearmament movement in Japan and to conciliate anti-Japanese feelings abroad. Moreover, this image in turn bolstered the US demand for rapid Japanese rearmament, and induced more American aid in return for Japan's reluctant defense contribution. The United States also needed this "peaceful" image of Japan to extenuate fear of the rise of Japanese militarism among Asia-Pacific neighbors. As the result of this compromise of interests, the Japanese Government continued to implement a gradual rearmament program without open and thorough discussion at home or any clear public explanation of its position. In other words, this deliberate vagueness was necessary to achieve Japanese gradual rearmament.

HEGEMON'S AGONY

The Korean War accelerated the polarization of international relations between the communist and capitalist blocs. It acted as a double-edged sword for US diplomacy. On the one hand, it became easier for the United States to consolidate the Western bloc because of the existence of the clear enemy. This polarization facilitated Washington's efforts to obtain the base rights and Yoshida's pledge for rearmament. On the other hand, the United States had to make a continuous commitment to provide benefits to the bloc members, especially those in the unstable region, in order to keep them in the Western bloc. Dulles asserted that there would be no middle road for Japan: Japan would have to become an enemy or a friend.[51] The State Department Intelligence asserted, "Failure to secure positive Japanese cooperation ... would be a significant weakening in the Western position, implicit in the strengthening of Communist China and in the possibility of an extension of Communist influence in Asia through the integration of Japanese industry and skills with mainland resources and manpower; and in the possibility of the release of Soviet power to focus increasingly on Europe."[52] In March 1951, the NSC senior staff members predicted that since the USSR would certainly try to exploit Japan's political and military weaknesses, Washington had to commit itself to create "a Japan with a rapidly and soundly developing economy, internal political stability, and an adequate military capability for self-defense."[53] NSC 48/5 of May 1951 argued that "the most immediate overt threats to United States security are currently presented in that area [Asia]."

Assuming that the Soviet Union with the cooperation of PRC sought to expand its influence in the Asia-Pacific region, NSC 48/5 anticipated that the Soviet control of this region including Japan would constitute "an unacceptable threat to the security of the United States."[54] NSC 125/1 concluded: "The security of Japan is of such importance to the United States position in the Pacific area that the United States would fight to prevent hostile forces from gaining control of any part of the territory of Japan."[55]

The State Department was especially concerned about maintaining US prestige in its relations with Japan: "All post-Treaty arrangements with Japan must be conducted in such a way as to maintain and advance the prestige of the United States and its representatives in Japan since such prestige is fundamental to satisfactory United States-Japanese relations."[56] Dulles feared that Japan might have a doubt about the US credibility in Asia.[57] Logic of a zero-sum game of the Cold War convinced Dulles that if "Japan is left bereft of any other help and has to stand alone, it would be absolutely certain that Soviet power would move in just as it moved into the vacuums of power that were left after the war in Central Europe." Consequently, he regarded it necessary for the United States to defend Japan even after its independence."[58]

Since Japan was an undependable former enemy, the United States could not just trust Tokyo's good will but had to stimulate its self-interest to side with the West, and at the same time, to prevent Japan from becoming a menace to other Asian nations. Charles Spinks of GHQ recognized, "[The] Japanese are essentially realists and their present general tendency to seek or accept an orientation toward the United States is inspired more by pragmatic considerations than any innate or compelling affection for the United States." NSC 125 of July 1951 indicated that Japan's future orientation would "depend in large degree upon maintenance by the United States of a strong military posture in the Pacific and the pursuance of policies by the United States and other free nations which encourage the growth in Japan of basic economic strength." In the long run, the NSC expected, "Japan's access to raw materials and markets for her exports will significantly affect Japan's basic operation." Sebald also reported that the US "security objectives can only be attained if Japan is convinced that it has a stake in the free world and that it is to its own self-interest to cooperate with the West." Dean Rusk insisted that US policy should lead Japan to make a voluntary and strong commitment to staying with the free, capitalist world-system.[59] General Ridgway, MacArthur's successor, believed that it was of "vital importance to retain Japan on side of free world," arguing that the United States had to "depend on self-interests of Japan to join with us."[60] Acting Secretary of State James Webb and Secretary of Defense Robert Lovett advised President Harry S. Truman that the "United States can attain its long-range security objectives in the Far East to the fullest extent only if Japan, in its own self-interest, fully recognizes its stake in the free world, develops close political, military and economic cooperation with the United States and other free nations."[61] In February 1952, the NSC concluded that the "overriding requirement for United States policy ... is the necessity for preserving and strengthening the voluntary and strong commitment" of Japan and the Japanese people to the West.[62] The CIA predicted that Japan's "pro-Western orientation [will last] at least during the next two or three years." Economic prosperity, however, would be essential to maintain this orientation: "If, however, Japan is unable to solve its economic problems, it will be particularly vulnerable to economic and diplomatic pressures from the Soviet Bloc and will be tempted to seize opportunities for closer economic and political relations with the Bloc."[63] The CIA concluded that the United States would need to provide two conditions to retain Japan on its side: maintenance of Japan's security and assurance of its economic prosperity.[64] Not a single-shot policy but an ongoing process of policies was necessary to attain this objective.

The Japanese government's primary task was to find the very minimum defense contribution line that would not jeopardize its ties with the United States. Tokyo endeavored to acquire security without wasting scarce resources for defense. The Japanese officials were excellent at exploiting the hegemon's Achilles' heel: They used the US security anxiety in Japan as a bargaining chip to induce greater US engagement in Japan's economic recovery. The PRC's intervention in the Korean War significantly raised the strategic importance of Japan, which gave the Japanese government more bargaining power in dealing with the United States. In March 1951, the ESB requested that the United States provide $150 million worth of assistance, imports of US capital and technology, and credit for food and assistance for 1952.[65] Although Yoshida agreed to the rearmament program, he told Watanabe of the Finance Ministry, prior to his visit to the United States, to make it clear that Japan could not implement the rearmament program immediately. When Japan became a little richer, it might be able to do so, but it could not do so yet.[66] Yoshida tried to induce aid from the United States in exchange for Japan's rearmament. As a weak ally in an unstable area surrounded by two giant communist countries, Japan found its weakness the best asset to deal with the United States. Watanabe told Dulles that in order to get Japan to stay within the free world, the United States should provide it with a sense of security.[67]

The CIA emphasized the unpredictable nature of the Japanese rearmament: "Even if Japan's military defenses were re-established, however, there would be no assurance that those forces would be used in opposition to Communism, if there were compelling economic reasons for an accommodation with the Communist world."[68] The US decision to strengthen Japan in the

Cold-War power struggle narrowed the range of policy options toward Japan: Washington could no longer afford to allow Tokyo to join the Communist bloc, and it had to implement Japan's economic recovery and assure its dependence on the United States. The Japanese rearmament decreased US flexibility while it greatly increased Japan's maneuvering power. NSC 48/1 warned that Japan would exaggerate its strategic importance and exploit US security concerns in order to obtain more aid from the United States.[69]

Global commitment was the requirement for US hegemony in the world-system and for its continuing active policy toward Asia. The conservative-minded Congress, however, sought to reduce pure economic aid to foreign countries. John Allison believed that actual fighting in Korea and Indo-China required more and more aid to Asia and in order to continue this flow of aid to Asia, he had to combine security with economic assistance: "It seems to me that all aid to any of these countries in the Far East under present world conditions must be justified on security grounds." The magic word was "security" in a broader sense: "I do not mean that the word 'security' should be interpreted in a narrow sense and certainly the provision of economic and technical assistance is one of the most effective methods of insuring that security."[70] The Truman Administration justified its commitment to Asia in the name of "security." The JCS planned to use bases in Japan for unilateral US military operations in Asia-Pacific including "the mainland of China ... the USSR, and on the high seas, regardless of whether such use is under United Nations aegis."[71] Assistant Secretary of State U. Alexis Johnson made a statement at the Hearings of the 91st Congress in January 1970 that the primary mission of the US forces and bases in Japan was not only to protect Japan but also to "support our commitments elsewhere" in Asia.[72] Nishimura Kumao of the JMFA also explained that the United States could take military action outside the Far East in order to secure peace and stability in the Far East.[73] The retention of the US bases and armed forces in Japan had an inherent tendency to expand the US mission in Asia. Security had no limits and no matter how deeply Washington became involved, it could not find the end, and each step of engagement would require another step. It was just like an Asian quagmire.

Even though the United States seemed to be the hegemonic power that almost unilaterally controlled Japan, in reality, the Cold War polarization, Cold War mentality in Washington, Asian instability, and the US Congressional constraints set limits on US power. The NSC feared that because of the cold-war structure, "Japan's flexibility of maneuver and freedom of choice will increase ... [and] Japan may try to take advantage of the United States-USSR conflict."[74] According to the State Department's analysis, Japan's weakness ironically increased its bargaining power: "Japan's bargaining situation vis-à-vis that of the United States is going to be extremely strong, since there is always the pull of closer relations with the Communist areas of Asia."[75] In addition, the retention of bases in Japan constituted another double-edged sword. Freeman Matthews, Deputy Undersecretary of State, emphasized the importance of Japan's role as a showcase to other Asian countries. On the one hand, since many Asian countries suffered Western colonialism and unequal treaties with the West for a long time, Japan's spontaneous ties with the United States and voluntary acceptance of stationing US troops would greatly increase "United States prestige and influence throughout Asia."[76] On the other hand, "it will be disastrous if it should develop that the presence of the United States forces in Japan is contrary to the wishes of the Japanese themselves and appears to the people of Asia to be an expression of 'western imperialism.'"[77] Consequently, the United States had to prevent the base issue from becoming an agenda of a heated debate at the Diet.

The United States seemed to obtain everything it wanted from the peace treaty negotiations with Japan, but this very achievement, in turn, restricted its options later. Washington could not push Japan too hard concerning Japan's rearmament program fearing that this topic might lead to a sensitive issue of amending Article Nine and US bases in Japan. Although security was one of the most important aspects in the US policy toward Japan, it was a Pandora's box: Nobody would dare touch it in an open and frank manner. Even though the United States acquired what it wished, the base rights and Japan's promise of future rearmament, this very success restrained the American freedom of behavior. Washington had to continue providing Japan with security and economic prosperity, but it also had to be careful not to make the security issue a subject of hot political debate in the Diet.

On 8 September 1951, 49 nations signed the San Francisco Peace Treaty, and it became effective on 28 April 1952. Japan and the United States also signed the Japan-US Security Treaty on 8 September 1951, which came into effect on 28 April 1952. The US occupation of Japan seemed to be quite successful on surface and the end of the occupation marked a new page of US-Japan relations that was full of high expectations, but the very success of US occupation policies had already planted seeds of its deep involvement in Asian affairs.

CONCLUDING OBSERVATIONS

The primary purpose of this book is to explain the limits and the ironies of American hegemonic power in occupied Japan. The US, wielding its dominant power, was successful in the early stages of the occupation, but this very success caused the United States to take on more burdens. Japan initiated the process of returning to the Anglo-American bloc in order to preserve its *kokutai* (national polity). This process, along with SCAP's zeal for remaking Japan, led swiftly to demilitarization and democratization. This achievement, however, left two major problems. First, Japan would have to produce an economic recovery in order to establish a new economic structure. Secondly, and moreover, since Article Nine of the new constitution made Japan defenseless, Japan would have to resolve post-occupation security issues.

Washington gradually took over occupation policy initiatives from SCAP. George Kennan's long telegram precipitated the intensification of a Cold War mentality in Washington after 1947. It was at this very moment that General MacArthur made it public that the United States would soon be ready to conclude a peace treaty. This announcement stimulated Washington's interest in Japan, and occupation policy initiatives began to shift from SCAP to Washington. The United States sought to absorb Japan into the Western camp. Punitive sentiment overshadowed US occupation policy immediately after the war, but this gradually eased and gave way to a more moderate disposition by 1948. In addition, because China remained in a chaotic state, the United States had to abandon its 'divided-core strategy' and it gradually fostered Japan as a single regional power in the unstable Asia-Pacific region. Washington faced two critical issues: It had to strengthen Japan as the primary stabilizing force in the region, while at the same time it had to make sure that the Communist bloc would not absorb Japan.

The adverse effects of inflation and a controlled economy were critical issues in Japan. The Japanese financial community effectively used Joseph Dodge to establish a liberal, market-oriented economic system. Equally, during the transitional period, the community channeled the direction of the Japanese discontent resulting from the country's economic depression toward the United States. The Dodge Line was the turning point in the US occupation of Japan, shifting the focus from a "production-first" strategy to an "export-first" program. The Japanese financial community positively assisted Joseph Dodge to break the ground for a Japanese liberal economic system managed by the financial community. He was successful in developing this system, but its fate depended on the expansion of Japanese exports. Japanese resistance to Dodge's severe austerity program urged the United States to increase Japanese exports. Japan's uncompetitiveness convinced US officials that Japan could penetrate only the Asian market, not the world market, but Asia was so unstable that the United States would have to intervene in this area in order to fend off communism and to bring stability to the region.

Security, after the termination of the US occupation of Japan, became a significant issue. Japan reluctantly accepted the US decision to maintain its military bases in Japan. This decision came after the occupation removed the security issue as the major obstacle to concluding a peace treaty, even as it restricted US policy options regarding Japan. Prime Minister Yoshida publicly declared that Japan's economic conditions would prohibit any rapid and large-scale rearmament. US officials could not reach a consensus on the Japanese rearmament issue. In contrast, Japan and the United States shared the opinion that the retention of American bases would be the most practical way to maintain Japan's security. This solution, however, was politically and psychologically sensitive for Japan. Because of this sensitivity, Washington hesitated in pushing Japan too hard toward rearmament after the occupation. In short, the successful acquisition of rights to bases in Japan in turn restricted American pressure for Japan's rearmament.

The Korean War made the United States sensitive to the communist menace and the importance of maintaining US prestige in Asia, although the war did not significantly alter the course of Japanese development. The Dodge-Ikeda-Ichimada Nexus firmly established the groundwork for the new economic structure led by the finance community, and they successfully defeated those who favored the remilitarization of the Japanese economy. This outcome restricted the US pressure for Japanese rearmament even as the American perception of the rise of communism in Asia propelled the United States to make a deeper commitment in Asian affairs.

The Yoshida-Dulles negotiation in early 1951 was a critical event that shaped Japan's development in the post-occupation era. Security was the major concern throughout the talks. Yoshida and Dulles shared the fundamental position that Japan would have to make at least a nominal commitment to rearmament and that it would also allow the Untied States to maintain its military bases after the occupation. The United States stationed its armed forces in Japan, and in compensation for its broad military protection, it forced Tokyo to agree to a rearmament program despite its reluctance. As the United States strengthened Japan, it had to worry about Japan's neutralist orientation which might lead to its abandoning of the Western bloc. Such developments further increased Washington's involvement in Japan, as achieving economic prosperity and national security was an perpetual process. The more Washington became involved in this process, the deeper its commitment became.

Notes

INTRODUCTION

1. Thomas McCormick, *America's Half-Century: United States Foreign Policy in the Cold War* (Baltimore: The Johns Hopkins University Press, 1989), p. 5.

2. Herbert Passin, *The Legacy of the Occupation–Japan* (New York: East Asian Institute, Columbia University, 1968); Edwin Reischauer, *The United States and Japan* (Cambridge: Harvard University Press, 1965); Kenneth Latourette, *The American Record in the Far East, 1945-1951* (New York: MacMillan, 1952); Robert E. Ward, "Reflections on the Allied Occupation and Planned Political Change in Japan," in Robert E. Ward ed., *Political Development in Modern Japan* (Princeton: Princeton University Press, 1968); Robert E. Ward, "The American Occupation of Japan: Political Retrospect," in Grant K. Goodman comp., *The American Occupation of Japan: A Retrospective View* (New York: Paragon Book Gallery, 1968); Robert E. Ward, "Conclusion," in Robert E. Ward and Sakamoto Yoshikazu eds., *Democratizing Japan: The Allied Occupation* (Honolulu: The University of Hawaii Press, 1987); Theodore Cohen, *Remaking Japan: The American Occupation As New Deal* (New York: The Free Press, 1987); Theodore Cohen, *Nihon Senryo Kakumei [The Third Turn: MacArthur, the Americans and the Rebirth of Japan]* (Tokyo: TBS Britannica, 1983); Akira Iriye, *After Imperialism: The Search for a New Order in the Far East, 1921-1931* (Cambridge: Harvard University Press, 1965); Akira Iriye, *Across the Pacific: An Inner History of American-East Asian Relations* (New York: Harcourt, Brace & Jovanovich, 1967); Akira Iriye, "Continuities in U.S.-Japanese Relations, 1941-49," in Yonosuke Nagai and Akira Iriye, eds., *The Origins of the Cold War in Asia* (New York: Columbia University Press, 1977); Iriye Akira, *Nichibei Senso [The Japan-U.S. War]* (Tokyo: Chuo Koronsha, 1978); Akira Iriye, *Power and Culture: the Japanese-American War, 1941-1945* (Cambridge: Harvard University Press, 1981).

3. T. A. Bisson, *Zaibatsu Dissolution in Japan* (Berkeley: University of California Press, 1954); Thomas Bisson, *Nihon Senryo Kaisoki [Reform Years in Japan 1945-47: An Occupation Memoir]* (Tokyo: Sanseido, 1983); Owen Lattimore, *The Situation in Asia* (Boston: Little Brown, 1949).

4. Ohkurasho Zaiseishishitsu [Office of Financial History, Ministry of Finance], ed., *Showa Zaiseishi [Economic and Financial History of the Showa Era, hereafter SZ]* Vol. 3 (Tokyo: Toyo Keizai Shimposha, 1976); Watanabe Akio, "Sengo Nihon no Shuppatsu," ["A New Start of Postwar Japan,"] in Watanabe Akio, ed., *Sengo Nihon no Taigai Seisaku [Foreign Policies of Postwar Japan]* (Tokyo: Yuhikaku, 1985); John W. Dower, "Occupied Japan as History and Occupation History as Politics," *Journal of Asian Studies*, XXXIV (1975); John W. Dower, *Empire and Aftermath: Yoshida Shigeru and the Japanese Experience, 1878-1954* (Cambridge: Harvard University Press, 1988); John W. Dower, "Occupied Japan and the American Lake, 1945-1950," in Edward Friedman and Mark Selden, eds., *America's Asia: Dissenting Essays on Asian-American Relations* (New York: Pantheon, 1971); John W. Dower, "The Superdomino in Postwar Asia: Japan In and Out of the Pentagon Papers," in Noam Chomsky and Howard Zinn, eds., *The Senator Gravel Edition of The Pentagon Papers Vol. 5* (Boston: Beacon Press, 1972); William Borden, *The Pacific Alliance: United States Foreign Economic Policy and Japanese Trade Recovery, 1947-1955* (Madison: University of Wisconsin Press, 1984); Igarashi Takeshi, *Tainichi Kowa to Reisen: Sengo Nichibei Kankei no Keisei [The Japanese Peace Treaty and the Cold War: The Formation of Postwar Japan-U.S. Relations]* (Tokyo: Tokyo Daigaku Shuppankai, 1986); Howard Schonberger, *Aftermath of War: Americans and the Remaking of Japan, 1945-1952* (Kent: The Kent State University Press, 1989).

5. Ronald L. McGlothlen, *Controlling the Waves: Dean Acheson and U.S. Foreign Policy in Asia* (New York: W.W. Norton & Company, 1993); William Guttman, "Miracles of Power: America and the Making of East Asian Economic Growth," (D. Phil., University of Oxford, 1989).

6. John Dower, *Embracing Defeat: Japan in the Wake of World War II* (New York: W.W. Norton & Company, 2000); Herbert Bix, *Hirohito and the Making of Modern Japan* (New York: HarperCollins, 2000).

CHAPTER ONE: SETTING THE STAGE

1. Stuart to the Secretary of State, 20 August 1946, the Department of State, *Foreign Relations of the United States* (hereafter *FR*) 1946, VIII, The Far East (Washington, D.C.: Government Printing Office, 1971), pp. 301-04.

2. George Kennan, "Problems of Far Eastern Policy," 14 January 1948, *George Kennan Papers*, Mudd Manuscript Library, Princeton University.

3. Chae-Jin Lee and Hideo Sato, *U.S. Policy Toward Japan and Korea* (New York: Praeger, 1982), p. 1.

4. Ballantine to Secretary of State, *FR* 1944, China (Washington, D.C.: Government Printing Office, 1967), p. 32.

5. Memorandum of Telephone Conversation by Joseph Grew, 4 August 1945, *FR* 1945 VI, The British Commonwealth, The Far East, China (Washington, D.C.: Government Printing Office, 1969), pp. 586, 588.

6. As for wartime internal affairs of China, see Himeda Mitsuyoshi et. al., *Chugoku Kingendai Shi [Chinese Modern History]* (Tokyo: Tokyo Daigaku Shuppankai, 1982), Vol. 2; Tatsumi Okabe, "The Cold War and China," in Nagai and Iriye eds., *Cold War in Asia*; Kenneth Shewmaker, *Americans and Chinese Communists, 1927-1945* (Ithaca: Cornell University Press, 1971); Chalmers Johnson, *Peasant Nationalism and Communist Power* (Stanford: Stanford University Press, 1962); Shun-hsi Chou, *The Chinese Inflation 1937-1949* (New York: Columbia University Press, 1963); Chang Kia-ngau, *The Inflationary Spiral* (Cambridge, MA: The Technology Press of Massachusetts Institute of Technology, 1958); Lloyd Eastman, *Seeds of Destruction* (Stanford: Stanford University Press, 1984); Yu Kwei Cheng, *Foreign Trade and Industrial Development of China* (Westport: Greenwood Press, 1978).

7. Donald Nelson's Report, 1947, *FR* 1944, China, p. 262.

8. David Steinberg, *Philippine Collaboration in World War II* (Ann Arbor: University of Michigan Press, 1967); Harry Benda, *The Crescent and the Rising Sun* (The Hague: W. van Hoeve, 1958); Christopher Thorne, *Allies of a Kind: The United States, Britain and the War Against Japan, 1941-1945* (New York: Oxford University Press, 1978); Iriye, *Nichibei Senso*, p. 258.

9. Sugita Yoneyuki, "'Kanri Sareta Kakumei' Koso: Beikoku no Tai Chugoku Seisaku 1941-1945 nen,"["An idea of 'Managed Revolution': American Policies toward China, 1941-1945,"]*Seiyo Shigaku [The Occidental History]* Vol. 157 (June 1990).

10. Judd to Truman, 6 July 1945, Official File 197, *Papers of Harry S Truman* [Hereafter *PHST*], Truman Library, Independence, Missouri.

11. John Lewis Gaddis, "Reconsiderations: Was the Truman Doctrine a Real Turning Point?" *Foreign Affairs,* Vol. 52, No. 2 (January 1974), p. 391.

12. Robert M. Blum, *Drawing the Line: The Origin of the American Containment Policy in East Asia* (New York: W. W. Norton & Company, 1982), p. 4.

13. NSC Draft, 12 September 1947, Records of the National Security Council, *PHST,* Truman Library, Independence, Missouri.

14. Blum, *Drawing the Line,* p. 4; Catherine Edwards, "U.S. Policy towards Japan, 1945-1951: Rejection of Revolution," (Ph.D. dissertation, University of California, Los Angeles, 1977), p. 10.

15. Iokibe Makoto, *Beikoku no Nihon Senryo Seisaku [U.S. Occupation Policy of Japan]* Vol. 1, pp. 256-82; *SZ* Vol. 3, p. 26; Marlene Mayo, "American Economic Planning for Occupied Japan," in Lawrence Redford ed., *The Occupation of Japan: Economic Policy and Reform* (Norfolk: The MacArthur Memorial, 1980), p. 208.

16. Robert A. Pollard, *Economic Security and the Origins of the Cold War, 1945-1950* (New York: Columbia University Press, 1985), p. 174; Takemae Eiji and Amakawa Akira, *Nihon Senryo Hishi [Secret History of Occupation of Japan]* Vol. 1 (Tokyo: Asahi Shinbunsha, 1977), p. 51.

17. Richard Finn, *Makkasa to Yoshida Shigeru [Winners in Peace]* (Tokyo: Dobunshoin International, 1993) Vol. 1, p. 64.

18. JCS1380/15, JCS to SCAP, *SZ*, Vol. 20 (Tokyo: Toyo Keizai Shimposha, 1982), p. 163.

19. John Dower, *Yoshida Shigeru to Sono Jidai [Empire and Aftermath]* (Tokyo: TBS Buritanika, 1981), Vol. 2, pp. 11, 22; T. J. Pempel, *Policy and Politics in Japan*

(Philadelphia: Temple University Press, 1982), p. 53.

20. The Konoe Memorial, February 1945, cited in Dower, *Empire and Aftermath*, p. 260.

21. Masumi Junnosuke, "Sengoshi no Kigen to Isou," ["Origins and Phases of Postwar History,"] Nakamura Masanori et. al., eds., *Sengo Nihon: Senryo to Sengo Kaikaku [Postwar Japan: Occupation and Postwar Reforms]* Vol. 2 (Tokyo: Iwanami Shoten, 1995), p. 13.

22. Richard J. Barnet, *Allies: America, Europe, Japan Since the War* (London: Jonathan Cape, 1984), p. 67; Michael Yoshitsu, *Nihon ga Dokuritsushita Hi [Japan and the San Francisco Peace Settlement]* (Tokyo: Kodansha, 1984), p. 19.

23. William R. Nester, *Japan's Growing Power over East Asia and the World Economy: Ends and Means* (Basingstoke: The MacMillan Press, 1990), p. 49.

24. William Chapman, *Inventing Japan: The Making of a Postwar Civilization* (New York: Prentice Hall Press, 1991), pp. 83-84.

25. Igarashi, *Tainichi Kowa to Reisen*, p. 181.

26. For the construction of racial imagery in nationalist propaganda, see John Dower, *War Without Mercy* (New York: Pantheon Books, 1986); Theodore Cohen, *Nihon Senryo Kakumei* (Tokyo: TBS Buritanika, 1983)Vol. 1, p. 97. In October 1945, Karl Compton, President of Massachusetts Institute of Technology, wrote to Truman that "there was initially very great uncertainty as to what would happen when the first handful of American troops entered Atsugi Airport and what would happen when the initial small detachments of Americans entered Yokohama, Tokyo, and other cities." October 4, 1945, Iokibe Makoto ed., *The Occupation of Japan Part 2 U.S. and Allied Policy 1945-1952* (Tokyo: Maruzen, 1989), 1A-21.

27. Amakawa Akira "'Minshuka' Katei to Kanryo no Taiou," ["'Democratization' Process and Bureaucrats' Responses,"] Nakamura Masanori, et.al. eds., *Sengo Nihon* Vol. 2 , p. 241.

28. Seimukyoku [The Political Bureau], 31 January 1946, *Nihon Gaiko Monjo [Documents of Japanese Foreign Relations]* (hereafter *NGM*) B'4.0.0.1 Vol. 1, #0056 Gaiko Shiryokan [Archives of the Ministry of Foreign Affairs], Tokyo.

29. Clayton James, *The Years of MacArthur,* Vol. 3 (New York: Houghton Mifflin Company, 1985), p. 7; Kazuo Kawai, *Japan's American Interlude* (Chicago: The University of Chicago Press, 1960), pp. 4, 6.

30. "Dilemma in Japan," *The Economist*, 26 February 1949, p. 357.

31. Shiraishi Takashi, *Sengo Nihon Tsusho Seisakushi [History of Postwar Japanese Trade Policy]* (Tokyo: Zeimu Keiri Kyokai, 1983), p. 3.

32. Warren S. Hunsberger, *Japan and the United States in World Trade* (New York: Harper & Row, Publishers, Inc., 1964), p. 80.

33. *SZ*, Vol. 17 (Tokyo: Toyo Keizai Shimposha, 1981), p. 502.

34. Nakamura Takafusa ed., *Shiryo: Sengo Nihon no Keizaiseisaku Koso [Documents: Postwar Japan's Idea of Economic Policies]* Vol. 1 (Tokyo: Tokyo Daigaku Shuppankai, 1990), pp. 18, 94.

35. Foreign Minister Yoshida Shigeru insisted that Japan introduce Anglo-American capital and technology and liberalize domestic economic system. Yoshida Shigeru Kinen Jigyoukai [Yoshida Shigeru Memorial], ed., *Yoshida Shigeru Shokan [Letters of Yoshida Shigeru]* (Tokyo: Chuo Koron, 1994), pp. 175-76, 553-54. The JMFA agreed that

Japan "should belong to the Anglo-American bloc." Nakamura ed., *Shiryo*, Vol. 1, pp. 18, 94, 100.

36. Igarashi, *Tainichi Kowa to Reisen*, p. 181.

37. Nakamura ed., *Shiryo*, Vol. 1, vi, pp. 65, 121, 135.

38. *Ibid.*, pp. 121-22, 133; Arisawa Hiromi and Inaba Shuzo eds., *Shiryo: Sengo 20nen Shi [Documents: Postwar 20-Year History]* (Tokyo: Nihon Hyoronsha, 1966), p. 21.

39. Nakamura ed., *Shiryo*, Vol. 1, p. 252. In the United States, an important national body of engineers shared the same view. In a report to the Secretaries of State, War and Navy, they warned that "the complete elimination of Japanese industry, leaving the nation to eke out a living on agriculture and fishing, if possible, would create social chaos and suffering of such magnitude that enforcement would be impossible, and world opinion would repudiate the action." Anticipating that Asian nations would soon have a competitive edge in textiles and daily miscellaneous goods because of their lower labor costs, they recommended a Japanese shift to the export of machinery and chemicals. In other words, the Japanese economic recovery would require heavy industrial development. *SZ*, Vol. 20, p. 436.

40. Iriye, *After Imperialism*; Iriye, *Across the Pacific*.

41. Iriye, *Nichibei Senso*, p. 262.

42. Donald P. Ray to the Secretary of State, 20 July 1945, the Department of State, *Records of the U.S. Department of State Relating to the Internal Affairs of Japan (hereafter IAJ) 1945-1949* (Wilmington: Scholarly Resources, 1986), Reel #20.

43. Memorandum of Telephone Conversation by Joseph Grew, 4 August 1945, *FR* 1945 VI, The British Commonwealth, The Far East, p. 586.

44. Iriye, *Nichibei Senso*, p. 262.

45. James, *The Years of MacArthur* Vol. 3, p. 57.

46. 27 January 1948, Study Group Reports, "Japan," *Papers of Council on Foreign Relations*, Council on Foreign Relations Archives, New York, NY.

47. Masumi, "Sengoshi no Kigen to Iso," p. 13.

48. Yoshihara Koichiro and Kubo Ryozo eds., *Nichibei Ampo Joyaku Taiseishi [History of the Japan-US Security Pact System]* Vol. 1 (Tokyo: Sanseido, 1970), p. 126; Yui Daizaburo, *Mikan no Senryo Kaikaku [Unfinished Occupation Reforms]* (Tokyo: Tokyo Daigaku Shuppankai, 1989), p. 268.

49. Mikuriya Takashi, "'Teikoku' Nihon no Kaitai to 'Minshu' Nihon no Keisei,"["Dissolution of 'Imperial' Japan and Creation of 'Democratic' Japan,"] Nakamura et. al., eds., *Sengo Nihon* Vol. 2, pp. 172-73.

50. *FR* 1945, VI, The British Commonwealth, The Far East, p. 102.

51. G. C. Allen, *Japan's Economic Recovery* (London: Oxford University Press, 1958), p. 33; Edwards, "U.S. Policy," p. 163.

52. Guttman, "Miracles of Power," Vol. 1, p. 72.

53. G. C. Allen, *Japan's Economic Recovery*, p. 28.

54. 24 April 1946, Memorandum for the Chief, Public Administration Division of Government Section, *Hussey papers* (University of Michigan) in *John Dower Collection* (Professor John Dower's personal collection of documents at Massachusetts Institute of Technology, hereafter *JDC*).

55. Herbert Bix portrayed Emperor Hirohito as a shrewd, active, and energetic leader who aggressively animated Japan's war system. Bix, however, seems to exag-

gerate the power and role of Hirohito and undermines the Japanese militarists as an independent and uncontrolled force. Bix, *Hirohito.*

56. United States Department of State, *Department of State Bulletin* (1 January 1944) in Yamagiwa Akira and Nakamura Masanori eds., *Shiryo Nihon Senryo 1: Tennosei [Documents of Japanese Occupation 1: the Imperial System]* (Tokyo: Ohtsuki Shoten, 1990), pp. 219-32.

57. *New York Times*, 2 January 1944 in *Ibid.*, pp. 234-35.

58. Edward Hunter, "Can We Make Use of Hirohito?" *Nation* (4 March 1944) in *Ibid.*, pp. 240-43.

59. *FR*, Vol. VI, 1945 (Washington D.C.: Government Printing Office, 1969), pp. 587-90.

60. Iokibe Makoto, *Beikoku no Nihon Senryo Seisaku [US Occupation Policy of Japan]* Gekan [Vol. 2] (Tokyo: Chuo Koron, 1985), p. 167.

61.*Congressional Record* Vol. 92, 79th Congress, 1st Session, 18 September 1945, in SWNCC 55 series in Yamagiwa and Nakamura eds., *Shiryo Nihon Senryo 1: Tennosei*, pp. 416-17.

62. *The New York Post*, 24 September 1945 in Hasegawa Masayasu, *Showa Kemposhi [History of Showa Constitution]* (Tokyo: Iwanami, 1971), p. 212.

63. Hornbeck Papers in *Ibid.*, pp. 193-98.

64. Hurley to the Secretary of State, 28 July 1945, *FR* 1945 VI, The British Commonwealth, The Far East, pp. 901-02.

65. The Australian Legation to the Department of State, 13 August 1945, *Ibid.*, pp. 650-54; Patton to the Secretary of State, 20 September 1945, *Ibid.*, pp. 719-20; Winant to the Secretary of State, 7 January 1946, *FR* 1946 VIII, The Far East (Washington D.C.: Government Printing Office, 1971), p. 384.

66. *FR* 1945, Vol. 1, Conference of Berlin, in Yamagiwa Akira and Nakamura Masanori eds., *Shiryo Nihon Senryo 1: Tennosei [Documents of Japanese Occupation 1: the Imperial System]* (Tokyo: Ohtsuki Shoten, 1990), p. 311.

67. *The Liberation Daily*, 14 September 1945, in *Ibid.*, pp. 411-13.

68. Notter File, 30 December 1943 - 23 February 1944 in *Ibid.*, pp. 49-67.

69. *FR* Vol. VI, 1945, p. 545.

70. *Ibid.*, pp. 924-26.

71. Iokibe, *Beikoku*, Jokan [Vol. 1], pp. 256-82; Hornbeck Papers in Yamagiwa and Nakamura eds., *Tennosei*, pp. 131-41.

72. Iokibe, *Beikoku*, Gekan [Vol. 2], pp. 5, 62-69.

73. Ray Moore, "Reflections on the Occupation of Japan," *Journal of Asian Studies*, Vol. XXXVIII, No. 4 (1979), p. 732.

74. This message was prepared jointly by the Departments of State, War, and Navy, and approved by the President on 6 September 1945 and released to the public on 22 September 1945. President's Secretary's File (hereafter PSF) Subject File #182, Japan, *PHST*, Harry S Truman Library, Independence, Missouri; SWNCC 150/4/A, 21 September 1945, Martin P. Claussen ed., *State-War-Navy Coordinating Committee and State-Army-Navy-Air Force Coordinating Committee, Case Files 1944-1949* (Wilmington, Delaware: Scholarly Resources, 1978).

75. The Department of State, *The Far Eastern Commission* (Hereafter *FEC*)

(Washington D.C.: Government Printing Office, 1953), pp. 20-21.

76. Dower, *Embracing Defeat*, pp. 282, 298, 283.

77. Memorandum for the Secretary, SWNCC by SFE, 5 October 1945, Claussen ed., *Case Files 1944-1949*.

78. SWNCC 55/6, 26 October 1945, *Ibid.*

79. SWNCC 209, RG353, in Yamagiwa and Nakamura eds., *Tennosei*, pp. 460-61.

80. Memorandum of the first Emperor-MacArthur meeting by Okumura, 27 September 1945, *Ibid.*, pp. 512-14.

81. Memorandum to the Commander-in-Chief by Bonner F. Fellers, 2 October 1945, *Ibid.*, pp. 515-16.

82. Roger Buckley, *Occupation Diplomacy* (Cambridge: Cambridge University Press, 1982), p. 62. He informed Navy Minister Yoneuchi on 26 November 1945 that GHQ would not alter the Emperor's status. Sumimoto Toshio, *Senryo Hiroku [Secret History of Occupation]* (Tokyo: Mainichi Shimbun, 1965), p. 133.

83. Included in SWNCC 209/1, 7 March 1946, Claussen ed., *Case Files 1944-1949*.

84. Sumimoto, *Senryo Hishi*, p. 135; Yoshida Naikaku Kankokai [Association of the Yoshida Cabinet Publication] *Yoshida Naikaku [The Yoshida Cabinet]* (Tokyo: Yoshida Naikaku Kankokai, 1954), p. 32.

85. Mikuriya, "'Teikoku' Nihon," p. 176.

86. Atcheson to Truman, 4 January 1946, *FR* 1946 VIII, The Far East, pp. 90-91.

87. *Ibid.*, pp. 102-03.

88. *Ibid.*, pp. 90-91.

89. *Ibid.*, p. 100.

90. National Archives Record Group 353, SWNCC 209 in Yamagiwa and Nakamura eds., *Tennosei*, pp. 460-61.

91. MacArthur to Eisenhower, 25 January 1946, *FR* 1946 VIII, The Far East, pp. 396-97.

92. Sodei Rinjiro and Takemae Eiji eds., *Sengo Nihon no Genten [The Origins of Postwar Japan]* Vol. 1 (Tokyo: Eiko, 1992), p. 244. The *Stars and Stripes* reported on 15 February 1946 that both the United States and Great Britain agreed provide the Emperor with immunity from prosecution. Sumimoto, *Secret Occupation History*, p. 137.

93. Report by Blakeslee, 26 December 1945 - 13 February 1946, *FR* 1946 VIII, The Far East, p. 166.

94. The Secretary of State to Winant, 18 February 1946, *Ibid.*, p. 415.

95. Memorandum by SWNCC to the Secretary of State, 13 April 1946, *Ibid.*, p. 200.

96. International Military Tribunal for the Far East, *Record of the proceedings of the International Military Tribunal for the Far East, [1946-1948]: Court House of the Tribunal, War Ministry Building, Tokyo, Japan / the United States of America. . .[et al.] against Araki, Sadao. . .[et al.].* (Washington D.C.: Library of Congress, 1946-1948), pp. 1540, 1545.

97. *Ibid.*, pp. 30795-96.

98. *Ibid.*, pp. 31329-30.

99. *Ibid.*, pp. 36381-83.

100. *Asahi Shimbum [The Asahi Newspaper]*, 29 September 1945.

101. *FR* Vol. VI, 1945, p. 781.

102. *FR* 1946, Vol. VIII, p. 166; US Department of State, *The Far Eastern Commission*

(Washington, D.C.: Government Printing Office, 1953), p. 26.

103. *FR* 1946, Vol. VIII, p. 138.

104. *Asahi Shimbun*, 29 September 1945.

105. *Ibid.*, 1 January 1946.

106. *Ibid.*, 3 January 1946.

107. Matsumoto Joji, Tokyo University professor, was one of the most prominent scholars in commercial law. After he left the university, he joined the managerial board of the Southern Manchurian Rail Road Company and later became its Vice President. In 1945, he became a national minister of the Shidehara Cabinet and played a key role in revising the Japanese imperial constitution.

108. Memorandum by Whitney for MacArthur, 2 February 1946, in Takayanagi Kenzo, Ohtomo Ichiro, and Tanaka Hideo eds., *Nihonkoku Kempo Seitei no Katei [The Making of the Constitution of Japan]* Vol. I, Documents (Tokyo: Yuhikaku, 1978), pp. 40-43.

109. Memorandum by Whitney for MacArthur, 1 February 1946, *Ibid.*, pp. 94-95.

110. Three basic points stated by Supreme Commander to be "Musts" in constitutional revision. Government Section paper prepared about 4 Feb 1946 *Ibid.*, pp. 98-101.

111. Memorandum of the first MacArthur-Emperor meeting by Okumura, 27 September 1945, Yamagiwa and Nakamura eds., *Tennosei*, p. 512.

112. Ohtake Hideo, *Sengo Nihon Boei Mondai Shiryoshu [Documents of Postwar Japanese Defense Issues]* Vol. 1 (Tokyo: Sanichi Shobo, 1991), p. 14. On 8 October 1945, George Atcheson presented his own 12 principles of a new constitution to Prince Konoye that did not mention the elimination of military forces. Hasegawa Masayasu, *Showa Kemposhi [Showa Constitutional History]* (Tokyo: Iwanami Shoten, 1971), pp. 213-14.

113. Iriye Memo of the Cabinet Council, 30 January 1946, Ohtake ed., *Sengo Nihon Boei*, Vol. 1, pp. 39-41.

114. Draft as submitted to the Japanese Government by the General Headquarters, SCAP, 13 February 1946, in Takayanagi, et. al. eds., *Nihonkoku Kempo Seitei*, Vol. I, pp. 266-73; Suzuki Akinori, *Nihonkoku Kempo wo Unda Misshitsu no Kokonokakan [Nine Days in a Closed Room for the Creation of the Japanese Constitution]* (Osaka: Sogensha, 1995), p. 125; Draft Constitution of Japan submitted to the Japanese Government by the General Headquarters, SCAP, 13 February 1946, Takayanagi et al. eds., *Nihonkoku Kempo Seitei*, Document #14, pp. 272-73. The final Chapter II reads "the Japanese people forever renounce war as a sovereign right of the nation and the threat or use of force as means of settling international disputes."

115. Record of Events on 13 February 1946 when proposed new constitution for Japan was submitted to the Foreign Minister, Mr. Yoshida, in behalf of the Supreme Commander, in Takayanagi, et. al. eds., *Nihonkoku Kempo Seitei*, Vol. I, pp. 328-29.

116. Takayanagi, et. al. eds., *Nihonkoku Kempo Seitei*, Vol. II, pp. 82-84.

117. Meeting of Whitney and Matsumoto, 22 February 1946, Takayanagi, et. al. eds., *Nihonkoku Kempo Seitei I*, Document #23, pp. 392-94.

118. Ohtake ed., *Sengo Nihon Boei*, Vol. 1, p. 12.

119. Howard Schonberger, *Senryo 1945-1952 [Aftermath of War]* (Tokyo: Jijitsushinsha, 1994), p. 73.

120. Takemae Eiji and Amakawa Akira, *Nihon Senryo Hishi [Secret History of*

Occupation of Japan] Vol. 2 (Tokyo: Asahi Shinbunsha, 1977), p. 8.

121. The *New York Times,* 6 March 1946, Yoshida Naikaku Kankokai, *Yoshida Naikaku,* p. 43.

122. Ishibashi Tanzan, "Kempo Kaisei Soan wo Hyosu," ["Comments on the Draft of Revised Constitution," *Toyo Keizai Shimpo [The Oriental Economist],* 16 March 1946 in Ohtake ed., *Sengo Nihon Boei Mondai Shiryoshu,* Vol. 1, p. 103.

123. Inoki Masamichi, *Hyoden Yoshida Shigeru, [Biography: Yoshida Shigeru]* Vol. 3, (Tokyo: Yomiuri Shimbun, 1981), p. 197; Nakamura Akira, *Sengo Seiji ni' Yureta Kempo Kyujo [Article Nine in Postwar Politics]* (Tokyo: Chuo Keizaisha, 1996), p. 61.

124. Inoki, *Yoshida Shigeru,* Vol. 2, p. 199.

125. Hata Ikuhiko, *Shiroku Nihon Saigunbi [Documentary History: Japanese Rearmament]* (Tokyo: Bungei Shunju, 1976), p. 68.

126. Gaimusho Seimukyoku [The Political Bureau of the JMFA], "Heiwa Joyaku Mondai Kenkyu Shiryo" ["Documents of the Peace Treaty Study"], 26 January 1946, Vol. 1, *NGM,* B'.4.0.0.1.

127. Hata, *Saigunbi,* p. 68.

128. The United States Department of State, *Records of the U.S. Department of State Relating to United States Political Relations With Japan* (hereafter *PRJ*) *1945-1949* (Wilmington, Delaware: Scholarly Resources, 1988), Reel #1.

129. Section I reads: "Aspiring sincerely to an international peace based on justice and order, the Japanese people forever renounce war as a sovereign right of the nation and the threat or use of force as means of settling international disputes." Section II reads: "In order to accomplish the aim of the preceding paragraph, land, sea, and air forces, as well as other war potential, will never be maintained. The right of belligerency of the state will not be recognized."

130. Iriye Toshiro at the House of Peers, 6 May 1946, Ohtake, *Sengo Nihon Boei Mondai,* Vol. 1, p. 106.

131. The mainstream of the JMFA led by the Treaty Bureau abandoned neutrality and sought to return to an international community by participating in the United Nations. *NGM,* B'0014, 9 May 1946 cited in Inouye Juichi, "Kokuren to Sengo Nihon Gaiko," ["The United Nations and Postwar Japanese Diplomacy,"] *Nenpo: Kindai Nihon Kenkyu [Annual Report: Modern Japanese Studies]* 16 (Tokyo: Yamakawa Shuppansha, 1994), p. 192.

132. Prime Minister Yoshida Shigeru at the House of Representatives Committee, 26 June 1946, in Ohtake, *Sengo Nihon Boei Mondai,* Vol. 1, p. 138.

133. Kanamori Tokujiro at the House of Representatives, 1 July 1946, *Ibid.,* p. 138.

134. Yoshihisa Hara, "The Significance of the U.S.-Japan Security System to Japan: The Historical Background," *Peace and Change,* Vol. 12, #314 (1987), p. 33.

135. Yoshida Shigeru at the House of Peers, 29 May 1946, Ohtake, *Sengo Nihon Boei Mondai,* Vol. 1, p. 107.

136. Hara at the Constitutional Reform Committee, 29 July 1946, *Ibid.,* p. 117.

137. Yoshida Shigeru at the House of Representatives Committee, 26 June 1946, *Ibid.,* p. 138.

138. Yoshida Shigeru at the House of Peers, 6 September 1946, *Ibid.,* p. 140.

139. Prime Minister Yoshida Shigeru on radio, 14 August 1946, Yoshida Naikaku

Kankokai ed., *Yoshida Naikaku,* p. 16.

140. Ohtake, *Sengo Nihon Boei Mondai,* Vol. 1, p. 442.

141. Dower, *Yoshida Shigeru,* Vol. 2, p. 26.

142. Nakamura ed., *Shiryo* Vol. 1, pp. 120–21.

143. Nakamura Takafusa, *Nihon Keizai: Sono Seicho to Kozo [The Japanese Economy: Its Growth and Structure]* (Tokyo: Tokyo Daigaku Shuppankai, 1993), pp. 136-37.

144. Sodei Rinjiro and Takemae Eiji eds., *Sengo Nihon no Genten [The Origins of Postwar Japan]* Vol. 2 (Tokyo: Eiko, 1992), p. 165.

145. Barnet, *Allies,* p. 67.

146. Shiso no Kagaku Kenkyukai, *Nihon Senryogun: Sono Hikari to Kage [Occupation Army in Japan: Its Light and Shadow]* Vol. 1 (Tokyo: Gendaishi Shuppankai, 1978), p. 15.

147. Dower, *Yoshida Shigeru to Sono Jidai,* Vol. 2, p. 29; Sodei Rinjiro, "Senryo to Iu Na no Seiji," ["Politics by the Name of Occupation"] in Sodei Rinjiro ed., *Sekaishi no Nakano Nihon Senryo [Japanese Occupation in the Context of World History]* (Tokyo: Nihon Hyoronsha, 1985), p. 130.

148. 23 January 1947, *Papers of the Council on Foreign Relations* (hereafter *PCFR*) Council on Foreign Relations Archives, New York.

149. JCS to MacArthur, 6 September 1945, "U.S. Initial Post-Surrender Policy for Japan," PSF, *HSTP,* Truman Library, Independence, Missouri.

150. *Ibid.*

151. Kashima Heiwa Kenkyujo ed., *Nihon Gaikoshi [Japanese Diplomatic History]* Vol. 26 (Tokyo: Kashima Kenkyjo Shuppankai, 1973), p. 421.

152. SCAP to JCS, 20 October 1945, *SZ* Vol. 20, p. 331.

153. Sumimoto Toshio, *Senryo Hiroku [Secret History of Occupation]* (Tokyo: Mainichi Shimbun, 1965), p. 158.

154. Higuchi Hiroshi, *Zaibatsu no Fukkatsu [Revival of Zaibatsu]* (Tokyo: Naigai Keizaisha, 1953), p. 4; SCAP to JCS, 20 October 1945, *SZ,* Vol. 20, pp. 332-33.

155. Yasuhara Kazuo and Yamamoto Tsuyoshi, *Sengo Nihon Gaikoshi [Postwar Japanese Diplomatic History]* IV (Tokyo: Sanseido, 1984), p. 44.

156. War Department to SCAP, 22 October 1945, *SZ* Vol. 20, p. 333.

157. Michael Schaller, *Douglas MacArthur* (New York: Oxford University Press, 1989), p. 137.

158. Report of the Mission on Japanese Combines to the Department of State and War Department, March 1946, *SZ* Vol. 20, p. 339.

159. "Report of the Mission on Japanese Combines: Part 1 Analytical and Technical Data," *JDC;* Higuchi, *Zaibatsu,* p. 6.

160. Ohkurasho Zaiseishishitsu ed., *Tai Senryogun Kosho Hiroku: Watanabe Takeshi Nikki [Secret Documents of Negotiations with Occupation Forces: Watanabe Takeshi Diary]* (Tokyo: Toyo Keizai Shimposha, 1983), p. 706; 18 April 1948, ESS, GHQ, *JDC.*

161. Edwards, "U.S. Policy," p. 64.

162. Nishi Toshio, *Makkasa no "Hanzai" [MacArthur's "Crime"]* Vol. 1 (Tokyo: Nihon Kogyo Shinbunsha, 1983), p. 100.

163. 3 November 1947, *IAJ 1945-1949,* Roll #30.

164. Marquat to JCS, 17 May 1946, *SZ* Vol. 20, p. 348.

165. Comments by SCAP, undated, 1946, *Ibid.*, p. 349.

166. Edwards, "U.S. Policy," pp. 65, 105, 195.

167. Yasuhara and Yamamoto, *Sengo Nihon Gaikoshi* IV, p. 44.

168. Guttman, "Miracles of Power," Vol. 1 p. 88; Eleanor M. Hadley, "From Deconcentration to Reverse Course in Japan," in Robert Wolfe ed., *Americans as Proconsuls* (Carbondale: Southern Illinois University Press, 1984), pp. 170-71; Nakamura, *Nihon Keizai*, p. 142.

169. Miyajima Hideaki, "Zaibatsu Kaitai," ["Zaibatsu Dissolution,"] in Hashimoto Juro and Takeda Haruhito eds., *Nihon Keizai no Hatten to Kigyo Shudan [Development of Japanese Economy and Business Groups]* (Tokyo: Tokyo Daigaku Shuppankai, 1993), pp. 203-16; Guttman, "Miracles of Power," Vol. 1, pp. 88-89.

170. G. C. Allen, *Japan's Economic Recovery* (London: Oxford University Press, 1958), p. 152.

171. 18 March 1947, *Papers of Douglas MacArthur*, RG5, MacArthur Memorial Bureau of Archives, Norfolk, VA.

172. Documents of meeting between Vice Foreign Minister and the members of the FEC, 30 January 1946, *NGM* B'4.0.0.1 Vol. 3 #0016.

173. Yoshida Naikaku Kankokai, *Yoshida Naikaku*, p. 60.

174. Record of the Third Emperor-MacArthur Meeting by Terasaki, 16 October 1946, Yamagiwa and Nakamura eds., *Shiryo Nihon Senryo I: Tennosei*, pp. 570-74.

175. Atcheson to Secretary of State, 14 March 1947, *FR* 1947, VI, The Far East (Washington, D.C.: Government Printing Office, 1972), p. 188.

176. 18 March 1947, *Douglas MacArthur Papers* RG 5, Reel #24, MacArthur Memorial Bureau of Archives.

177. Atcheson to Secretary of State, 14 March 1947, *FR* 1947 VI, The Far East, p. 188.

178. G.H.Q. draft, 1 March 1946, Hussey Papers, *JDC.*

179. Dower, *Yoshida Shigeru*, p. 70; Yoshida Shigeru, *Kaiso Junen [Memoirs]* Vol. 2 (Tokyo: Tokyo Shirakawa Shoin, 1982), p. 229.

180. *SZ* Vol. 3 (Tokyo: Tokyo Keizai Shimposha, 1976), p. 202; Kajima Morinosuke, *Nihon Gaikoshi [Japanese Diplomatic History]* (Tokyo: Kajima Kenkyujo Shuppankai, 1965), Vol. 26, p. 431.

181. Shiratori Rei ed., *Nihon no Naikaku [Japanese Cabinet]* (II) (Tokyo: Shinhyoron, 1981), p. 95.

182. Supreme Commander for the Allied Powers, *The Political Reorientation of Japan, September 1945-September 1948* (Washingto, D.C.: Government Printing Office, 1948), p. 780, Appendix F: 42.

183. The Allied Council for Japan is an advisory body consisting of representatives of the United States, the U.S.S.R., Britain and the Commonwealth, and China. They convened in Tokyo to advise General MacArthur on the best way to implement occupation policies and to monitor his adherence to their advice.

184. *SZ* Vol. 3, pp. 202-06.

185. Hiromitsu Kaneda, "Structural Change and Policy Response in Japanese Agriculture after the Land Reform," and comment by Richard B. Rice in Redford ed., *The Occupation of Japan*, pp. 141, 150-51; Allen, *Recovery*, p. 62.

186. Dower, *Yoshida Shigeru*, Vol. 2, p. 31.

187. James, *The Years of MacArthur* Vol. III, p. 184.

188. Edwards, "U.S. Policy," p. 280.

189. Rekishigaku Kenkyukai, *Nihon Dojidaishi 1: Haisen to Senryo [Japanese Contemporary History 1: Defeat and Occupation]* (Tokyo: Aoki Shoten, 1990), p. 202; Frank Sackton, "The Transfer of Land Ownership to the Peasants: The Priceless Economic Reform," in Redford ed., *The Occupation of Japan*, p. 141.

190. G. C. Allen, *Recovery*, p. 65; Kawagoe Toshihiko, "Nochi Kaikaku," ["Land Reform,"] in Kosai Yutaka and Teranishi Juro, eds., *Sengo Nihon no Keizai Kaikaku: Shijo to Seifu [Economic Reform in Postwar Japan: Market and Government]* (Tokyo: Tokyo Daigaku Shuppankai, 1993), p. 171; James, *MacArthur*, p. 189; Keizai Saiken Kenkyukai [Association of Economic Recovery], ed., *Pore Kara Daresu he [From Pauley to Dulles]* (Tokyo: Diamondsha, 1952), p. 22; William M. Gilmartin and W. I. Ladejinsky, "The Promise of Agrarian Reform in Japan," *Foreign Affairs*, Vol. 26 #2 (January 1948), p. 320.

191. *SZ* Vol. 3, p. 206.

192. SWNCC 162/2, 8 January 1946, *FR* 1946 VIII, The Far East, p. 107.

193. William Sebald and C. Nelson Spinks, *Japan: Prospects, Options, and Opportunities* (Washington, D.C.: American Enterprise Institute, 1967), p. 26.

194. Report by Blakeslee, 26 December 1945 - 13 February 1946, *FR* 1946 VIII, The Far East, p. 167.

195. Atcheson to the Secretary of State, 12 August 1946, *Ibid.*, p. 287.

196. Stuart to the Secretary of State, 20 August 1946, *Ibid.*, pp. 302-03.

197. Memorandum by MacArthur, 21 March 1947, *FR* 1947 VI, The Far East, p. 454.

198. Russell Brines, *MacArthur's Japan* (Philadelphia: J.B. Lippincott Company, 1948), p. 70; Roger Buckley, *Occupation Diplomacy* (Cambridge: Cambridge University Press, 1982), p. 124.

199. Cohen, *Nihon Senryo Kakumei*, Vol. 2, p. 97.

CHAPTER TWO: SHIFT IN AMERICAN
OCCUPATION POLICIES

1. David Mayers, *George Kennan and the Dilemmas of US Foreign Policy* (New York: Oxford University Press, 1988), p. 116; Wilson Miscamble, *George F. Kennan and the Making of American Foreign Policy, 1947-1950* (Princeton: Princeton University Press, 1992), p. 349.

2. George Kennan, *Memoirs 1929-1950* (Boston: Little, Brown and Company, 1967), pp. 294-95.

3. John Gaddis, *The Long Peace* (New York: Oxford University Press, 1987), p. 284.

4. Walter LaFeber, *The American Age* (New York: W.W. Norton & Company, 1989), pp. 449-452.

5. Joint Staff Planners, 31 October 1946, Office of the Secretary of State, Committee and Subject Files 1943-53, 60D240, RG 59, National Archives.

6. Central Intelligence Agency (CIA), 12 September 1947, Records of the National Security Council, *PHST*, Harry S Truman Library, Independence, Missouri.

7. For example, Kojima Noboru, *Kowa Joyaku [The Peace Treaty]* Vol. 2 (Tokyo: Shinchosha, 1995); Bruce Cumings, *The origins of the Korean War* Vol. 2 (Princeton, N.J. : Princeton University Press, 1992).

8. Louis Hartz, *The Liberal Tradition in America* (New York: Horcourt, Brace and Company, 1955); Saito Makoto, *Amerika towa Nanika [What is America?]* (Tokyo: Heibonsha, 1995); Saito Makoto, *Amerikashi no Bunmyaku [Context of American History]* (Tokyo: Iwanami Shoten, 1981); Gordon S. Wood, *The Creation of the American Republic 1776-1787* (New York: W. W. Norton & Company, 1969).

9. Gaddis, *The Long Peace*, pp. 20-47.

10. Makino Hiroshi, *Reisen no Kigen to Amerika no Haken [Origins of the Cold War and American Hegemony]* (Tokyo: Ochanomizu Shobo, 1993), p. 303.

11. NSC 7, 30 March 1948, Paul Kesaris ed., *Documents of the National Security Council*, (Washington, D.C.: University Publications of America, 1980) Reel #1.

12. Nagai Yonosuke *Reisen no Kigen [Origins of the Cold War]* (Tokyo: Chuo Koronsha, 1978), pp. 15-27.

13. Babcock to McCoy, 10 February 1946, *FR* 1946 Vol. VIII, The Far East, p. 161.

14. Council on Foreign Relations, 23 January 1947, *PCFR*, Council on Foreign Relations Archives, New York.

15. Dennis Merrill ed., *Documentary History of the Truman Presidency* Vol. 5 (Frederick, MD: University Publications of America, 1996), p. 210.

16. The Supreme Commander for the Allied Powers (SCAP) recommended that the Japanese government establish a board to deal with overall economic issues with the higher authorities in each ministry. It had to be a temporary board (one-year term and renewable) to overcome the current economic crisis, and had to formulate stable economic policies regardless of any unforseen changes in administration. The Japanese government established the Economic Stabilization Board (ESB), a technocratic organization, in August 1946. In line with SCAP's recommendation, the Japanese government strengthened the ESB's authority. The ESB had been able to send orders to related ministries through the Prime Minister, but this revision allowed the ESB to order them sent directly. This revision also established a comprehensive coordinating committee above the ESB to which SCAP dispatched Shigeto Tsuru to act as vice chairman. *SZ* Vol. 4 (Tokyo: Toyo Keizai Shimposha, 1976), p. 400.

17. Sebald, 19 March 1948, *IAJ 1945-1949*, Reel #21.

18. Nagai, *Reisen no Kigen*, p. 38; Sebald to the Secretary of State, 3 April 1948, *IAJ 1945-1949*, Reel #21.

19. *SZ* Vol. 3, pp. 293-95.

20. According to Howard Schonberger, "the Japan Lobby was a small, loosely-knit group of individuals who operated largely behind-the-scenes." *New Republic* explained that the Japan Lobby was a group "aided by *Newsweek* Magazine, led by old Japanese hands of the State Department, and backed by major corporations with investments in Japan and friends among the Zaibatsu." Their organizational umbrella was the American Council on Japan (ACJ). The ACJ included Harry F. Kern, foreign affairs editor of *Newsweek*, W. Averell Harriman, Secretary of Commerce, Compton Pakenham, *Newsweek*'s Tokyo bureau chief, William Veazie Pratt, Retired Admiral, James Lee Kauffman, a well-know attorney, and others. *New Republic*, CXX (30 May

1949) in Howard Schonberger, "The Japan Lobby in American Diplomacy, 1947-1952," *Pacific Historical Review* 46 (1977).

21. *SZ* Vol. 2 (Tokyo: Toyo Keizai Shimposha, 1982), p. 456; James Kauffman, "Report on Conditions in Japan As of September 6, 1947" *JDC.*

22. *SZ* Vol. 2, pp. 481, 485.

23. Okurasho Zaiseishishitsu ed., *Watanabe Takeshi Nikki,* pp. 149, 709.

24. Lovett to Roayll, 25 November 1947, *FR* 1947 Vol. VI, The Far East, p. 319.

25. Okurasho Zaiseishishitsu ed., *Watanabe Takeshi Nikki,* pp. 504, 709.

26. Council on Foreign Relations, 27 January 1948, *PCFR,* Council on Foreign Relations Archives, New York.

27. Congressional Record, Senate, 19 December 1947, *JDC.*

28. Congressional Record, Senate, 19 December 1947 and 19 January 1948, *JDC.*

29. Borden, *The Pacific Alliance,* p. 84.

30. Edwards, "U.S. Policy," p. 179.

31. Statement to be made to Far Eastern Commission, 22 January 1948, *FR* 1948 VI, The Far East and Australasia (Washington, D.C.: Government Printing Office, 1974), p. 655.

32. Draper was an investment banker and vice president of Dillon Read & Company. He was Chief of the Economic Section of the Allied Control Council in Germany and Economic Adviser to the new Occupation commander, General Lucius Clay, working with Joseph M. Dodge. He later became Under Secretary of Army (August 1947) and a chief architect of the Japanese economic recovery.

33. Kennan to Lovett, 24 February 1948, Iokibe ed., *The Occupation of Japan* Part 2, 3H-15.

34. *SZ* Vol. 2, p. 518.

35. Conversation between MacArthur and Kennan, 5 March 1948, *FR* 1948 VI, The Far East and Australasia, p. 703; *SZ* Vol. 2, pp. 511, 522; SCAP to the Department of Army, 27 April 1948, *LAJ 1945-1949* Reel #30.

36. *SZ* Vol. 2, pp. 485-87, 511, 518, 520-22.

37. Saltzman to McCoy, 29 September 1948, *FR* 1948 VI, The Far East and Australasia, pp. 1023-24.

38. Memorandum by Douglas MacArthur, 21 March 1947, *FR* 1947 VI, The Far East, p. 454.

39. Igarashi, *Tainichi Kowa to Reisen,* pp. 64-65; General Douglas MacArthur had his own sort of realist thinking: Because the Soviet Union did not want to see Japan as an American military outpost, he reasoned it would accept a disarmed and neutral Japan. At the same time, he insisted on continuing to control Okinawa after concluding a peace treaty, which, he believed, would be a sufficient measure to maintain Japan's security. Conversation between MacArthur and Kennan, 5 March 1948, *FR* 1948 VI, The Far East and Australasia, pp. 700-01.

40. James, *MacArthur* Vol. III, p. 18.

41. Nester, *Japan's Growing Power,* p. 24; Borden, *The Pacific Alliance,* p. 86.

42. Michael Schaller, "MacArthur's Japan: The View from Washington," *Diplomatic History* Vol. 10, No. 1 (Winter, 1986), pp. 10, 15.

43. Masuda Hiroshi, *Nichibei Kankeishi Gaisetsu [Survey of Japan-US Relations]*

(Tokyo: Nansosha, 1977), p. 145.

44. Michael M. Yoshitsu, *Nihon ga Dokuritsu shita Hi [Japan and the San Francisco Peace Settlement]* (Tokyo: Kodansha, 1984), p. 15; Hata, *Saigunbi*, p. 56.

45. Yoshitsu , *Nihon ga Dokuritsu shita Hi*, pp. 15, 17; Watanabe Akio and Miyazato Seigen eds., *Sanfuranshisuko Kowa [San Francisco Peace Treaty]* (Tokyo: Tokyo Daigaku Shuppankai, 1986), p. 113; Hata, *Saigunbi*, p. 56.

46. Kojima Noboru, *Kowa Joyaku: Sengo Nichibei Kankei no Kiten [Peace Treaty: The Starting Point of Postwar Japan-US Relations]* Vol. 1 (Tokyo: Shinchosha, 1995), pp. 107, 297; James, *MacArthur Vol. III*, p. 337.

47. James, *MacArthur*, Vol. III, p. 337.

48. Atcheson to Truman, 19 June 1947, *FR* 1947 VI, The Far East, p. 233.

49. Bishop to Penfield, 14 August 1947, *Ibid.*, p. 493.

50. Butterworth to the Secretary of State, 22 September 1947, *Ibid.*, p. 523.

51. McGlothlen, *Controlling the Waves*, p. 41; Igarashi Takeshi, "Reisen to Kowa [Cold War and Peace Treaty]," in Watanabe Akio ed., *Sengo Nihon no Taigai Seisaku [Postwar Japanese Foreign Policies]* (Tokyo: Yuhikaku Sensho, 1985), p. 38; PPS/10, 14 October 1947, United States Department of State Policy Planning Staff, *The State Department Policy Planning Staff Papers 1947-1949* [Hereafter *PPSP*] Vol. 1 (New York: Garland Publishing, Inc., 1983), pp. 108-115.

52. PPS/10, 14 October 1947, *PPSP* Vol. 1, pp. 108-15.

53. Memorandum of Conversation, by the Secretary of State, 9 October 1947, *FR* 1947 VI, The Far East, p. 527.

54. Memorandum of Conversation, by Sebald, 26 October 1947, *Ibid.*, p. 550.

55. Stuart to the Secretary of State, 5 February 1948, *FR* 1948 VI, The Far East and Australasia, p. 661.

56. Hussey's Report on Washington's Attitude Regarding Aspects of the Occupation, 6 December 1947, *SZ* Vol. 20, p. 181.

57. OIR #4553, 15 December 1947, Paul Kesaris ed., *O.S.S./State Department Intelligence and Research Reports PartII Postwar Japan, Korea, and Southeast Asia* (Washington, D.C.: University Publications of America, 1977). The American Ambassador to the Soviet Union insisted that an "early Japanese peace conference will have little if any deterrent effect on Kremlin's plans for Far East." Smith to the Secretary of State, 21 February 1948, *FR* 1948 VI, The Far East and Australasia, p. 665.

58. PPS/10, 14 October 1947, *PPSP* Vol. 1, pp. 108-15.

59. 19 May 1948, *Kennan Papers*, Mudd Manuscript Library, Princeton University.

60. NSC 13, 2 June 1948, Kesaris ed., *Documents of the National Security Council*, Reel #1.

61. Memorandum by Kennan, 14 October 1947, *FR* 1947 VI, The Far East, pp. 536-37.

62. PPS 28, 25 March 1948; Conversation Between MacArthur and Kennan, 5 March 1948, *FR* 1948 VI, The Far East and Australasia, pp. 694, 703.

63. Conversation Among MacArthur, Draper, and Kennan, 21 March 1948 (Amended 23 March 1948); PPS 28, 25 March 1948, *Ibid.*, pp. 691, 706.

64. Memorandum of Conversations with MacArthur, 1 March 1948, *Ibid.*, p. 697.

65. Explanatory Notes by Kennan, 25 March 1948, *Ibid.*, p. 712.

66. Explanatory Notes by Kennan, 25 March 1948; Conversation Among MacArthur, Draper, and Kennan, 21 March 1948 (Amended 23 March 1948); Conversation Between MacArthur and Kennan, 5 March 1948; Conversation Among MacArthur, Draper, Kennan, 21 March 1948 (Amended 23 March 1948), *Ibid.*, pp. 701, 708, 709, 712.

67. PPS 28, 25 March 1948, *Ibid.*, p. 692.

68. *Ibid.*, p. 694.

69. Kennan, *Memoirs*, pp. 380, 393-94.

70. PPS 28, 25 March 1948, *FR* 1948 VI, The Far East and Australasia, p. 694.

71. CIA, 28 September 1948, ORE 46-48, PSF, *PHST*, Harry S. Truman Library, Independence, Missouri.

72. Nishimura Kumao, *Nihon Gaikoshi 27: San Francisco Heiwa Joyakuk [Japanese Diplomatic History 27: San Francisco Peace Treaty]* (Tokyo: Kashima Kenkyujo Press, 1971), p. 21.

73. Hagiwara Toru, "On Timing and Procedure of a Japanese Peace Treaty,"1 June 1947, *NGM*, B'4.0.0.1 Vol. 2, #0022.

74. Nishimura, *Nihon Gaikoshi 27*, p. 22; Iokibe Makoto, *Nichibei Senso to Sengo Nihon [Japan-US War and Postwar Japan]* (Osaka: Osaka Shoseki Press, 1989), p. 5.

75. Watanabe and Miyazato, eds., *Sanfuranshisuko Kowa*, p. 22; Iokibe, *Nichibei Senso*, p. 5.

76. Nihon Gaimusho, 31 January 1946, *NGM*, B'4.0.0.1

77. By then, the JMFA recognized that US policy toward Japan had shifted to moderation. Joyakukyoku [Treaty Bureau], "Tainichi Heiwa Joyaku no Gendankai," ["Current Stage of a Peace Treaty with Japan"] 25 June 1948, Tainichi Heiwa Joyaku Kankei Junbi Kenkyu Kankei [Documents Concerning Preparations for Peace Treaty] Vol. 3, *NGM*, B'4.0.0.1.

78. *SZ*, Vol. 20, p. 168.

79. G.H.Q. Operational Policy, 1 March 1946, *JDC*.

80. Edwin Pauley was in oil business in California.

81. Borden, *Pacific Alliance*, p. 65; Takushi Ohno, *War Reparations and Peace Settlement: Philippines-Japan Relations 1945-1956* (Manila: Solidaridad Publishing House, 1986), pp. 9-10.

82. Statement by Pauley, 31 October 1945, *FR* 1945 VI, The British Commonwealth, The Far East, pp. 997-98.

83. Maxwell to Pauley, 26 December 1945, *JDC*.

84. Ohno, *War Reparations*, p. 9; *FEC*, p. 125.

85. Ohno, *War Reparations*, p. 10.

86. Guttman, "Miracles of Power," Vol. 1, p. 100.

87. *FEC*, p. 125.

88. SWNCC 302, 25 May 1946, *IAJ 1945-1949*, Reel #29.

89. Nakamura Takafusa ed., *Shiryo* Vol. 1, pp. 120-28.

90. Pauley replied that "We can allow filling of this vacuum . . . by encouraging in all Asia industries able to live in a competitive world." Borden, *The Pacific Alliance*, pp. 66-67.

91. Memorandum by Nelson Johnson, 30 January 1946, *FR* 1946 VIII, The Far East, p. 124.

92. Report by SWNCC Subcommittee for the Far East, 15 May 1946, *Ibid.*, pp. 502-03.

93. Ohno, *War Reparations*, p. 14.

94. *FEC*, p. 125.

95. Guttman, "Miracles," pp. 100-01; *FEC*, p. 20.

96. Pauley, 1 April 1946, *JDC.*

97. Howard Schonberger, "Zaibatsu Dissolution and the American Restoration of Japan," *Bulletin of Concerned Asian Scholars* Vol. 5, No. 2 (September 1973), p. 21.

98. Tsusho Sangyosho [The Ministry of International Trade and Industry] ed, *Tsusho Sangyo Seisaku Shi [History of Policies of Trade and Industry]* Vol. 4, (Tokyo: Research Institute of Trade and Industry, 1990), p. 15.

99. Council on Foreign Relations, 22 October 1947, *PCFR,*

100. The Strike Committee, 18 February 1947 and 24 February 1947, *JDC.*

101. Borden, *The Pacific Alliance,* pp. 66, 74.

102. Cheseldine Report, 17 February 1947, *JDC.*

103. PPS/10, 14 October 1947, *FR* 1947 VI, The Far East, p. 542.

104. Overseas Consultants, Inc., "Report on Industrial Reparations Survey of Japan to the United States of America," 26 February 1948 *JDC.*

105. Conversation between MacArthur and Kennan, 5 March 1948, *FR* 1948 VI, The Far East and Australasia, p. 705.

106. PPS 28, 25 March 1948, *Ibid.*, p. 695.

107. Ohno, *War Reparations*, p. 22. The mission consisted of such prominent businessmen as Johnston, chairman of Chemical Bank; William Draper, former Wall Street banker, Robert Loree, former vice-president of Morgan Guaranty Trust and chairman of the National Foreign Trade Council; and Paul Hoffman, former president of Studebaker and head of the Economic Cooperation Administration.

108. Johnston Report, 26 April 1948, *PCFR.*

109. Atcheson to Truman, 5 January 1947, *FR* 1947 VI, The Far East, p. 157.

110. Atcheson to Byrnes, 5 January 1947, Ryoichi Miwa ed., *The Occupation of Japan Economic Reform 1945-1952* (hereafter *OJER*) Part 1: Deconcentration and Modernization of Economic Power, 4-106-77 (Washington D.C.: Congressional Information Service, Inc., 1994), 6-301-02.

111. Report by R. M. Cheseldine, 17 February 1947, *JDC.*

112. The Strike Report, 24 February 1947, *Ibid.*

113. SWNCC 236/43, 7 April 1947, *FR* 1947 VI, The Far East, p. 383.

114. PPS/10, 14 October 1947, *Ibid.*, p. 542.

115. Department of State, Memorandum of Conversation, 12 November 1947, *OJER,* 6-301-11.

116. Overseas Consultants, Inc., "Report on Industrial Reparations Survey of Japan to the United States of America," 26 February 1948 *JDC.*

117. The Johnston mission, 26 April 1948, *Ibid.*

118. R. Reid to Undersecretary of Army, 18 October 1948, *Ibid.*

119. Saltzman to Draper, 22 January 1948, *FR* 1948 VI, The Far East and Australasia, p. 947.

120. Thorp to Butterworth, 6 April 1948, *Ibid.*, p. 964.

121. Saltzman to the Secretary of State, 5 June 1948, *Ibid.*, p. 973.

122. Memorandum of Conversation by Ely, 15 March 1948; Thorp to Butterworth, 6 April 1948, *Ibid.,* pp. 683, 965.

123. *FEC,* p138.

124. Marshall to Royall, 26 August 1948, *FR* 1948 VI, The Far East and Australasia, p. 998.

125. Royall to Marshall, 31 August 1948, *Ibid.,* pp. 1002-03.

126. Thorp to Butterworth, 6 April 1948, *Ibid.,* p. 965.

127. NSC13/2, 7 October 1948, *Ibid.,* p. 862.

128. Nitze to Thorp, 7 January 1949, *FR* 1949 VII, The Far East and Australasia part II (Washington D.C.: Government Printing Office, 1976), p. 610.

129. Borden, *The Pacific Alliance,* pp. 82, 108; Bishop to Butterworth, 6 January 1949; Bishop to Butterworth, 25 January 1949; Butterworth to the Secretary of State, 27 January 1949, *Ibid.,* pp. 608-09, 625, 637.

130. Bishop to Butterworth, 17 December 1948, *FR* 1948 VI, The Far East and Australasia, p. 1065.

131. Memorandum by the Secretary of State, 1 February 1949, *FR* 1949 VII, The Far East and Australasia Part 2, pp. 641-42.

132. K.V. Kesavan, *Japan's Relations with Southeast Asia: 1952-60* (Bombay: Somaiya Publications PVT LTD, 1972), p. 44.

CHAPTER THREE: THE ROAD TO ECONOMIC STABILITY

1. Drafted by Fearey, G. Atcheson to Secretary of State, 17 April 1946, *SZ,* Vol. 20 (Tokyo: Toyo Keizai Shimposha, 1982), p. 218.

2. SWNCC 162/2, 8 January 1946, *FR* 1946 VIII, The Far East, p. 108.

3. Report by Blakeslee, 26 December 1945–13 February 1946, *Ibid.,* p. 167.

4. Memorandum by Fearey, 17 April 1946, *Ibid.,* p. 209.

5. G.H.Q. Operational Policy, 1 March 1946, *JDC.*

6. The War Depratment Report, 17 February 1947, *JDC.*

7. Rapporteur's Report on Round Table C Dealing with American Policy Toward Japan National Conference, American Institute of Pacific Relations, Inc., 13 April 1947, Royal Institute of International Affairs, Far Eastern Files, School of Oriental and African Studies, London, p. 5.

8. Atcheson to the Secretary of State, 19 June 1947, *FR* 1947 VI, The Far East, p. 231.

9. Address by Senator Elbert D. Thomas, 5 August 1947, Official Files 197 Misc., *HSTP,* Truman Library, Independence, Missouri.

10. Barnett to Martin, 4 November 1947, *JDC.*

11. Memorandum of Conversation with SCAP Political Adviser, 12 November 1947, *OJER* Part 2, 4-109-02.

12. Ikuhiko Hata, "Japan Under the Occupation," *The Japan Interpreter,* Vol. 10, Nos. 3-4 (winter 1976), p. 17.

13. Records of the Executive Secretariat (Dean Acheson), 2 March 1948, 53D444, RG 59, National Archives.

14. Schonberger, *Aftermath of War,* p. 201.

15. The Reconstruction Finance Bank, a quasi-public bank, was established in October 1946 and issued 44 billion yen in loans through 1947. Government-appropriated funds were the only resources for the RFB, which helped increase production, but also promoted hyper inflation.

16. *SZ* Vol. 3, p. 261.

17. Dick Nanto, "The Dodge Line: A Reevaluation," in Lawrence H. Redford, ed., *The Occupation of Japan: Economic Policy and Reform,* Symposium Proceedings (Norfolk: The MacArthur Memorial, 1980), pp. 45-46.

18. Economic and Scientific Section, "Essentials of the ESS Economic Stabilization Program," 20 May 1947, *JDC.*

19. SWNCC, 3 October 1947, *IAJ 1945-1949,* Reel #21.

20. Memorandum for the Secretary, State, Army, Navy, Air Force Coordinating Committee by William H. Draper, Jr., 12 December 1947, *IAJ 1945-1949,* Reel #21.

21. Speech by Royall to the Commonwealth Club, San Francisco, 6 January 1948, *Documents concerning the Allied Occupation and Control of Japan,* Vol. II (Political, Military and Cultural), pp. 4-10, compiled by the Division of Special Records, Foreign Office, Japan, 1949.

22. Economic Stabilization Board, January 1948, *JDC.*

23. Records of the Executive Secretariat (Dean Acheson), 2 March 1948, 53D444, RG 59, National Archives.

24. Hiwatari Nobuhiro, *Sengo Nihon no Shijo to Seiji [Market and Politics of Postwar Japan]* (Tokyo: Tokyo Daigaku Shuppankai, 1991), p. 36.

25. Fujiwara Akira ed., *Nihon Gendaishi [Modern Japanese History]* Vol. 6 (Tokyo: Nihon Hyoronsha, 1979), pp. 18-19.

26. Keizai Saiken Kenkyukai ed., *Polei kara Daresu he [From Pauley to Dulles]* (Tokyo: Diamond sha, 1952), p. 54.

27. The NAC consisted of representatives from the State, Army, Commerce, and Treasury Departments, as well as from the Federal Reserve Board. The NAC had the authority to examine and approve all foreign aid budget requests after the implementation of the Marshall Plan.

28. Borden, *The Pacific Alliance,* pp. 89-90.

29. The Young Report, 12 June 1948, *OJER* Part 1, 4-106-77.

30. Report of Special Mission on Yen Foreign Exchange Policy (Young Report), 12 June 1948, *OJER* Part 1: Deconcentration and Modernization of Economic Power, 4-106-77 (Tokyo: Maruzen, 1994).

31. Tsusho Sangyosho, *Tuusho Sangyo Seisaku Shi* Vol. 4, p. 305.

32. Nanto, "The United States' Role," p. 213; The Young Report, 12 June 1948, *OJER* Part 1, 4-106-77.

33. McDiarmid, "The Dodge and Young Missions," p. 64.

34. Incoming Message to SCAP, 3 July 1948, *JDC.*

35. Treasury Department memo, 1 July 1948, Department of Treasury 67-A-245 cited in Borden, *The Pacific Alliance,* p. 90.

36. *SZ* Vol. 3, pp. 396-99.

37. Saltzman to General Noce, 14 July 1948, *IAJ 1945-1949,* Reel #27.

38. *SZ* Vol. 17, p. 1068.

39. The ten-point principles included production increases, an effective allocation/rationing system, effective food collection, rigorous adherence to official price schedules, wage stabilization, efficient tax collection, the introduction of a new tax, reduction of deficits in the Special Account, foreign trade and exchange control, and credit control. *SZ* Vol. 20, p. 542; Hiwatari Nobuhiro, *Sengo Nihon*, p. 36.

40. Ohkurasho Zaiseishishitsu ed., *Watanabe Takeshi Nikki*, p. 242.

41. Nakamura Takafusa ed., *"Keikakuka" to "Minshuka" ["Planning" and "Democratization"]* (Tokyo: Iwanami Shoten, 1989), p. 151.

42. Nakamura Takafusa ed., *Nihon Keizaishi*, Vol. 7 (Tokyo: Iwanami Shoten, 1989), p. 151.

43. Tessa Morris-Suzuki and Takuro Seiyama eds., *Japanese Capitalism since 1945: Critical Perspectives* (Armonk, NY: M.E. Sharpe, Inc., 1989), pp. 42, 72.

44. NSC 13, 2 June 1948, PSF, *PHST*, Harry S Truman Library, Independence, Missouri.

45. CIA, "Japan" SR-38, 14 September 1948, PSF, *PHST*, Harry S Truman Library, Independence, Missouri.

46. NSC 13/1, 24 September 1948, *Ibid.*

47. This economic assistance financed the provision of industrial raw materials and it was limited to one country, not a regional economic aid. *SZ* Vol. 3, p. 407.

48. *Ibid.*, pp. 407-08; Borden *The Pacific Alliance*, p. 90.

49. 10 December 1948, PSF, *PHST*, Harry S. Truman Library, Independence, Missouri.

50. *SZ* Vol. 3, p. 397.

51. Press Release by MacArthur, 19 December 1948, *FR*, 1948 VI, p. 1066.

52. 19 December 1948, *Joseph Dodge Papers* (hereafter *JDP*), Detroit Public Library, Detroit, Michigan.

53. *SZ* Vol. 3, p. 414.

54. Nakamura, *Nihon Keizaishi* 7, p. 154.

55. 16 September 1948, *PRJ 1945-1949*, Reel #1.

56. Douglas MacArthru's announcement, 24 January 1949, Yoshida Naikaku Kankokai, *Yoshida Naikaku*, pp. 167-68.

57. Hayashi Shigeru & Tsuji Kiyoaki eds., *Nihon Naikaku Shiroku [History of Japanese Cabinets]* Vol. 5 (Tokyo: Daiichi Hoki, 1981), p. 172; *Ibid.*, p. 120.

58. OIR 5022, 1 September 1949, Kesaris ed., *O.S.S./State Department*, Reel #5.

59. Hayashi & Tsuji eds., *Nihon Naikaku Shiroku*, Vol. 5, pp. 172, 180; Yoshida Naikaku Kankokai, *Yoshida Naikaku*, p. 120.

60. Rekishigaku Kenkyukai ed., *Nihon Dojidaishi* Vol. 2 (Tokyo: Aoki Shoten, 1990), pp. 52-53. Yoshida selected Ikeda Hayato, the first-year representative and former Vice Minister of Finance, as Finance Minister and Sato Eisaku, another first-year representative and former Vice Minister of Transportation, as the DLP's secretary general.

61. Mikuriya Takashi, "'Teikoku' Nihon," p. 189.

62. Shiratori ed., *Nihon no Naikaku* II, p. 104; Dower, *Yoshida Shigeru*, pp. 48-51.

63. Hiwatari Nobuhiro, *Sengo Nihon*, pp. 36-37; 4 February 1949, Iokibe ed., *The Occupation of Japan*, 4D 76.

64. Kern to Butterworth, 26 March 1949, *PRJ 1945-1949,* Reel #1.

65. Paul Kesaris ed., *Documents of the National Security Council,* Fourth Supplement (Frederick, MD: University Publications of America, 1987), Reel #3.

66. Acheson to Patterson, 14 April 1947, *FR,* 1947 VI, pp. 200-01.

67. Office Memorandum by Green for the Director of Office of Far Eastern Affairs, 27 April 1948, *IAJ 1945-1949,* Reel #21.

68. Conversation between MacArthur and Kennan, 5 March 1948, *FR* 1948 VI, The Far East and Australasia, p. 702.

69. Borden, *The Pacific Alliance,* p. 86.

70. Joseph M. Dodge was a successful commercial banker who had increased the assets of the Detroit Bank from $60 million in 1936 to $550 million in 1948. He was President of the American Bankers Association between 1947 and 1948. Dodge served the government as chairman of the War Contracts Board and the Price Adjustment Board during the war and as deputy finance advisor to Military Governor General Lucius Clay to bring about a deflationary currency reduction in occupied Germany. Then, he went to Vienna to represent the State Department as U.S. Representative on the Austrian Treaty Commission and returned to Washington to advise Secretary of State George Marshall on Austrian affairs. In Washington, he was one of the members of the advisory committee on fiscal and monetary problems in the Economic Cooperation Administration handling the Marshall Plan funds between 1947 and 1951. By 1948, Dodge was one of the most prominent and competent persons involved in the attempt to solve the difficult problems of the international economy. William Draper, Dodge's colleague in the War Department and occupied Germany, recommended Dodge to Truman and contacted Dodge in spring 1948 about going to Japan.

71. Dodge to Board of Directors, the Detroit Bank, 13 December 1948, *JDP,* Detroit Public Library, Detroit, Michigan.

72. Contract from Harry S. Truman to appoint Joseph M. Dodge, January 17, 1949, *JDP.*

73. Lucius Clay, Letter to Joseph Dodge, January 26, 1949, *JDP.*

74. Nanto, "The Dodge Line: A Reevaluation," p. 47.

75. Suzuki Takeo, *Kinyu Kinkyu Sochi to Dodge Line [The Emergency Financial Measures and the Dodge Line]* (Tokyo: Seimeikai Shuppanbu, 1960); Keizai Kikakucho, *Sengo Keizaishi (Zaisei Kinyu) [Postwar Economic History (Volume on Finance and Public Finance)]* (Tokyo: Ohkaurasho Insatsu Kyoku, 1959); G. C. Allen, *Japan's Economic Expansion* (New York: Oxford University Press, 1965).

76. Nanto, "The United State's Role"; Borden, *The Pacific Alliance.*

77. Shinjo Hiroshi, *History of the Yen* (Tokyo: Kinokuniya Bookstore Co., Ltd., 1962); Joyce and Gabriel Kolko, *The Limits of Power* (New York: Harper and Row, 1972); William J. Sebald with Russell Brines, *With MacArthur in Japan* (New York: W. W. Norton & Company, 1965); Ohtake Hideo, *Adenauer to Yoshida Shigeru [Adenauer and Yoshida Shigeru]* (Tokyo: Chuo Koron, 1986).

78. Hiwatari Nobuhiro, *Sengo Nihon,* p. 35; Ohtake, *Adenaua,* p. 247.

79. 17 January 1949, Kesaris, ed., *National Security Council, Fourth Supplement.*

80. Ohkurasho Zaiseishishitsu ed., *Watanabe Takeshi Nikki,* p. 314.

81. Ohtake, *Adenaua,* p. 242.

82. *Ibid.*, pp. 243-48

83. *SZ* Vol. 3, p. 424; Tokyo Daigaku Shakai Kagaku Kenkyujo [Tokyo University Institute of Social Science], *Sengo Kaikaku [Postwar Reform]* Vol. 7, p. 20.

84. Inoki Masamichi, *Hyoden Yoshida Shigeru [Critical Biography Yoshida Shigeru]* Vol. 4 (Tokyo: Chikuma Shobo, 1995), p. 323.

85. Itoh Masaya, *Ikeda Hayato* (Tokyo: Jiji Tsushinsha, 1985), p. 47.

86. Guttman, "Miracles of Power,", p. 111; Nanto, "The United States' Role," p. 290.

87. ESB Analysis, 12 March 1949, *JDP*, Detroit Public Library, Detroit, Michigan.

88. Redford ed., *The Occupation of Japan,* p. 58.

89. Schonberger, *Senryo 1945-1952,* p. 264.

90. Nester, *Japan's Growing Power,* p. 25.

91. Major General William Frederic Marquat, Letter to Joseph Dodge, September 11, 1949, *JDP*, Detroit Public Library, Detroit, Michigan.

92. Ohkurasho Zaiseishishitsu ed., *Watanabe Takeshi Nikki,* p. 197.

93. *SZ* Vol. 3, p. 421.

94. ESB, 9 March 1949, *JDC.*

95. ESB Analysis, 12 March 1949, *JDP*, Detroit Public Library, Detroit, Michigan.

96. Keizai Antei Honbu [Economic Stabilization Board] *Nihon Keizai Fukkou Keikaku [Japanese Economic Recovery Plan]* (Tokyo: Kokumin Keizai Kenkyukai, 1949), p. 11.

97. Joseph Dodge, Comment on Credit and Budget Policy, 27 April 1949, *JDP*, Detroit Public Library, Detroit, Michigan.

98. Joseph Dodge, Summary of meeting with Mr. Ikeda, 22 April 1949, *Ibid.*

99. Memorandum by Joseph Dodge, 27 April 1949, *Ibid.*

100. Comment by Joseph Dodge, 1949 (no date), *Ibid.*

101. Memorandum by Joseph Dodge, 16 April 1949, *Ibid.*

102. Recommendations by Joseph Dodge, 7 March 1949, *Ibid.*

103. Ohkurasho, *Watanabe Takeshi Nikki,* p. 330.

104. Rekishigaku Kenkyukai, *Nihon Dojidaishi* Vol. 2, p. 153; Ohtake, *Adenauer,* pp. 264-65.

105. Miyazawa Kiichi, *Tokyo-Washington no Mitsudan [Secret Talks between Tokyo and Washington]* (Tokyo: Jitsugyo no Nihonsha, 1956), p. 26; Jacques Hersh, *The USA and the Rise of East Asia since 1945* (New York: St. Martin's Press, Inc., 1993), p. 22.

106. Borden, *The Pacific Alliance,* p. 99; Dodge to Ikeda, 9 August 1949, JDP, Detroit Public Library, Detorit, Michigan.

107. Major General William Frederic Marquat, Letter to Joseph Dodge, September 11, 1949, *JDP* Detroit Public Library, Detorit, Michigan.

108. Hiwatari Nobuhiro, *Sengo Nihon,* p. 38. The RFB funds into industries were categorized as loans, but in fact they were virtual subsidies: the RFB allocated 108,421 million yen by December 1948, but collected only 13,329 million yen, or 12.2% of the total amount of loans outstanding. Nanto, "The United States' Role" pp. 234-35.

109. Yoshida Shigeru, *Nihon wo Kettei Shita 100nen [One Hundred Years that Gave Great Impact to Japan]* (Tokyo: Chuo Koron Shinsha, 1999), p. 95.

110. Joseph Dodge, Summary of meeting with Finance Minister Ikeda, 4 March 1949, *JDP*, Detroit Public Library, Detroit, Michigan.

111. Miyazawa, *Tokyo to Washington*, pp. 24-25.

112. Finance Address by Ikeda, No Date (1949), *JDP*, Detroit Public Library, Detroit, Michigan.

113. Statement by Ikeda, July 1949, *Ibid.*

114. Nakamura Takafusa ed., *Shiryo/Sengo Nihon* Vol. 3 (Tokyo: Tokyo Daigaku Shuppankai, 1990), pp. 281, 285. The ERPC consisted of Prime Minister as chairman, vice ministers, and other important officials.

115. Observations by Ichimada, 9 January 1950, *PRJ 1945-1949*, Reel #1.

116. Ohtake, *Adenaua*, pp. 240, 247. As part of this economic liberalization of the Japanese economic system, many Japanese industries worked hard to try to adopt American-style quality, production, and labor management know-how to their production schemes. Kosai Yutaka & Teranishi Juro eds., *Sengo Nihon no Keizai Kaikaku: Shijo to Seifu [Postwar Japan's Economic Reform: Market and Government]* (Tokyo: Tokyo Daigaku Shuppankai, 1993), p. 221.

117. The Finance Ministry to SCAP, 15 July 1949, *JDC.*

118. Ito Masaya, *Ikeda Hayato* (Tokyo: Jiji Tsushinsha, 1985), p. 44.

119. Hiwatari Yumi, *Sengo Seiji to Nichibei Kankei [Postwar Politics and Japan-US Relations]* (Tokyo: Tokyo Daigaku Shuppankai, 1990), pp. 15,18.

120. Cohen, *Nihon Senryo Kakumei*, Vol. 2, p. 316.

121. Ohtake Hideo, *Nihon Seiji no Soten [Controversial Points in Japanese Politics]* (Tokyo: Sanichi Shobo, 1984), pp. 42-43; Ohtake, Adenaua, pp. 224-26.

122. Ichimada Naoto, *Genka no Keizai Kinyu Mondai ni Tsuite [A Discussion on Current Economic and Financial Condition]* (Lecture at the Kobe Chamber of Commerce, 1950).

123. Ichimada to Dodge, 5 October 1949, *JDP*, Detroit Public Library, Detroit, Michigan.

124. *SZ* Vol. 3, p. 369; Miyajima Hideaki "Zaibatsu Kaitai," ["Zaibatsu Dissolution,"] in Hashimoto Juro & Takeda Haruhito eds., *Nihon Keizai no Hatten to Kigyou Shudan [Development of Japanese Economy and Industrial Group]* (Tokyo: Tokyo Daigaku Shuppankai, 1992), p. 230.

125. Nakamura Takafusa, *Nihon Keizai*, p. 154.

126. Hiwatari Yumi, *Sengo Seiji*, pp. 20-21.

127. Okazaki Tetsuji and Okuno Masahiro eds., *Gendai Nihon Keizai Shisutemu no Genryu [Origins of the Modern Japanese Economic System]* (Tokyo: Nihon Keizai Shimbunsha, 1993), pp. 81, 125.

128. *Ibid.*, pp. 230-38.

129. *Ibid.*, p. 133. Monitoring by the financial community forced companies to streamline their management by reducing excess labor and closing down inefficient factories. This rationalization process, however, did not lead to new plant investment and the introduction of new technologies due to a lack of financial resources. Shiraishi, *Sengo Nihon*, p. 71.

130. Nakamura, *Nihon Keizai*, p. 154. The industrial community criticized the Dodge Line while the financial community was in favor of it. Ohtake, Adenaua, p. 253.

131. Dower, *Yoshida Shigeru*, Vol. 2, p. 80.

132. Nanto, "The United States' Role" p. 235; Guttman, "Miracles of Power,"p. 111.

133. The counter part fund was the yen equivalent of the dollar value of wheat, raw cotton, and other imports provided by the United States under GARIOA and EROA aid programs that were deposited in a special account for redemption and loans at low interest rates to major industries.

134. Dodge announcement on budget, 15 April 1949, Keizai Saiken Kenkyukai ed., *Pauley kara Dulles he,* p. 268.

135. Rekishigaku Kenkyukai ed., *Nihon Dojidaishi* Vol. 2, p. 135.

136. Yoshida Naikaku Kankokai, *Yoshida Naikaku,* p. 475.

137. Hata, "Japan Under the Occupation," pp. 21,34.

138. Chalmers Johnson, *Tsusansho to Nihon no Kiseki [MITI and the Japanese Miracle: The Growth of Industrial Policy, 1925-1975]* (Tokyo: TBS Britanica, 1982), pp. 192-94.

139. *Ibid.,* p. 209.

140. Ohtake, *Adenauer,* p. 259. The Ministry of Finance also drastically cut the size of the MITI personnel from 13,822 (1949) down to 3,257 (1952) in order to decrease its influence.

141. Robert A. Scalapino ed., *The Foreign Policy of Modern Japan* (Berkeley: University of California Press, 1977), p. 261; MITI, Tsusho Sangyo Seisakushi, Vol. 4, p. 429.

142. Tsusho Sangyosho, *Tsusho Sangyo Seisakushi,* Vol. 4, p. 427.

143. Yoshida Shigeru's Press statement, 27 December 1949, Yoshida Naikaku Kankokai, *Yoshida Naikaku,* p. 131.

144. Ikeda Analysis, July 1949, *JDP,* Detroit Public Library, Detroit, Michigan.

145. Robert Fearey, *The Occupation of Japan: Second Phase, 1948-1958.* (New York: Macmillan, 1950), p. 135.

146. Memorandum by R. Reid for the Under Secretary of the Army, 18 October 1948, *JDP,* Detroit Public Library, Detroit, Michigan. William Sebald reported in December 1948 that "most of the Commonwealth representatives were of the opinion that the establishment of a single exchange rate for Japan might well be considered by their governments as an essential prerequisite to the extension of most favored nation treatment to Japan." Bane to Sebald, No date, 1948, *FR,* 1948 VI, The Far East and Australasia, p. 1051.

147. Dodge's announcement, 7 March 1949, Keizai Saiken Kenkyukai, *Pauley kara Dulles he,* p. 259.

148. Dodge to Ikeda, 9 August 1949, *JDP,* Detroit Public Library, Detroit, Michigan.

149. "Report of the Special Mission on Yen Foreign Exchange Policy," 12 June 1948, *OJER* Part 2, 4-106-77.

150. Yoshida Naikaku Kankokai, *Yoshida Naikaku,* p. 199; Tsusho Sangyosho, *Tsusho Sangyo Seisakushi,* VI, pp. 334, 341.

151. Ichimada to Royall, 1 February 1949, *JDP,* Detroit Public Library, Detroit, Michigan.

152. Ichimada Naoto, *Kyu Gensoku to Keizai Antei [Nine-Point Program and Economic Stabilization]* (Tokyo: Rodo Bunkasha, 1949), pp. 36, 38.

153. Joseph Dodge Press Statement, 7 March 1949, *JDC.*

154. NAC Staff Committee to NAC, 25 March 1949, *IAJ 1945-1949,* Reel #27; Shiraishi, *Sengo Nihon,* p. 63.

155. Memorandum by Joseph Dodge, 30 March 1949, *JDC.*

156. Voorhees to Dodge, 30 March 1949, *IAJ 1945-1949*, Reel #27. The NAC insisted on its proposal not only because it was favorable to export industries but also because it had secret information that England was poised to devalue the pound. Nanto, "The United States' Role," p. 256; *SZ* Vol. 3, p. 430; Schonberger, *Aftermath of War,* p. 258.

157. Dodge's future Press Statement, 4 December 1949, *JDP,* Detroit Public Library, Detroit, Michigan; Nanto, "The United States' Role," p. 247.

158. Ikeda Hayato, *Kinko Zaisei[Balanced Budget]* (Tokyo: Chuo Koron Shinsha, 1999), p. 21.

159. CIA, 14 September 1948, PSF, *PHST,* Harry S Truman Library, Independence, Missouri.

160. Butterworth to the Acting Secretary of State, 16 September 1948, *PRJ,* Reel #1.

161. The Department of the Army and Coordinated with the State Department, *Economic Rehabilitation Occupied Areas,* 4/1/48 - 6/30/49, *OJER,* Part 1, 4-112-18.

162. ESS, "Self Supporting," November 1948, *JDC.*

163. Nakamura Takafusa, *Shiryo: Sengo Nihon* Vol. 3, p. 195.

164. Memorandum by Welsh, Chief of Antitrust and Cartels Division, ESS, 20 August 1949, *OJER,* 4-101-04.

165. Joseph M. Dodge, "Economic Problems of Japan," *Michigan Business Review,* November 1949, *JDP,* Detroit Public Library, Detroit, Michigan.

166. Bruce Cumings, "Japan and Northeast Asia into the Twenty-first Century," in Peter J. Katzenstein and Takashi Shiraishi, eds., *Network Power: Japan and Asia* (Ithaca: Cornell University Press, 1997), pp. 151-52.

167. ESS, "A Possible Program for a Balanced Japanese Economy," 27 March 1947, *JDC.*

168. Borden, *The Pacific Alliance,* p. 110.

169. Memorandum to Marquat, 24 December 1947, *OJER,* Part 1, 4-107-16.

170. Andrew Rotter, *The Path to Vietnam* (Ithaca: Cornell University Press, 1987), p. 128.

171. ESS, "Program for a Self Supporting Japanese Economy," November 1948, *JDC.*

172. Barnett to Martin, 9 June 1947, *PRJ* 1945-1949, Reel #1. Acting Secretary of State Dean Acheson began to lobby for a softening of the US Initial Post Surrender Policy for Japan "which sets forth the ultimate objectives of the United States in regard to Japan, envisages resumption of peaceful economic activity in Japan as rapidly as possible." Acheson to Patterson, 14 April 1947, *FR* 1947 VI, The Far East, p. 200. Since the built-in ambiguity of the initial surrender policy gave Washington flexibility, Acheson was able to apply a more lenient interpretation of the same policy guidance on which the earlier punitive occupation policies had relied. Washington gradually shifted its position toward a milder stance.

173. Davies to Kennan, 11 August 1947, *FR* 1947 VI, The Far East, pp. 485-86.

174. Hilldring to Petersen, 25 July 1947, *Ibid.,* p. 265.

175. Allison to Butterworth, December 17, 1947, *IAJ 1945-1949*, Reel #21.

176. Dower, *Empire and Aftermath*, p. 419.

177. Guttman, "Miracles of Power," p. 162; Rotter, *Vietnam*, pp. 45, 128; Borden, *The Pacific Alliance*, pp. 120-22.

178. Butterworth to the Acting Secretary of State, 16 September 1948, *PRJ 1945-1949*, Reel #1.

179. CIA, 12 September 1949, ORE 69-49, PSF, *PHST*, Harry S Truman Library, Independence, Missouri.

180. CIA, 14 September 1948, *Ibid.*

181. Martin to Hilldring, 12 March 1947, *FR* 1947 VI, The Far East, p. 184.

182. Barnett to Martin, 13 May 1947, *IAJ 1945-1949*, Reel #21.

183. SANACC 381/2, 12 February 1948 *JDC.*

184. The Johnston Report, 26 April 1948, *JDP*, Detroit Public Library, Detroit, Michigan.

185. Sebald to Butterworth, 30 September 1948, *FR* 1948 VI the Far East and Australasia, p. 1028.

186. Joseph Dodge Memorandum for the Under Secretary of Army, 18 October 1948, *JDP*, Detroit Public Library, Detroit, Michigan.

187. Testimony of Dodge, 24 March 1950, *Papers of Douglas MacArthur*, RG5, MacArthur Memorial Bureau of Archives, Norfolk, VA.

188. Address by Draper, Jr., 9 November 1948, *JDC.*

189. Jessup to Acheson, 14 November 1949 and 27 October 1949, Rotter, *Path to Vietnam*, p. 118.

190. Guttman, "Miracles of Power," p. 162.

191. Report by ESS, No date (1950), *JDP*, Detroit Public Library, Detroit, Michigan.

192. Yoshida, *Nihon wo Kettei Shita 100nen*, p. 95.

193. Akio Watanabe, "Southeast Asia in U.S.-Japanese Relations," in Akira Iriye and Warren Cohen eds., *The United States and Japan in the Postwar World* (Lexington, Kentucky: The University Press of Kentucky, 1989), pp. 84-85.

194. ESB, January 1948, *JDC.*

195. ESB, 17 May 1948, Nakamura Takafusa ed., *Shiryo: Sengo Nihon no Keizai Seisaku Koso Vol. 3, Keizai Fukko Keikaku [Documents: Economic Policy Planning in Postwar Japan Vol. 3, Economic Rehabilitation Planning]* Document #1 (Tokyo: Tokyo Daigaku Shuppankai, 1990), p. 30.

196. Nakamura ed., *Shiryo: Sengo Nihon no Keizai Seisaku Koso* Vol. 3, pp. 30, 132, 134.

197. Ichimada to Royall, 1 February 1949, *JDP*, Detroit Public Library, Detroit, Michigan.

198. Memorandum for record by Reid, 24 March 1949, *Ibid.*

199. Memorandum from Fine for Marquat, 29 June 1950, *OJER*, Part 1, 4-101-68.

200. Nakamura ed., *Shiryo: Sengo Nihon no Keizai Seisaku Koso* Vol. 3, pp. 245, 252.

201. ESB, 20 June 1950, *JDC.*

202. The JMFA, 8 December 1949, *NGM* B'.4.0.0.1. Vol. 5.

203. The Japanese Ministry of Finance, Reference for Finance Minister Ikeda, 5 May 1950, *JDC.*

204. Sebald to the Secretary of State, 16 September 1947, *FR* 1947 VI, The Far East, p. 294.

205. Sebald to the Secretary of State, 24 October 1947, *Ibid.*, p. 310.

206. 24 December 1947, Memorandum to Marquat, *OJER*, Part 1, 4-107-16.

207. Borden, *The Pacific Alliance,* pp. 109, 125.

208. November 1949, *JDP,* Detroit Public Library, Detroit, Michigan.

209. Conversation between MacArthur and Kennan, 5 March 1948, *FR* 1948 VI, The Far East and Australasia, p. 702.

210. Department of the Army and Cooperated with the State Department, Economic Rehabilitation Occupied Areas, 1 April '48 - 30 June '49, *OJER*, Part 1,, 4-112-18.

211. Rotter, *Path to Vietnam,* p. 45.

212. NSC51, 1 July 1949, Kesaris ed., *Documents of the National Security Council,* Reel #2.

213. James S. Lay, Jr., 26 October 1949, NSC Meeting No. 50; NSC 48/1, 23 December 1949, PSF, *PHST,* Harry S Truman Library, Independence, Missouri.

214. NSC 48/2, 30 December 1949, Paul Kesaris ed., *Documents of the National Security Council: Second Supplement* (Frederick, MD: University Publications of America, 1983), Reel #1.

215. CIA, 25 July 1949, Intelligence Memorandum No. 197, Records of the National Security Council, *PHST,* Harry S Truman Library, Independence, Missouri.

216. Voorhees, 29 December 1949, *Tracy Voorhees Papers* F, Spcial Collections/Archives Rutgers University Library.

217. NSC 61, 27 January 1950, Kesaris ed., *Documents of the National Security Council,* Reel #2.

218. CIA 2-50, 15 February 1950, PSF, *PHST,* Harry S. Truman Library, Independence, Missouri.

219. NSC 64, 27 February 1950, Kesaris ed., *Documents of the National Security Council,* Reel #2.

220. Reid Memo for Voorhees, 27 February 1950, *JDC.*

221. Borden, *The Pacific Alliance,* p. 140.

222. Memorandums from Voorhees for Gray, 25 February 1950, *Tracy Voorhees Papers* M, Special Collections/Archives, Rutgers University.

223. Memorandum from Reid for Voorhees, 5 April 1950, Japan Papers 1950, *JDP,* Detroit Public Library, Detroit, Michigan.

224. Doherty to Allison, 29 March 1950, *IAJ 1950-1954,* Reel #21.

225. Cleveland to Hoffman, 11 April 1949, RG469, National Archives.

226. Memorandum by Reid for Voorhees, 5 April 1950, *JDC.*

227. Memorandum by Andrews & West for Voorhees, 22 April 1950, *JDC;* Borden, *The Pacific Alliance,* pp. 126-27.

228. Memo to Marquat from the Programs and Statistics Division of ESS, 14 January 1950, *JDC.*

229. Keizai Doyukai [Japan Association of Corporate Executives] *Keizai Doyukai Junenshi [Ten-Year History of Japan Association of Corporate Executives]* (Tokyo: Keizai Doyukai, 1956).

230. Marquat to Dodge, 7 April 1950, *JDC.*

231. Summary of the Department of State, 23 May 1950, *JDC.*

232. NSC 51, 1 July 1949, PSF, *PHST,* Harry S Truman Library, Independence,

Missouri.

233. NSC 48/2, 30 December 1949, Paul Kesaris ed., *Documents of the National Security Council: Second Supplement*, Reel #1.

CHAPTER FOUR: JAPAN'S SECURITY

1. Memorandum by Davies, 10 August 1946, *FR* 1946 VIII, The Far East, p. 285.

2. Memorandum by Emmerson, 9 October 1946, *Ibid.*, pp. 337-38.

3. Cheseldine, 17 February 1947, *JDC.*

4. The Central Intelligence Agency, ORE 43-48, 24 May 1948, PSF, *PHST*, Harry S Truman Library, Independence, Missouri.

5. Dower, *Empire and Aftermath*, p. 419.

6. Cheseldine, 17 February 1947, *JDC.*

7. Stuart to the Secretary of State, 20 August 1946, *FR* 1946 VIII, The Far East, p. 303.

8. Hata, *Saigunbi*, p. 75.

9. Memorandum by Davies, 10 August 1946, *FR* 1946 VIII, The Far East, p. 286.

10. PPS/10, 14 October 1947, *FR* 1947 VI, The Far East, p. 541.

11. Kennan, 19 May 1948, *Kennan Papers*, Mudd Manuscript Library, Princeton University.

12. CIA, 14 September 1948 and 25 July 1949, PSF, *PHST*, Harry S Truman Library, Independence, Missouri.

13. Hata, *Saigunbi*, p. 73.

14. Frank Kowalski Jr., *Nihon Saigunbi [The Rearmament of Japan]* (Tokyo: The Simul Press, 1969), p. 32; Eichelberger reported to the JCS that American forces in Japan consisted of four division (47,000 men), 20,000 out of which were non combat men. Japanese police had approximately 100,000 men but only 18,000 men carried pistols. Hata, *Saigunbi*, pp. 94-99.

15. Jon Halliday, *A Political History of Japanese Capitalism* (New York: Pantheon Books, 1975), pp.197-198.

16. Finn, *Makkasa to Yoshida Shigeru* Vol. 1, pp. 184-85; Kowalski, *Nihon Saigunbi*, p. 32; Takamasa Ohtsuka, *Gaiko to Nihonkoku Kempo [Foreign Policy and the Japanese Constitution]* (Tokyo: Bunshindo, 1992), pp. 163-64; *SZ* Vol. 3, pp. 404, 435-36.

17. Explanatory Notes by Kennan, 25 March 1948, *FR* 1948 VI, The Far East and Australasia, p. 713.

18. Memorandum by the Joint Chiefs of Staff for the Undersecretary of Army, 12 October 1949, *IAJ 1945-1949*, Reel #38.

19. Memorandum on Reactivation of Japanese Armed Forces by the Department of Defense, 7 November 1949, *IAJ 1945-1949*, Reel #12.

20. J.C.S. 1380/77, 10 December 1949, *Records of the Joint Chiefs of Staff*, Part II, 1946-53 Europe and NATO, Reel #6.

21. Memo by Royall to Forrestal, 20 February 1948, RG 218, National Archives; memo from Ohley to Royall, 24 February 1948, RG 330, National Archives cited in Kan Hideki, "Amerika no Ajia ni okeru Shudan Anzen Hosho Koso to Nihon Saigunbi Mondai, 1948-51 (1)," [American Scheme of Collective Security in Asia and Japanese Rearmament Issues, 1948-51 (1)] *Kitakyushu University Gaiokugo Gakubu Kiyo* Vol. 62

(March 1988), p. 28; Limited Military Armament for Japan, JCS 1380/48, 24 February 1948, RG 218, National Archives, cited in Kan, "Amerika no Ajia ni okeru," p. 28.

22. Kojima, *Kowa Joyaku* Vol. 1, p. 596. In December 1948, he insisted that Japan adopt one of the following measures to increase its defense capabilities: (1) arm the existing police force of 125,000 men and increase the number to 150,000 (2) create a new constabulary of 150,000 men in addition to the existing police force. Eichelberger, 14 December 1948, Ohtake *Sengo Nihon Boei Mondai*, Vol. 1, p. 257.

23. Nishi, *Makkasa no "Hanzai"* Vol. 2, pp. 252-53.

24. Memorandum by Emmerson, 9 October 1946, *FR*, 1946, VIII, The Far East, pp. 337-39.

25. Saltzman to Butterworth, 9 April 1948, *FR* 1948 VI, The Far East and Australasia, p. 728.

26. Butterworth and Howard to the Secretary of State, 15 November 1949, *IAJ 1945-1949*, Reel #12.

27. 13 March 1948, *Eichelberger Diary* in Ohtake, *Sengo Nihon Boei Mondai*, Vol. 1, p. 250; Hata, *Saigunbi*, p. 94; MacArthur to the Secretary of State, 1 September 1947, *FR* 1947 VI, The Far East, pp. 512-13.

28. Hata, *Saigunbi*, p. 95; Conversation Among MacArthur, Draper, and Kennan, 21 March 1948 (Amended March 23, 1948), *FR* 1948 VI, The Far East and Australasia, pp. 708-09; GHQ to JCS, 23 December 1948, PSF, *PHST*, Harry S Truman Library, Independence, Missouri.

29. GHQ to JCS, 23 December 1948, PSF, *PHST*, Harry S. Truman Library, Independence, Missouri.

30. Memorandum by Muler for JCS, 23 December 1948, Ohtake, *Sengo Nihon Boei Mondai*, Vol. 1, pp. 258-61.

31. American Council on Japan, 24 January 1949, *JDC*.

32. CIA, 25 July 1949, Intelligence Memorandum No. 197, Records of the National Security Council, *PHST*, Harry S Truman Library, Independence, Missouri.

33. Royall to the Secreatary of Defense, 18 May 1948, PSF, *PHST*, Harry S Truman Library, Independence, Missouri.

34. Memorandum by the JCS for Secretary of Defense Jamese Forrestal, 1 March 1949, Ohtake, *Sengo Nihon Boei Mondai*, Vol. 1, pp. 261-62.

35. Royall to the Secretary of Defense, 18 May 1948, p. 254.

36. Hata, *Saigunbi*, p. 107.

37. Memorandum of Conversation, by the Charge in Japan (Huston), 16 July 1949, *FR* 1949 VII, The Far East and Australasia, Part 2, p. 806.

38. Memorandum on Reactivation of Japanese Armed Forces by the Department of Defense, 7 November 1949, *IAJ 1945-1949*, Reel #12.

39. Nishimura, *Nihon Gaikoshi* Vol. 27, pp. 12-13.

40. Miura Yoichi, *Yoshida Shigeru to San Furanshisuko Kowa [Yoshida Shigeru and the San Francisco Peace Treaty]* Vol. 1, (Tokyo: Ohtsuki Shoten, 1996), p. 116; Paul M. Kattenburg, *The Vietnam Trauma in American Foreign Policy, 1945-75.* (New Brunswick: Transaction Books, 1980), p. 10.

41. Hata, *Saigunbi*, p. 128.

42. Memorandum of Conversation, 24 April 1950, Merrill ed., *Documentary History of the Truman Presidency* Vol. 5, p. 562.

43. NSC 13/3, 5 May 1950, *FR* 1950 VI, East Asia and the Pacific (Washington, D.C.: Government Printing Office, 1976), p. 1189.

44. Memorandum by SCAP, 14 June 1950, *Ibid.*, p. 1216.

45. Report by the JCS, 9 June 1949, *FR* 1949 VII, The Far East and Australasia, part 2, p. 776.

46. Memorandum by Butterworth to Webb, 19 May 1949, *Ibid.*, p. 752.

47. Memorandum from the Undersecretary of State for Souers, 23 May 1949, PSF, *PHST,* Harry S. Truman Library, Independence, Missouri.

48. Sebald to the Secretary of State, 20 August 1949, *FR* 1949 VII, The Far East and Australasia, Part 2, pp. 839-40.

49. Yoshida Naikaku Kankokai, *Yoshida Naikaku,* pp. 175-76.

50. Memo of Conversations, 9 September 1949, *Confidential U.S. State Department Special Files Japan 1947-1956* (hereafter *SFJ*) (Washington, D.C.: UPA, 1990) Reel #8.

51. Yoshida Naikaku Kankokai, *Yoshida Naikaku,* p. 397.

52. NSC 49/1, 4 October 1949, *Documents of the National Security Council,* Reel #2.

53. Miura, *Yoshida Shigeru* Vol. 1, p. 142.

54. J.C.S. 1380/75, 30 November 1949, *Records of the Joint Chiefs of Staff,* Part II, 1946-53 Europe and NATO, Reel #7.

55. Miura, *Yoshida Shigeru* Vol. 1, p. 129.

56. Hata, *Saigunbi,* p. 128.

57. Memorandum by Allison to Butterworth, 11 April 1950, *FR* 1950 VI, East Asia and the Pacific, p. 1169.

58. Memorandum of Conversation by Howard, 24 April 1950, *Ibid.*, p. 1180.

59. PPS Draft Paper, 28 June 1949, Iokibe ed., *The Occupation of Japan Part 2,* 3H-40.

60. Jessup to Howard, 14 November 1949, *IAJ 1945-1949,* Reel #12.

61. Butterworth and Howard to the Secretary of State, 15 November 1949, *Ibid.*

62. J.C.S. 1380/77, 10 December 1949, *Records of the Joint Chiefs of Staff* Part II, 1946-53, Reel #6.

63. Memorandum by Bradley for the Secretary of Defense, 22 December 1949, *SFJ,* Reel #3.

64. Informal Memorandum by Dean Acheson for the British Ambassador, 24 December 1949, *SFJ,* Reel #8.

65. Howard to Rusk, 1 February 1950, *SFJ,* Reel #11.

66. Memorandum by Conversation, by Howard, 24 April 1950, *FR* 1950 VI, East Asia and the Pacific, p. 1180.

67. Memorandum of Conversation, 24 April 1950, Merrill ed., *Documentary History of the Truman Presidency,* Vol. 5, p. 562.

68. Memorandum for the record by Sebald, 19 June 1950, *William Joseph Sebald Papers,* (hereafter *Sebald Papers*) Manuscript Collection, United States Naval Academy, Nimitz Library, Annapolis.

69. Miyake Masaki et. al., *Sengo Sekai to Nihon Saigunbi [Postwar World and Japanese Rearmament]* (Tokyo: Daiichi Hoki Shuppan, 1983), p. 45.

70. Memorandum of Conversation, by Fearey, 2 November 1949, *FR* 1949 VII, The Far East and Australasia, p. 891.

71. Miura, *Yoshida Shigeru,* Vol. 1, p. 127.

72. Memorandum of Conversation, MacArthur and Sebald, 6 April 1950, *FR* 1950 VI, East Asia and the Pacific, p. 1170.

73. Memorandum by MacArthur, 23 June 1950, *Ibid.,* pp. 1227-28.

74. Miura, *Yoshida Shigeru,* Vol. 1, pp. 211, 227.

75. Memorandum by Dulles to the Secretary of State, 27 July 1950, *FR* 1950 VI, East Asia and the Pacific, p. 1259.

76. Memorandum of Telephone Conversation, by Dulles, 3 August 1950, *Ibid.,* pp. 1264-65.

77. Memorandum for the President, 7 September 1950, *Ibid.,* pp. 1293-94.

78. Seimukyoku [Political Bureau] of the JMFA, "Heiwa Joyaku no Naiyo ni Kansuru Gensokuteki Hoshin," ["Basic Policy toward a Peace Treaty"] 26 January 1946, Tainichi Heiwa Joyaku Kankei Junbi Kenkyu Kankei [Documents Concerning Preparations for Peace Treaty] Vol. 1, *NGM,* B'.4.0.0.1.

79. Nishimura, *Nihon Gaikoshi,* Vol. 27, p. 31.

80. The JMFA, Anzen Hosho Mondai [Security Issues] 12 June 1947, Tainichi Heiwa Joyaku Kankei Junbi Kenkyu Kankei [Documents Concerning Preparations for Peace Treaty] Vol. 2, *NGM,* B'.4.0.0.1.

81. Inouye Juichi, "Kokuren to Sengo Nihon Gaiko," ["The United Nations and Postwar Japanese Diplomacy,"] *Nenpo Kindai Nihon Kenkyu [Annual Report Modern Japan]* Vol. 16 (1994), pp. 84, 192-94.

82. Igarashi, *Tainichi Kowa to Reisen,* p. 181.

83. The JMFA, 20 July 1947, *NGM,* B'0010 in Inouye, "Kokuren," p. 195.

84. Miyake et. al., *Sengo Sekai to Nihon Saigunbi,* p. 44.

85. Toyoshita Narahiko, *Ampo Joyaku no Seiritsu [Process of the Japan-US Security Treaty]* (Tokyo: Iwanami Shoten, 1997), p. 156.

86. Suzuki-Eichelberger Meeting, 13 September 1947, Tainichi Heiwa Joyaku Kankei Junbi Kenkyu Kankei [Documents Concerning Preparations for Peace Treaty] Vol. 3, *NGM,* B'.4.0.0.1. After securing approval from both Prime Minister Katayama and Secretary General Nishio, Suzuki submitted this memorandum to Robert Eichelberger. This memo also stated that if American-Soviet relations improved in the future, "Japan's independence can be fully guaranteed by the United Nations."

87. Hata, *Saigunbi,* p. 87.

88. *Asahi Shimbun,* 19 March 1947 in Miura, *Yoshida Shigeru,* Vol. 1, p. 167.

89. Hatano Sumio, "'Saigunbi' wo Meguru Seijirikigaku," ["The Politics of Japanese Rearmament,"] *Nenpo Kindai Nihon Kenkyu [Journal of Modern Japanese Studies],* No. 11, 1989, p. 187.

90. The JMFA, "Tainichi Heiwa Joyaku no Shomondai," ["Issues about Japanese Peace Treaty"] 15 November 1949, *NGS* B'.4.1.0.11, Vol. 2.

91. The JMFA, "Prospect of International Conditions and a Japanese Peace Treaty," 23 December 1949, *NGM* B'.4.0.0.1, V.

92. Watanabe and Miyazato eds., *Sanfuranshisuko Kowa,* p. 40; The JMFA, "Heiwa Joyaku Kankei Sagyo ni tsuite," ["Memo on Works concerning a Peace Treaty"], 28 December 1949, *NGS,* B'.4.0.0.1, Vol. 5.

93. Inoue Toshikazu, "Kokuren to Sengo Nihon Gaiko," ["The United Nations and Postwar Japanese Diplomacy,"] *Nenpo Kindai Nihon Kenkyu [Journal of Modern Japanese*

Studies], No. 16, 1994, p. 197.

94. Yoshida Shigeru's statement at Governors' Conference, 2 May 1950, Yoshida Naikaku Kankokai, *Yoshida Naikaku,* p. 180.

95. Joyakukyoku Kyokucho [Director of the Treaty Bureau], "On Studies Relating to a Peace Treaty," 28 December 1949, *NGM* B'.4.0.0.1, Vol. 5.

96. The JMFA, "Majority Peace ni okeru Anzenhosho ni Kansuru Kihon Hoshin," ["Basic Policy concerning Security in case of a Majority Peace"], 3 December 1949, *NGS,* B'.4.0.0.1, Vol. 5.

97. Yoshida statement in his interview with the Reuter correspondent, 7 May 1949, Ohtake, *Sengo Nihon Boei Mondai,* Vol. 1, p. 331.

98. The JMFA, "Heiwa Mondai ni Kansuru Kihonteki Tachiba," ["Basic Sance on Peace Issues,"], 31 May 1950, *NGS,* B'.4.0.0.1., Vol. 6.

99. Memorandum of Conversation, by Huston, 8 April 1950, *FR* 1950 VI, East Asia and the Pacific, p. 1166.

100. Summary of a Recent Conversation with Ikeda, 2 May 1950, *Ibid.,* pp. 1195-96; Yoshitsu, *Nihon ga Dokuritsushita Hi,* p. 67; Ohkurasho [The Japanese Ministry of Finance], "Daijin Tobei Shiryo," ["Reference for the Minister's trip to the United States,"], 5 may 1950, *JDC;* Miyazawa, *Tokyo-Washington,* pp. 54-55.

101. Miura, *Yoshida Shigeru,* Vol. 1, p. 200.

102. Yoshida, *Kaiso Junen,* Vol. 1, p. 179.

103. Memorandum of Conversation between Shirasu and Butterworth, 1 May 1950, *SFJ,* Reel #8.

104. Butterworth to the Secretary of State, 3 May 1950, *Ibid.*

105. Memorandum by Green to Allison, 2 August 1950, *FR* 1950 VI, East Asia and the Pacific, pp. 1262-63.

106. Sebald to the Secretary of State, 9 August 1950, *Ibid.,* pp. 1270-71.

107. Memorandum of Conversation with Ohta Ichiro (Vice Minister of Foreign Affairs) by Sebald, 7 August 1950, *Ibid.,* note 3, p. 1271.

108. Howard B. Schonberger, *Senryho 1945-1952: Sengo Nihon wo Tsukuriageta 8nin no Amerikajin [Aftermath of War: Americans and the Remaking of Japan, 1945-1952]* (Tokyo: Jiji Tsushinsha, 1994), p. 304; Ohtake, *Sengo Nihon Boei Mondai,* Vol. 1, p. 344.

109. Toyoshita, *Ampo Joyaku no Seiritsu,* pp. 126, 170-75.

110. NSC 34, 13 October 1948, PSF, *PHST,* Harry S. Truman Library, Independence, Missouri.

111. CIA, 20 July 1948, Records of the National Security Council, CIA File, *PHST;* CIA, 3 November 1948, PSF, *PHST,* Harry S Truman Library, Independence, Missouri.

112. CIA, 15 December 1948, PSF, *PHST,* Harry S. Truman Library, Independence, Missouri.

113. CIA, 16 December 1948, CIA 12-48, *Ibid.*

114. Kennan, 11 October 1948, *Kennan Papers,* Mudd Manuscript Library, Princeton University.

115. Kennan, 8 November 1948, *Ibid..*

116. Kennan, 21 December 1948, *Ibid.*

117. NSC 34/1, 11 January 1949, PSF, *PHST,* Harry S. Truman Library, Independence, Missouri.

118. NSC Meetings Memorandum for the President, 4 February 1949, *Ibid.*

119. Nancy Bernkopf Tucker, *Patterns in the Dust: Chinese-American Relations and the Recognition Controversy, 1949-1950* (New York: Columbia University Press, 1983), p. 14.

120. PPS39/2, 25 February 1949, Paul Kesaris ed., *Documents of the National Security Council Fifth Supplement* (Frederick, MD: University Publications of America, 1989), Reel 1..

121. NSC 34/2, 28 February 1949, PSF, *PHST,* Harry S. Truman Library, Independence, Missouri; NSC 34/2 was based on George Kennan's recommendation in PPS 39/2 of 25 February 1949, *Ibid.*

122. NSC 34, 13 October 1948, *Documents of the National Security Council,* PSF, *PHST,* Harry S. Truman Library, Independence, Missouri.

123. NSC 41, 28 February 1949, PSF, *PHST,* Harry S. Truman Library, Independence, Missouri.

124. *Ibid.*

125. NSC 34/2, 28 February 1949, *Ibid..*

126. Kennan, 13 June 1949, *Kennan Papers,* Mudd Manuscript Library, Princeton University.

127. Alsops, 5 August 1949, *Joseph and Stewart Alsops Papers,* Library of Congress.

128. Lapham and Griffin to Jessup, 14 September 1949, RG 469, National Archives.

129. CIA, Memorandum No. 209, 20 September 1949, Records of the National Security Council, *PHST,* Harry S. Truman Library, Independence, Missouri.

130. Edwin Martin, *Divided Counsel* (Kentucky: The University Press of Kentucky, 1986).

131. CIA, Memorandum No. 209, 20 September 1949, Records of the National Security Council, *PHST,* Harry S. Truman Library, Independence, Missouri.

132. CIA, "Review of the World Situation," 17 November 1948, *Ibid.*

133. Kennan, 9 January 1949, *Kennan Papers,* Mudd Manuscript Library, Princeton University.

134. Memorandum by Lay, Jr., 26 October 1949, PSF, *PHST,* Harry S. Truman Library, Independence, Missouri.

135. For NSC Staff Discussion Only, 31 August 1949, *Documents of the National Security Council* Fourth Supplement.

136. Lay, Jr., 26 October 1949, NSC Meeting No. 50; NSC 48/1, 23 December 1949, PSF, *PHST,* Harry S. Truman Library, Independence, Missouri.

137. NSC 51, 1 July 1949, *Documents of the National Security Council,* PSF, *PHST,* Harry S. Truman Library, Independence, Missouri.

138. Koo, 19 October 1949, *Wellington Koo Papers,* Butler Library, Columbia University.

139. The Secretary of State to Certain Diplomatic Offices, 8 May 1949, *FR* 1949 VII, The Far East and Australasis, Part 2, p. 737.

140. Draft for NSC Staff, 25 October 1949, PSF, *PHST,* Harry S. Truman Library, Independence, Missouri. The NSC also apprehended a possible domino scenario. "If Indochina fell into Communist hands, the way would be paved for Communist control over Thailand and Burma." CIA, CIA 2-50, 15 February 1950, PSF, *PHST,* Harry S. Truman Library, Independence, Missouri.

141. Kennan, 17 April 1950, *Kennan Papers*, Mudd Manuscript Library, Princeton University.

142. Kennan, 19 September 1949, *Ibid.*

143. CIA, 22 September 1949, ORE 74-46, PSF, *PHST*, Harry S. Truman Library, Independence, Missouri.

144. Dodge, 19 January 1950, *JDC.*

145. CIA, 17 November 1948, CIA 11-48, PSF, *PHST*, Harry S. Truman Library, Independence, Missouri.

146. Kern to Dodge, 24 January 1949, *JDC.*

147. NSC 125/1, 18 July 1952, RG 273 National Archives.

148. Tucker, *Patterns*, p. 36.

149. Memorandum for SCAP by Dodge, 28 April 1949, *JDC.*

150. Study Group Reports, Japanese Peace Treaty Problems, 23 October 1950; Same, 27 November 1950, *CFRP*, Council on Foreign Relations Archives, New York.

151. Study Group Reports, Japanese Peace Treaty Problems, 23 October 1950; Same, 27 November 1950, *Ibid.*

152. Memorandum by Marquat for Senator Smith, 17 December 1951, *H. Alexander Papers*, Mudd Manuscript Library, Princeton University.

153. Nester, *Japan's Growing Power*, p. 53.

154. Inoki, *Hyoden Yoshida Shigeru* Vol. 3, p. 408; Dulles to Allison, 14 December 1951, *SFJ*, Reel #2; Kagawa Takaaki, Yoshida's private secretary remembered that "Mr. Yoshida always said that . . . China and the Soviets were quite different from one another and someday would part." William Chapman, *Inventing Japan: The Making of a Postwar Civilization* (New York: Prentice Hall Press, 1991), p. 83.

155. Memorandum for SCAP by Dodge, 28 April 1949, *JDC.*

156. Ichimada to West, 23 March 1950, *JDC.*

157. ESB to SCAP, 18 April 1950, *JDC.*

158. NSC 41, 28 February 1949, PSF, *PHST*, Harry S. Truman Library, Independence, Missouri.

159. *Ibid..*

160. Tucker, *Patterns*, p. 37.

161. Iriye and Cohen eds., *The United States and Japan*, p. 89.

162. CIA, NIE-52, 29 May 1952, PSF, *PHST*, Harry S. Truman Library, Independence, Missouri.

163. The big business community was rather cool about the future of the Chinese market for Japan. Ota Tadayuki, Chief of the Public Relations Department of the Keidanren, indicated that he did not expect any large volume of trade between Japan and the PRC. Instead, he focused his attention more on Southeast Asia. Boehringer to the Department of State, 20 January 1950, *IAJ 1950-1954*, Reel #21.

164. NSC 41, 28 February 1949, PSF, *PHST*, Harry S. Truman Library, Independence, Missouri.

165. CIA, 15 April 1949, ORE 29-49, PSF, *PHST*, Harry S. Truman Library, Independence, Missouri. In November 1948, the CIA wondered if "the Chinese Communist Party is an absolutely reliable instrument of Soviet policy." CIA, 17 November 1948, PSF, *PHST*, Harry S. Truman Library, Independence, Missouri. About

a month later, it acquired more concrete information that "the Chinese Communist Party has been and is an instrument of Soviet policy." It might have expected Sino-Soviet trouble once the Communists ruled over China. CIA, 10 December 1948, ORE 77-48, PSF, *PHST,* Harry S. Truman Library, Independence, Missouri. In September 1949, the CIA estimated that "it is estimated that the Communist regime in China is not immediately vulnerable in the sense of being deposed or altered, and that, for the next few years, the CCP's Stalinist leadership will continue to control the Party, while Moscow will continue to control the Party leadership." CIA, 20 September 1949, PSF, *PHST,* Harry S Truman Library, Independence, Missouri.

166. Koo, *Wellington Koo Papers,* 12 September 1949, Butler Library, Columbia University.

167. NSC 34, 13 October 1948, PSF, *PHST,* Harry S Truman Library, Independence, Missouri.

168. Kennan, 19 September 1949, *Kennan Papers,* Mudd Manuscript Library, Princeton University.

169. Kennan, 17 April 1950, *Ibid.*

170. Tucker, *Patterns,* p. 175.

171. Draft for NSC Staff, "The Position of the United States with Respect to Asia," 25 October 1949, PSF, *PHST,* Harry S. Truman Library, Independence, Missouri.

CHAPTER 5: IMPACT OF THE KOREAN WAR ON U.S. POLICY TOWARD ASIA

1. Morrow to Marquat, 14 January 1950, *JDC.*

2. Office of Intelligence Research, Report of 23 May 1950, *JDC.*

3. Nester, *Japan's Growing Power,* p. 39.

4. Warren S. Hunsberger, *Japan and the United States in World Trade* (New York: Council on Foreign Relations, 1964), p. 41; William L. Holland, "Japan and the New Balance of Power in the Far East," *International Affairs* Vol. XXVIII, No. 3 (July 1952), p. 292. It was, however, primarily a quantitative expansion, and except for a minority of large companies, very few industries made rationalized investments in order to overcome the technological disadvantages they faced. Rekishigaku Kenkyukai ed., *Nihon Dojidaishi* Vol. 2, pp. 144-45. The Dodge Line made it imperative for Japanese industries to rationalize themselves so as to compete in the world economy, but the Korean War induced them to chase short-term profits at the expense of long-term planning for things such as plant investment. Shiraishi, *Sengo Nihon,* pp. 90, 121. The economic significance of the Korean War lay not so much in how it necessitated structural changes in the Japanese economy but in how it legitimized the Dodge line.

5. Seiyama Takuro, "A Radical Interpretation of Postwar Economic Policies," in Morris-Suzuki and Seiyama eds., *Japanese Capitalism,* p. 45.

6. Tsuru, *Essays,* p. 77.

7. Nakamura, *Nihon Keizai,* pp. 156-57, 175; Redford, *The Occupation of Japan,* p. 282; Nester, *Japan's Growing Power,* p. 39.

8. Seiyama, "A Radical Interpretation," p. 45.

9. Nakamura Takafusa, *Nihon Keizai,* pp. 156-57, 175; Radford, *The Occupation of*

Japan, p. 282.

10. Rotter, *The Path to Vietnam*, p. 205.

11. Rekishigaku Kenkyukai, *Sengo Nihonshi [Postwar Japanese History]* Vol. 2 (Tokyo: Aoki Shoten, 1961), p. 72.

12. Nakamura Takafusa, *Nihon Keizai*, pp. 156-58.

13. ESB Report, March 1951, *JDC*.

14. Guttman, "Miracles of Power," pp. 137-38.

15. Richard J. Samuels, *"Rich Nation, Strong Army": National Security and the Technological Transformation of Japan*. (Ithaca: Cornell University Press, 1994), p. 141.

16. Tokyo Daigaku Shakai Kagaku Kenkyujo ed., *Sengo Kaikaku* Vol. 7, p. 26.

17. Unofficial Army Document, 6 July 1950, Japan Papers 1950, *JDP*, Detroit Public Library, Detroit, Michigan.

18. Extracts Reference Japan Contained in the Gray Dollar Gap Report, October 1950, *OJER* Part 1, 4-103-44.

19. Notes on Conversation between Dulles and Marquat, 5 February 1951; Report of the ESS, 7 February 1951, *IAJ 1950-1954*, Reel #20; Marquat Statement, 16 May 1951, *JDC*.

20. *The New York Times*, 22 July 1951, *JDC*.

21. Borden, *The Pacific Alliance*, p. 195.

22. Ohno, *War Reparations*, p. 65.

23. Statement by Dodge, 29 November 1951, *OJER*, Part 1, 4-102-37.

24. Borden, *The Pacific Alliance*, p. 196.

25. *FR* 1950, VI, East Asia and the Pacific, pp. 949-51.

26. NSC Staff Study in NSC 48/4, 17 May 1951, US Department of Defense, *United States-Vietnam Relations, 1945-67* (hereafter *Pentagon Papers*), Vol. 8 (Washington, D.C.: Government Printing Office, 1971), pp. 442-43.

27. CIA, NIE-43, 13 November 1951, PSF *PHST*, Harry S Truman Library, Independence, Missouri.

28. Borden, *The Pacific Alliance*, p. 141.

29. CIA, ORE 29-50, 13 October 1950, PSF, *PHST*, Harry S Truman Library, Independence, Missouri.

30. NSC64/1, 21 December 1950, *Documents of the National Security Council*, Reel #2.

31. NSC 64/1, 21 December 1950, *Ibid*.

32. Memorandum of Meeting with Rusk, 29 October 1951, RG 469, National Archives.

33. NSC 124, 13 February 1952, *Documents of the National Security Council: Second Supplement*, Reel #1.

34. JCS to the Secretary of Defense, 28 July 1952, JCS Files, 092 Japan, National Archives.

35. Statement by Dodge, 7 October 1950, *JDC*.

36. Jerome B. Cohen, *Japan's Postwar Economy* (Bloomington: Indiana University Press, 1958), pp. 87-89.

37. Meeting with Ichimada, Memorandum by Dodge, 9 November 1951, *OJER*,

Part 1, 4-102-41.

38. Memorandum by Dodge, 22 November 1951, *JDP*, Detroit Public Library, Detroit, Michigan.

39. William Adams Brown, Jr. and Redvers Opie *American Foreign Assistance* (Washington, D.C.: The Brookings Institution, 1953), p. 369.

40. Briefing Paper by Marquat for Subcommittee of House Committee on Expenditures in Executive Departments, 25 October 1951, RG 331, *OJER*, Part 1, 4-107-11.

41. Memorandum by Morrow for Harriman, RG 331, *OJER*, Part 1, 4-105-72.

42. Borden, *The Pacific Alliance*, pp. 156-57.

43. *Ibid.*, pp. 149-50.

44. Voorhees to MacArthur, 6 April 1950, *JDP*, Detroit Public Library, Detroit, Michigan.

45. Reid to Johnson, 8 March 1951, *IAJ 1950-1954*, Reel #35.

46. Memorandum by Marshall for the Secretaries of Army, the Navy, the Air Force and the Chairman of Munitions Board, 28 March 1951, *IAJ 1950-1954*, Reel #23.

47. Johnson to Rusk, 12 June 1951, *IAJ 1950-1954*, Reel #20.

48. Nakamura Takafusa, *Showashi [History of Showa]* (Tokyo: Toyo Keizai Shimposha, 1993),Vol. II, p. 444.

49. Amemiya Shoichi, "Sengo Taisei no Keisei," ["Formation of Postwar System,"] Nihon Gendaishi Kenkyukai [Association of Modern Japanese History] ed., *Sengo Taisei no Keisei [Formation of Postwar System]* (Tokyo: Ohtsuki Shoten, 1988), p. 5.

50. Samuels, *Rich Nation*, p. 137.

51. Opinion formulated by the Fourth Sub-Committee of the Committee on US-Japan Economic Cooperation, 24 July 1951, *JDP*, Detroit Public Library, Michigan.

52. Hiwatari Yumi, *Sengo Seiji*, p. 38.

53. Yoshida Naikaku Kankokai, *Yoshida Naikaku*, pp. 350-55.

54. Yoshida to Marquat, 1 August 1951, *OJER*, Part 1, 4-105-60.

55. Samuels, *Rich Nations*, pp. 142-43. John Foster Dulles and the Defense Department also supported the idea of fostering military-related industries in Japan. Johnson to Rusk, 12 June 1951, *IAJ 1950-1954*, Reel #20.

56. Samuels, *Rich Nations*, p. 145; Hiwatari Yumi, *Sengo Seiji*, p. 40; Hiwatari Nobuhiro, *Sengo Nihon*, pp. 38-40.

57. Watanabe Takeshi, *Senryoka no Nihon Zaisei Oboegaki [Memorandum of Japan's Finance under the Occupation]* (Tokyo: Nihon Keizai Shinbunsha, 1966), p. 319.

58. Johnson to Rusk, 12 June 1951, *IAJ 1950-1954*, Reel #20.

59. US Political Adviser in Tokyo to the Department of State, 9 July 1951, *IAJ 1950-1954*, Reel #22.

60. Nakamura, *Showashi*, Vol. II, p. 444.

61. Asahi Shimbun, 26 December 1952, in Ohtake, *Nihon Seiji no Soten*, p. 18.

62. Ohtake Hideo, *Sengo Nihon no Ideorogi Tairitsu [Ideological Confrontation in Postwar Japan]* (Tokyo: Sanichi Shobo, 1996), p. 262.

63. Ohtake, *Soten*, p. 41.

64. Memorandum by Kennan for Secretary of State, 26 June 1950, *Kennan Papers*,

Mudd Manuscript Library, Princeton University.

65. CIA, Intelligence Memorandum No. 300, 28 June 1950, Records of the National Security Council, Record of the National Security Council, *PHST,* Harry S Truman Library, Independence, Missouri.

66. Voorhees to Dulles, 30 June 1950, *SFJ* Reel #3.

67. Harry S Truman, *Memoirs by Harry S. Truman Vol. 2: Years of Trial and Hope* (New York: Doubleday & Company, 1956), p. 339.

68. The Department of State to Dulles, 13 December 1950, *SFJ,* Reel #3.

69. Memorandum by the Secretaries of the Navy, the Army, and the Air Force for Secretary of Defense Johnson, 1 August 1950, *Documents of the National Security Council Fourth Supplement,* Reel #4.

70. Speech by Wellington Koo for the Press, 7 July 1950, *Wellington Koo Papers,* Butler Library, Columbia University.

71. Telegram by the JCS to the Commander in Chief, Far East (CINCFE), 29 June 1950 *John Foster Dulles Papers* (hereafter *JFDP*), Mudd Manuscript Library, Princeton University.

72. David Allan Mayers, *Cracking the Monolith: U.S. Policy Against the Sino-Soviet Alliance, 1949-1955* (Baton Rough: Louisiana State University Press, 1986), p. 85.

73. Record of Conversation between Koo and Dulles, 20 October 1950, *Wellington Koo Papers,* Butler Library, Columbia University.

74. Dulles to Allison, 18 July 1950, *IAJ 1950-1954,* Reel #16.

75. Dulles to Nitze, 20 July 1950, *SFJ,* Reel #11; Council on Foreign Relations, 23 October 1950, *CFR Papers,* Council on Foreign Relations Archives, New York.

76. Report by Voorhees, 21 June 1950, *JDP,* Detroit Public Library, Detroit, Michigan.

77. Voorhees to Dulles, 30 June 1950, *SFJ,* Reel #3.

78. George Kennan lecture, "The Present International Situation," at National War College, Washington, D.C., No date, *Kennan Papers,* Mudd Manuscript Library, Princeton University.

79. The Department of State to Dulles, 13 December 1950, *SFJ,* Reel #3.

80. Council on Foreign Relations, 18 December 1950, *CFR Papers,* Council on Foreign Relations Archives, New York.

81. Office of Intelligence Research, the Department of State, 11 January 1951, *SFJ,* Reel #6.

82. Memorandum from Fearey for Dulles, 7 March 1951, *SFJ,* Reel #5.

83. Memorandum by MacArthur, 23 June 1950, *Douglas MacArthur Papers* RG 5, Reel #24, MacArthur Memorial Bureau of Archives.

84. John Welfield, *Empire in Eclipse : Japan in the Postwar American Alliance System* (London: Athlone Press, 1988), p. 72.

85. Ohtake, *Sengo Nihon Boei Mondai Shiryoshu* Vol. 1, pp. 432, 510.

86. Overton to Johnson, 19 September 1950, *IAJ 1950-1954,* Reel #20.

87. PPS, 26 July 1950, *FR* 1950 VI, East Asia and The Pacific, pp. 1255-57.

88. Dulles to Nitze, 20 July 1950, *Ibid.,* p. 1247.

89. *Asahi Shimbun* [The *Asahi Newspaper*], 19 August 1950, in Ohtake, *Sengo Nihon Boei Mondai,* Vol. 1, p. 430.

90. Council on Foreign Relations, 28 February 1951, *CFRP,* Council on Foreign Relations Archives, New York.

91. Overton to Johnson, *IAJ 1950-1954,* Reel #20.

92. Fearey to Dulles and Allison, 25 January 1951, *SFJ,* Reel #7.

93. Council on Foreign Relations, 23 October 1950, *CFRP,* Council on Foreign Relations Archives, New York.

94. Office of Intelligence Research of the Department of State, OIR Report No. 5375, 24 October 1950, *O.S.S./State Department Intelligence and Research Reports* Part VIII: Japan, Korea, Southeast Asia and the Far East Generally: 1950-1961 Supplement (Washington, D.C.: University Publications of America) Reel #3.

95. Yoshida Naikaku Kankokai, *Yoshida Naikaku,* pp. 181, 183.

96. Yoshida, *Kaiso Junen* Vol. 2, p. 166. Prime Minister Yoshida did not believe that the Korean War would become a third world war. Ohtake, *Sengo Nihon Boei Mondai,* Vol. 1, p. 415.

97. Shugiin Heiwa Joyaku oyobi Nichibei Anpo Tokubetsu Iinkai [House of Representatives, Special Committee for Peace Treaty and Japan-US Security], 18 October 1951, Suekawa Hiroshi, et.al., *Nihon Gendaishi Shiryo: Nichibei Anpo Joyaku Taiseishi [Documents of Modern Japanese History: History of the Japan-US Security Treaty System]* Vol. 2 1948-1960 (Tokyo: Sanseido, 1971), p. 188.

98. Shugiin Yosan Iinkai [House of Representatives, Budget Committee], 10 March 1952, *Ibid.,* p. 221.

99. Shugiin Yosan Iinkai [House of Representatives, Budget Committee], 11 March 1952, *Ibid.,* p. 376.

100. Rekishigaku Kenkyukai ed., *Nihon Dojidaishi Vol. 3: 55Nen Taisei to Ampo Toso [Japanese Contemporary History Vol. 3: The 1955 System and the Struggle against the Security Treaty]* (Tokyo: Aoki Shoten, 1990), pp. 10-11.

101. Ikeda, *Kinko Zaisei,* p. 74.

102. Draft Paper by the PPS, 28 June 1949, Iokibe ed., *The Occupation of Japan* Part 2, 3H-40.

103. Office of Intelligence Research of the Department of State, 27 December 1951, *IAJ 1950-1954,* Reel #1.

104. Yoshida used Tatsumi primarily as a contact person, behind the scene, with G2. Yoshida relied little on advice from the military group.

105. Hatano, "'Saigunbi' wo meguru,"pp. 181-86.

106. Rekishigaku Kenkyukai ed., *Nihon Dojidaishi* Vol. 2, p. 180.

107. Ohtake, *Sengo Nihon Boei Mondai,* Vol. 2 (Tokyo: Sanichi Shobo, 1992), p. 64.

108. *Ibid.,* p. 82.

109. Ashida Hitoshi, *Ashida Hitoshi Nikki [Ashida Hitoshi Diary]* Vol. 4 (Tokyo: Iwanami Shoten, 1986), p. 6.

110. Nishi, *Makkasa no "Hanzai"* Vol. 1, p. 157.

111. Hiwatari Yumi, *Sengo Seiji,* pp. 62, 75.

112. Bronfenbrenner to Dodge, 2 June 1950; Dodge to Bronfenbrenner, 12 June 1950, *JDP,* Detroit Public Library, Detroit, Michigan.

113. Hiwatari Yumi, *Sengo Seiji,* p. 100.

114. Shugiin Heiwa Joyaku oyobi Nichibei Anpo Tokubetsu Iinkai [House of

Representatives, Special Committee for Peace Treaty and Japan-US Security], 18 October 1951, Suekawa, et. al., *Nichibei Ampo* Vol. 2, p. 47.

115. Dulles's Press Conference, 15 September 1950, *JFDP*, Mudd Manuscript Library, Princeton University.

116. Memorandum by Chief of Staff, US Air Force for the Secretary of Defense, 12 December 1951, *IAJ 1950-1954*, Reel #16.

117. Robert A. Scalapino ed., *The Foreign Policy of Modern Japan* (Berkeley: University of California Press, 1977), p. 325.

118. Hara Yoshihisa, *Sengo Nihon to Kokusai Seiji [Postwar Japan and International Politics]* (Tokyo: Chuo Koron, 1988), p. 33.

119. Hara, "The Significance,"p. 36. Y. Takeno, Chief of the Repatriation Bureau of the JMFA, advocated a quid-pro-quo policy regarding Japan's rearmament: immediate rearmament without further hesitation in return for substantial assistance from the United States. Memorandum of Conversation, Y. Takeno and Stanley Carpenter, 22 December 1950, *IAJ 1950-1954*, Reel #1.

120. Yoshida, *Kaiso Junen* Vol. 4, p. 220.

121. Dulles to Acheson, 19 July 1950, *SFJ*, Reel #1.

122. Schonberger, *Senryo 1945-1952*, p. 304.

123. J.C.S. 1380/89, 18 August 1950, *Records of the Joint Chiefs of Staff*, Part II, 1946-53, The Far East, Reel #6.

124. Memorandum by Louis Johnson for the President, 7 September 1950, Merrill ed., *Documentary History of the Truman Presidency* Vol. 5, p. 575.

125. NSC Sr. Staff Paper, 13 March 1951, Records of the PPS 47-53, Working Papers 64D563, RG 59, National Archives.

126. Dulles to the Secretary of State, 30 November 1950, *JFDP*, Mudd Manuscript Library, Princeton University.

127. CIA, NIE-11, 5 December 1950, PSF, *PHST*, Harry S Truman Library, Independence, Missouri.

128. Council on Foreign Relations, Working Paper No. 3, 18 December 1950, *CFRP*, Council on Foreign Relations Archives, New York.

129. NSC Sr. Staff Paper, 13 March 1951, Records of the PPS 1947-1953, Working Papers 64D563, RG 59, National Archives. Recent studies, however, show that there existed a wide division between the Soviet Union and the PRC concerning the latter's intervention in the Korean War. Sergei N. Goncharov, John W. Lewis, and Xue Litai, *Uncertain Partners: Stalin, Mao, and the Korean War* (Stanford: Stanford University Press, 1993). It was an extremely bloody war for China, costing approximately 900,000 lives. Since the PRC had to rely solely on the Soviet Union for support in order to confront the United States, the war provided the Soviet Union with great leverage with which to deal with the PRC; consequently, no serious divisions came to the surface. Mayers, *Cracking the Monolith*, p. 99.

130. Mayers, *Cracking the Monolith*, pp. 106, 119.

131. NSC 48/5, 17 May 1951, PSF, *PHST*, Harry S Truman Library, Independence, Missouri.

132. NSC 114, 27 July 1951, *Documents of the National Security Council: First Supplement* Reel #1.

133. Memorandum for the President, Summary of the discussion at the 100th Meeting of the NSC, 23 August 1951, PSF, *PHST,* Harry S Truman Library, Independence, Missouri.

134. CIA, National Intelligence Estimate Number 10, 15 January 1951, PSF, *PHST,* Harry S. Truman Library, Independence, Missouri.

135. The Economic Cooperation Administration, February 1951, PSF, National Security Council Meetings, *PHST,* Harry S. Truman Library, Independence, Missouri.

136. Mayers, *Cracking the Monolith,* p. 100.

137. NSC Sr. Staff Paper, 13 March 1951, Records of the PPS 1947-1953, Working Papers, 64D563, RG 59, National Archives.

138. Address by John Allison for the Press, 4 March 1952, Office Files of Marshall D. Shulman, Special Assistant to the Secretary of State, 1950-1953, 53D403, RG 59, National Archives.

139. Mayers, *Cracking the Monolith,* p. 108.

140. NSC Sr. Staff Paper, 13 March 1951, Records of the PPS 1947-1953 Working Papers, 64D563, RG 59, National Archives.

141. Yamagiwa Akira ed., *Higashi Asia to Reisen [East Asia and the Cold War]* (Tokyo: Sanrei Shobo, 1994), p. 200.

142. Mayers, *Cracking the Monolith,* pp. 107-08.

143. Nester, *Japan's Growing Power,* p. 33.

144. Borden, *The Pacific Alliance,* p. 195.

145. Office of Intelligence Research, the Department of State, 27 December 1951, *IAJ 1950-1954* Reel #1.

146. NSC Staff Study, State-Defense Draft, 29 December 1951, PSF, National Security Council Meetings, *PHST,* Harry S Truman Library, Independence, Missouri.

147. Memorandum of Conversation, 4 January 1952, *IAJ 1950-1954,* Reel #2.

148. Memorandum from Lay, Jr. for the Senior NSC Staff, 1 February 1952, PSF, National Security Council Meetings, *PHST,* Harry S Truman Library, Independence, Missouri.

149. NSC 124, 13 February 1952, *Documents of the National Security Council: Second Supplement,* Reel #1.

CHAPTER 6: THE DULLES-YOSHIDA NEGOTIATIONS

1. Ohtake, *Sengo Nihon Boei Mondai Shiryoshu* Vol. 1, p. 351; Nishimura, *Nihon Gaikoshi* Vol. 27, pp. 64-65.

2. The JMFA documents, B'0010 in Inoue Toshikazu, "Kokuren to Sengo Nihon Gaiko," ["The United Nations and Postwar Japanese Diplomacy,"] *Nenpo Kindai Nihon Kenkyu [Journal of Modern Japanese Studies],* No. 16, 1994, p. 199.

3. The JMFA, "Beikoku no Tainichi Heiwa Joyakuan no Koso," ["US Ideas of a Peace Treaty with Japan,"], 2 October 1950, *NGM,* B'.4.0.0.2.

4. The JMFA, "Beikoku no Tainichi Heiwa Joyakuan no Koso ni Taiousuru Wagaho Yobo Hoshin (An)," ["Our Request Policy in response to US Ideas of a Peace Treaty with Japan (An Idea),"], 4 October 1950, *NGM,* B'.4.0.0.2.

5. The JMFA, "Beikoku no Tainichi Heiwa Joyakuan no Koso ni Taiousuru Wagaho

Yobo Hoshin (An)," ["Our Request Policy in response to US Ideas of a Peace Treaty with Japan (An Idea),"], 4 October 1950, *NGM,* B'.4.0.0.2.

6. The JMFA, "A Sagyo" ["Work A"], submitted to the Prime Minister on 5 October 1950, *NGM,* B'.4.0.0.2; Watanabe and Miyazato eds., *San Francisco Kowa,* p. 42; Nishimura, *Nihon Gaikoshi,* Vol. 27, p. 80; Ohtake, *Sengo Nihon Boei Mondai,* Vol. 1, pp. 351-54.

7. Watanabe and Miyazato eds., *Sanfuranshisuko Kowa,* p. 44.

8. Toyoshita, *Ampo Joyaku no Seiritsu,* pp. 19-20; The JMFA, "Anzen Hosho ni Kansuru Chinjutsu (Soan)" ["Statements on Security (Draft)"], 10 January 1950, *NGM,* B'.4.1.0.13.; Ohtake, *Sengo Nihon Boei Mondai* Vol. 2, pp. 21-22.

9. The JMFA, "Heiwa Joyaku Taisaku (An)," ["Suggestions for a Japanese Peace Treaty (An Idea),"], 13 October 1950, *NGM,* B'.4.1.0.11 Vol. 2.

10. 28 December 1950, Ohtake, *Sengo Nihon Boei Mondai,* p. 66.

11. Inoki, *Hyoden Yoshida Shigeru* Vol. 3, p. 394.

12. Watanabe and Miyazato eds., *San Francisco Kowa,* p. 44; Toyoshita, *Ampo Joyaku no,* pp. 25-30; Ohtake, *Sengo Nihon Boei Mondai,* Vol. 2, pp. 26-27. It was also probable that Yoshida created this forum to let military experts express their opinions on various issues. There is little evidence that Yoshida relied on Group B's recommendations except for his selective use of its recommendations.

13. Hatano, "'Saigunbi' wo meguru," pp. 193-94. Hotta was a liaison person between Yoshida and Group B. Considering his role, he reflected Yoshida's idea.

14. Toyoshita, *Ampo Joyaku,* p. 33; Watanabe and Miyazato eds., *San Francisco Kowa,* pp. 43, 73; Nishimura, *Nihon Gaikoshi,* Vol. 27, p. 84; Ohtake, *Sengo Nihon Boei Mondai,* Vol. 2, pp. 29-33.

15. Memorandum for the President, 7 September 1950, *FR 1950* VI, East Asia and the Pacific, p. 1294.

16. J.C.S. 2180/2, 28 December 1950, *Records of the Joint Chiefs of Staff,* Part II, 1946-53, The Far East, Reel #6.

17. Dulles to the Secretary of State, 4 January 1951, *FR 1951* VI, Asia and the Pacific, pp. 781-83.

18. Draft Letter to Dulles, 9 January 1951, *Ibid.,* p. 789.

19. Dulles to Allison, 11-12 January 1951, *Ibid.,* p. 791.

20. Fearey to Dulles, 25 January 1951, *Ibid.,* p. 810.

21. Memorandum of Fearey: Minutes-Dulles Mission Staff Meeting 26 January 1951, *Ibid.,* pp. 811-12.

22. Memorandum of Conversation, by Fearey, 27 January 1951, *Ibid.,* pp. 818-19.

23. Memorandum of Conversation, by Allison, 29 January 1951, *Ibid.,* pp. 827-30.

24. Memorandum of Conversation by Allison, 29 January 1951, *Ibid.,* p. 830.

25. Memorandum by Fearey, 30 January 1951: Minutes–Dulles Mission Staff Meeting, *Ibid.,* p. 832.

26. *Our View* consisted of six parts: Territorial, Security, Rearmament, Human Rights, Cultural Relations, and International Welfare. Ohtake, *Sengo Nihon Boei Mondai,* Vol. 2, pp. 40-41.

27. Ohtake, *Sengo Nihon Boei Mondai* Vol. 2, pp. 42-43.

28. The JMFA, "Beigawa ni Kofusareta 'WagaHo Kenkai'," ["'Our View' Submitted

to the United States,"], 30 January 1951, *NGM*, B'.4.0.0.3 Vol. 1.

29. Nishimura, *Nihon Gaikoshi*, Vol. 27, pp. 90-91.

30. The Second Yoshida-Dulles Talk, 31 January 1951, Ohtake, *Sengo Nihon Boei Mondai*, Vol. 2, p. 43; Inoki, *Yoshida Shigeru*, Vol. 3, p. 401.

31. The JMFA, "Dai Niji Kaidan Memo," ["Memo of the Second Talk,"], 31 January 1951, *NGM*, B'.4.0.0.3 Vol. 2.

32. Ohtake, *Sengo Nihon Boei Mondai* Vol. 2, p. 43.

33. Inoki, *Hyoden Yoshida Shigeru*, Vol. 3, p. 402.

34. The JMFA, "Formula Concerning Japanese-American Cooperation for Their Mutual Security," 1 February 1951, *NGM*, B'.4.0.0.3 Vol. 2.

35. The JMFA, "Dai Sanji Kaidan Memo," ["Memo of the Third Talk,"], 1 February 1951, *NGM*, B'.4.0.0.3 Vol. 2.

36. The JMFA, "Agreement Concerning Japanese-American Cooperation for Their Mutual Security," 2 February 1951, *NGM*, B'.4.0.0.3 Vol. 2.

37. Inoki, *Hyoden Yoshida Shigeru*, Vol. 3, p. 404.

38. Ohtake, *Sengo Nihon Boei Mondai* Vol. 2, pp. 44-45.

39. Nishimura, *Nihon Gaikoshi*, Vol. 27, p. 96.

40. Hata Ikuhiko, "Senryoka no Nihon Saigunbi," ["Japanese Rearmament under Occupation,"], Hata Ikuhiko and Sodei Rinjiro, *Nihon Senryo Hishi [Secret History of Japanese Occupation]* Vol. 2 (Tokyo: Asahi Shimbun, 1977), pp. 38-39; Inoki, *Hyoden Yoshida Shigeru*, Vol. 3, p. 397.

41. Watanabe and Miyazato, *San Francisco Kowa*, pp. 45, 56, 132.

42. Minutes-Dulles Mission Staff Meeting, 5 February 1951, *SFJ*, Reel #7.

43. Notes on Conversation between Dulles and British Ambassador, 6 February 1951, *SFJ*, Reel #14.

44. Dulles Press Conference, 19 April 1951, *NGM*, B'.4.1.0.17.

45. Council on Foreign Relations, 28 February 1951, *CFRP*, Council on Foreign Relations Archives, New York.

46. Raymond B. Allen to Ed Taylor, 9 February 1952, Psychological Strategy Board Files, Merrill ed., *Documentary History of the Truman Presidency* Vol. 5, p. 721.

47. NSC 125, A Report to the National Security Council, 21 February 1952, PSF, *PHST*, Harry S Truman Library, Independence, Missouri.

48. Address by Allison for the Press, 27 June 1952, 53D403, Office Files of Marshall D. Shulman, Special Assistant to the Secretary of State, 1950-53, RG 59, National Archives.

49. Transcript of Proceedings, Meeting of Washington Representatives of National Organizations on Japanese Peace Treaty, 23 August 1951, *JFDP*, Mudd Manuscript Library, Princeton University.

50. The JMFA, "Sori Ma Gensui Kaidan Memo," [Memo of the meeting between the Prime Minister and General MacArthur,"], 6 February 1951, *NGM*, B'.4.0.0.3. Vol. 2.

51. Notes on Conversation between Dulles and Marquat, 5 February 1951, *JDC*.

52. Office of Intelligence Research, the Department of State, 11 January 1951, *SFJ*, Reel #6.

53. NSC Sr. Staff Paper, 13 March 1951, Records of the PPS 1947-1953, Working

Papers 64D563, RG 59, National Archives.

54. NSC 48/5, 17 May 1951, *Documents of the National Security Council*, Reel #2.

55. NSC 125/1, 18 July 1952, *Documents of the National Security Council* Third Supplement (Frederick, MD: University Publications of America, 1985), Reel #1.

56. Matthews to Nash, 18 January 1952, *Records of the U.S. Department of State Relating to United States Political Relations With Japan* (hereafter *USPR) 1950-1954*, Reel #1.

57. Council on Foreign Relations, 25 May 1951, *CFRP*, Council on Foreign Relations Archives, New York.

58. Transcript of Proceedings, Meeting of Washington Representatives of National Organizations on Japanese Peace Treaty, 23 August 1951, *JFDP*, Mudd Manuscript Library, Princeton University.

59. Allison to Matthews, 16 November 1951, *IAJ 1950-1954*, Reel #16.

60. Ridgway to Bradley, C-65938, 22 January 1952, CJCS-092.2 Japanese Peace Treaty, RG 218, National Archives.

61. Memorandum by the President, No date (around 15 February 1952), White House Central Files-Confidential File, Merrill ed., *Documentary History of the Truman Presidency* Vol. 5, pp. 737-41.

62. NSC 125, 21 February 1952, *Documents of the National Security Council* Third Supplement, Reel #1.

63. CIA, NIE-52, 29 May 1952, PSF, *PHST*, Harry S Truman Library, Independence, Missouri.

64. Office of Intelligence Research, the Department of State, 27 December 1951, *IAJ 1950-1954* Reel #1.

65. Hiwatari Yumi, *Sengo Seiji*, p. 38.

66. Ohkurasho Zaiseishishitsu ed., *Watanabe Takeshi Nikki*, pp. 666.

67. Watanabe Takeshi, *Senryoka no Nihon Zaisei Oboegaki [Memorandum of Japan's Finance under the Occupation]* (Tokyo: Nihon Keizai Shinbunsha, 1966), p. 291.

68. CIA, 25 July 1949, Intelligence Memorandum No. 197, National Security Council File, *PHST*, Harry S Truman Library, Independence, Missouri.

69. NSC 48/1, 23 December 1949, *Documents of the National Security Council*, Reel #2.

70. Allison to Harlan, 27 November 1951, Office of Far Eastern Operations, Far East Subject Files 1950-1954, RG 469, National Archives.

71. Memorandum from the Joint Secretaries for the Secretary of Defense, 17 July 1951, *IAJ 1950-1954*, Reel #16.

72. U. Alexis Johnson, Hearings, 91st Cong, 2d session, 26-29 Jan., 1970.

73. Hara, *Sengo Nihon to Kokusai Seiji*, p. 24.

74. NSC 125, 21 February 1952, *Documents of the National Security Council* Third Supplement, Reel #1.

75. "Post-Treaty Financial Arrangements with Japan," 23 June 1951, *USPR 1950-1954*, Reel #1.

76. Matthews to Nash, 18 January 1952, *Ibid*.

77. NSC 125, 21 February 1952, RG 273, National Archives.

BIBLIOGRAPHY
(ENGLISH LANGUAGE SOURCES)

PRIMARY DOCUMENTS

Alexander Smith Papers, Mudd Manuscript Library, Princeton University, Princeton, New Jersey.

Blakeslee, George. *The Far Eastern Commission.* Department of State Publication 5138. Far East Series 60. Washington, D.C.: Government Printing Office, 1953.

Claussen, Martin P. and Evelyn Bills Claussen ed. *The State-War-Navy Coordinating Committee and State-Army-Navy-Air Force Coordinating Case Files, 1944-1949.* Wilmington: Scholarly Resources, 1977.

Confidential U.S. State Department Central Files, China: Internal Affairs, 1945-1949. Frederick: University Publications of America, 1984.

Confidential U.S. State Department Special Files, Japan 1947-1956 Lot Files. Bethesda, MD: University Publications of America, 1990.

Council on Foreign Relations. *Papers of Council on Foreign Relations.* Council on Foreign Relations Archives, New York.

Dean Acheson Papers, Harry S Truman Presidential Library, Independence, Missouri.

Division of Northeast Asian Affairs of Department of State. *United States Relations with Japan: 1945-1952.* New York: American Institute of Pacific Relations, January 1953.

Douglas MacArthur Papers, MacArthur Memorial Library, Norfolk, Virginia.

General Headquarters. *History of the Non-military Activities of the Occupation of Japan, 1945-1951.* Tokyo: National Diet Library, 1984.

George M. Elsey Papers, Harry S Truman Presidential Library, Independence, Missouri.

George F. Kennan Papers, Mudd Manuscript Library, Princeton University, Princeton, New Jersey.

Gray, Gordon. *Report to the President on Foreign Economic Policies.* Washington, D.C.: Government Printing Office, 10 November 1950.

Harry S Truman Oral History Collections. Harry S Truman Presidential Library, Independence, Missouri.

Harry S Truman Papers, Harry S Truman Presidential Library, Independence, Missouri.

The Holding Company Liquidation Commission. *Final Report on Zaibatsu Dissolution.* 10 July 1951.

Iokibe Makoto, ed. *The Occupation of Japan, Part 2: U.S. and Allied Policy, 1945-1952.* Bethesda: Congressional Information Service, 1989.

Iokibe Makoto, ed. *The Occupation of Japan, Part 3: Reform, Recovery, and Peace, 1945-1952.* Bethesda: Congressional Information Service, 1991.

Japanese Ministry of Foreign Affairs. *Economic Rehabilitation and Foreign Commerce of Japan.* Government of Japan, April 1953.

Japanese Ministry of Foreign Affairs. *Japan's Problems.* Government of Japan, March 1954.

Japanese Ministry of Foreign Affairs. *Nihon Gaiko Monjo [Documents of the Japanese Ministry of Foreign Affairs]* Gaiko Shiryokan [National Archives for the Japanese Ministry of Foreign Affairs] Tokyo, Japan.

Jessup, C. Philip Papers, Library of Congress, Washington, D.C.

John Foster Dulles Oral History Collection. Mudd Manuscript Library, Princeton University, Princeton, New Jersey.

John Foster Dulles Papers. Mudd Manuscript Library, Princeton University, Princeton, New Jersey.

John Snyder Papers. Harry S Truman Presidential Library, Independence, Missouri.

Joseph M. Dodge Papers, Detroit Public Library, Detroit, Michigan.

Joseph and Stewart Alsop Papers, Library of Congress.

Kesaris, Paul ed. *Postwar Japan, Korea, and Southeast Asia.* Washington, D.C.: University Publications of America, Inc., 1977.

Kesaris, Paul ed. *Records of the Joint Chiefs of Staff Part II: 1946-1953 The Far East.* Washington, D.C.: University Publications of America, Inc., 1979.

Kesaris, Paul ed. *The Presidential Documents Series: Official Conversations and Meetings of Dean Acheson, 1949-1953.* Frederick: University Publications of America, Inc., 1980.

Kesaris, Paul ed. *Documents of the National Security Council 1947-1977.* Frederick: University Publications of America, Inc., 1980.

Kesaris, Paul ed. *CIA Research Reports: Japan, Korea, and the Security of Asia, 1946-1976.* Frederick: University Publications of America, Inc., 1982.

Kesaris, Paul ed. *Documents of the National Security Council Second Supplement.* Frederick: University Publications of America, Inc., 1983.

Kesaris, Paul ed. *Documents of the National Security Council Third Supplement.* Frederick: University Publications of America, Inc., 1985.

Kesaris, Paul ed. *Documents of the National Security Council Fourth Supplement.* Frederick: University Publications of America, Inc., 1987.

Kesaris, Paul ed. *Documents of the National Security Council Fifth Supplement.* Frederick: University Publications of America, Inc., 1989.

Ministry of International Trade and Industry Japanese Government. *The Present Conditions of Japanese Foreign Trade.* 15 August 1949.

Miwa, Ryoichi ed. *The Occupation of Japan: Economic Reform 1945-1952.* Bethesda: Congressional Information Service, Inc., 1994-1995.

Murphy, Gregory ed. *Confidential U.S. State Department Special Files: Japan, 1947-1956.* Bethesda: University Publications of America, Inc., 1990.

O.S.S./State Department Intelligence and Research Reports Part II: Postwar Japan, Korea, and Southeast Asia (1945-1949). Washington, D.C.: University Publications of America, Inc, 1977.

O.S.S./State Department Intelligence and Research Reports Part III: China and India. Washington, D.C.: University Publications of America, Inc, 1977.

O.S.S./State Department Intelligence and Research Reports Part VIII: Japan, Korea, Southeast Asia and the Far East Generally: 1950-1961 Supplement. Washington, D.C.: University Publications of America, Inc., 1979.

Pauley, Edwin W. *Report on Japanese Reparations to the President of the United States, November 1945 to April 1946.* Department of State Publication 3174, Far Eastern Series 25, Washington, D.C.: Government Printing Office.

The Presidential Documents Series: Official Conversations and Meetings of Dean Acheson (1949-1953). Frederick, MD: University Publications of America, Inc., 1980.

Records of the U.S. Department of State Relating to the Internal Affairs of Japan 1945-1949. Wilmington: Scholarly Resources, Inc., 1986.

Records of the U.S. Department of State Relating to the Internal Affairs of Japan 1950-1954. Wilmington: Scholarly Resources, Inc., 1987.

Records of the U.S. Department of State Relating to United States Political Relations with Japan, 1930-1954. Wilmington: Scholarly Resources, Inc., 1988.

Stanley Andrews Papers, Harry S Truman Presidential Library.

Supreme Commander for the Allied Powers. *History of the Nonmilitary Activities of the Occupation of Japan Volumes 1-55. Historical Monographs 1945-1951.*

Supreme Commander fort the Allied Powers. *The Political Reorientation of Japan, September 1945 - September 1948: Report of the Government Section of SCAP.* Washington, D.C. 1948.

Tracy Voorhees Papers. Alexander Library, Rutgers University, New Brunswick, New Jersey.

The United States, *Official Records,* National Archives and Washington National Records Center.

The United States Department of State. *Department of State Bulletin, 1944-1952.*

The United States Department of State. *The Far Eastern Commission Second Report by the Secretary General.* 1948.

The United States Department of State. *Foreign Relations of the United States.* Annual volumes for 1944 - 1952, Washington, D.C.

The United States Department of State. *Occupation of Japan Policy and Progress,* Publication 2671 Far Eastern Series 17, Washington, D.C.: Government Printing Office, 1946.

The United States Department of State. *The Far Eastern Commission: A Study in International Cooperation 1945 to 1952.* Far Eastern Series 60, Washington, D.C.: Government Printing Office, December 1953.

The United States Department of State. *The State Department Policy Planning Staff Papers 1947-1949.* New York: Garland Publishing, Inc., 1983.

The United States House of Representatives. *United States Policy in the Far East Part 1 U.S. Policy and Japan, The Korean War and Peace Negotiations, South Asian and Related Problems.* Selected Executive Session Hearings of the Committee, 1951-56 Volume XVII. Washington, D.C.: Government Printing Office, 1976.

The United States House of Representatives. *United States Policy in the Far East Part 2 Korean Assistance Acts, Far East Portion of the Mutual Defense Assistance Act of 1950* Selected Executive Session Hearings of the Committee, 1943-50 Volume VIII. Washington, D.C.: Government Printing Office, 1976.

Wellington Koo Papers, Butler Library, Columbia University.

William Sebald Papers, United States Naval Academy, Nimitz Library, Annapolis.

SELECTED SECONDARY SOURCES: BOOKS

Acheson, Dean. *Present at the Creation: My Years in the State Department.* New York: Norton, 1969.

Acheson, Dean. *The Korean War.* New York: W. W. Norton, 1971.

Aduard, Barone. *Japan From Surrender to Peace.* The Hague: Martinus Nijhoff, 1953.

Alexander, Charles C. *Holding the Line: The Eisenhower Era, 1952-1961.* Bloomington: Indiana University Press, 1976.

Allen, G. C. *Japan's Economic Recovery.* London: Oxford University Press, 1958.

Allen, G.C. *Japan's Economic Expansion.* London: Oxford University Press, 1965.

Allen, G.C. *Japan As a Market & Source of Supply.* Oxford: Pergamon Press, 1967.

Allen, G.C. *A Short Economic History of Modern Japan 1867-1937 with a Supplementary Chapter on Economic Recovery and Expansion 1945-1970.* London: George Allen & Unwin Ltd., 1972.

Allen, G.C. *Japan's Economic Policy.* London: The Macmillan Press Ltd., 1980.

Allen, G.C. *The Japanese Economy.* London: Weidenfeld and Nicolson, 1981.

Allen, Louis. *The End of the War in Asia.* New York: Beekman/Esanu Publishing, Inc., 1976.

Allison, John. *Ambassador From the Prairie; or Allison Wonderland.* Boston: Houghton Mifflin, 1973.

The American Assembly, Graduate School of Business, Columbia University. *The United States and the Far East.* New York: December 1956.

Asada, Sadao. *Japan & the World 1853-1952: A Bibliographic Guide to Japanese Scholarship in Foreign Relations.* New York: Columbia University Press, 1989.

Asahi Shimbun. *The Pacific Rivals; A Japanese View of Japanese-American Relations.* New York: Weatherhill/Asahi, 1972.

Baerwald, Hans H. *The Purge of Japanese Leaders under the Occupation.* Berkeley: University of California Press, 1959.

Ball, William MacMahon. *Japan: Enemy or Ally?* New York: John Day, 1949.

Barnet, Richard. *Allies America Europe Japan Since the War.* London: Jonathan Cape, 1983.

Barnett, Doak. *China on the Eve of Communist Takeover.* New York: Frederick A. Praeger, 1963.

Beal, John Robinson. *John Foster Dulles, A Biography.* New York: Harper & Brothers Publishers, 1957.

Bernstein, Barton ed. *The Truman Administration: A Documentary History.* New York: Harper & Row, 1966.

Bert, Cochran. *Harry Truman and the Crisis Presidency.* New York: Funk & Wagnalls, 1973.

Bisson, Thomas. *Prospects for Democracy in Japan.* New York: Macmillan, 1949.

Bisson, Thomas. *Zaibatsu Dissolution in Japan.* Berkeley: University of California Press, 1954.

Bisson, Thomas. *Reform Years in Japan 1945-47: An Occupation Memoir.* Unpublished Manuscript, Japanese Translation, Tokyo: Sanseido, 1983.

Bix, Herbert. *Hirohito and the Making of Modern Japan.* New York: HarperCollins, 2000.

Blum, John Morton. *From the Morgenthau Diaries: Years of Urgency, 1938-41.* Boston: Houghton Mifflin, 1965.

Blum, Robert M. *Drawing the Line: The Origin of the American Containment Policy in East Asia.* New York: W.W. Norton & Co., 1982.

Board of Trade. *The Future Development of the Japanese Economy and the Opportunities for British Trade with Japan.* London: His Majesty's Stationery Office, 1948.

Boardman, Robert. *Britain and the People's Republic of China 1949-74.* London: The Macmillan Press Ltd., 1976.

Boltho, Andrea. *Japan: An Economic Survey 1953-1973.* London: Oxford University Press, 1975.

Borden, William S. *The Pacific Alliance: United States Foreign Economic Policy and Japanese Trade Recovery, 1947-1955.* Madison: The University of Wisconsin Press, 1984.

Borg, Dorothy and Waldo Heinrichs eds. *Uncertain Years: Chinese-American Relations, 1947-1950.* New York: Columbia University Press, 1980.

Borton, Hugh. *American Presurrender Planning for Postwar Japan.* New York: The East Asian Institute, Columbia University, 1967.

Brands, H.W., *Cold Warriors: Eisenhower's Generation and American Foreign Policy.* New York: Columbia University Press, 1988.

Brands, H. W. *The Specter of Neutralism: The United States and The Emergence of The Third World, 1947-1960.* New York: Columbia University Press, 1989.

Brines, Russell. *MacArthur's Japan.* Philadelphia and New York: J.B. Lippincott Company, 1948.

Bronfenbrenner, Martin. "The Road Not Taken: Reflections on the Minseito-Zaibatsu Alternative in Japan," Harry Johnson Memorial Lecture, University Teachers of Economics, York: England, March 1978.

Brown, William Adamas. *The United States and the Restoration of World Trade.* Washington, D.C.: The Brookings Institution, 1950.

Brown, William Adams and Redvers Opie. *American Foreign Assistance.* Washington, D.C.: The Brookings Institution, 1953.

Buckley, Roger. *Occupation Diplomacy: Britain, the United States and Japan 1945-1952.* Cambridge: Cambridge University Press, 1982.

Buckley, Roger. *US-Japan Alliance Diplomacy 1945-1990.* New York: Cambridge University Press, 1995.

Buhite, Russell. *Soviet-American Relations, 1945-54.* Norman: University of Oklahoma Press, 1981.

Burk, Robert. *Dwight D. Eisenhower: Hero and Politician.* Boston: Twayne Publishers, 1986.

Burkman, Thomas W. *The Occupation of Japan: The International Context.* Norfolk: the MacArthur Memorial, 1984.

Byrnes, James. *Speaking Frankly.* New York: Harper & Brothers Publishers, 1947.

Cameron, Meribeth E., Thomas H. Mahoney, and George E. McReynolds. *China, Japan and the Powers: A History of the Modern Far East.* New York: The Ronald Press Company, 1960.

Chang, Gordon H. *Friends and Enemies: The United States, China, and the Soviet Union, 1948-1972.* Stanford: Stanford University Press, 1990.

Chapman, William. *Inventing Japan: The Making of a Postwar Civilization.* New York: Prentice Hall Press, 1991.

Chay, John ed. *The Problems and Prospects of American-East Asian Relations.* Boulder: Westview Press, 1977.

Chen, Nai-Ruenn and Walter Galenson. *The Chinese Economy Under Communism.* Chicago: Aldine Publishing Company, 1969.

Chern, Kenneth. *Dilemma in China: America's policy debate, 1945.* Hamden, Conn.: Archon Books, 1980.

Chomsky, Noam and Howard Zinn, eds. *The Senator Gravel Edition of The Pentagon Papers,* Boston: Beacon Prress, 1972.

Cochran, Bert. *Harry Truman and the Crisis Presidency.* New York: Funk & Wagnalls, 1973.

Cohen, Bernard C. *The Political Process and Foreign Policy: The Making of the Japanese Peace Settlement.* Westport: Greenwood Press, 1980.

Cohen, Jerome. *Japan's Economy in War and Reconstruction.* Minneapolis: University of Minnesota, 1949.

Cohen, Jerome B. *Japan's Postwar Economy.* Bloomington: Indiana University Press, 1958.

Cohen, Theodore. *Remaking Japan: The American Occupation as New Deal,* ed. by Herbert Passin. New York: Free Press, 1987.

Cohen, Warren. *America's Response to China: An Interpretative History of Sino-American Relations.* New York: John Wiley & Sons, Inc., 1971.

Cohen, Warren I., ed. *New Frontiers in American-East Asian Relations: Essays Presented to Dorothy Borg.* New York: Columbia University Press, 1983.

Cohen, Warren I. and Akira Iriye eds. *The Great Powers in East Asia 1953-1960.* New York: Columbia University Press, 1990.

Cook, Blanche Wiesen. *The Declassified Eisenhower: A divided Legacy.* Garden City, NY: Doubleday & Company, Inc., 1981.

Council on Foreign Relations. *The United States in World Affairs.* Annual. New York: Harper, 1949-1952.

Cox, Robert W. *Production, Power, and World Order: Social Forces in the Making of History.* New York: Columbia University Press, 1987.

Cumings, Bruce. *The Origins of the Korean War: Liberation and the Emergence of Separate Regimes. 1945-47.* Princeton: Princeton University Press, 1981.

Cumings, Bruce ed. *Child of Conflict: The Korean-American Relationship, 1943-53.* Seattle: University of Washington Press, 1983.

Dallek, Robert. *Franklin D. Roosevelt and American Foreign Policy, 1932-1945.* New York: Oxford University Press, 1979.

Denison, Edward F. and William K. Chung. *How Japan's Economy Grew So Fast: The Sources of Postwar Expansion.* Washington, D.C.: The Brookings Institution, 1976.

Divine, Robert A. *Eisenhower and the Cold War.* New York: Oxford University Press, 1981.

Dore, R. P. *Land Reform in Japan.* London: Oxford University Press, 1959.

Dower, John. *War Without Mercy.* New York: Pantheon Books, 1986.

Dower, John. *Empire and Aftermath: Yoshida Shigeru and the Japanese Experience, 1878-1954.* Cambridge: Harvard University Press, 1988.

Dower, John. *Japan in War & Peace: Selected Essays.* New York: W.W. Norton & Company, 1993.

Dower, John. *Embracing defeat : Japan in the wake of World War II.* New York: W.W. Norton, 1999.

Drifte, Reinhard. *The Security Factor in Japan's Foreign Policy, 1945-1952.* East Sussex: Saltire Press, 1983.

Dunn, Frederick S. *Peace-Making and the Settlement with Japan.* Princeton: Princeton University Press, 1963.

Eckes, Alfred E., Jr. *A Search for Solvency: Bretton Woods and the International Monetary System, 1941-1971.* Austin: University of Texas Press, 1975.

Eckes, Alfred E., Jr. *The United States and the Global Struggle for Minirals.* University of Texas Press, 1980.

Eckstein, Alexander. *Communist China's Economic Growth and Foreign Trade: Implications for U.S. Policy.* New York: McGraw-Hill Book Company, 1966.

The Economist. *Consider Japan.* London: Gerald Duckworth & Co. Ltd., 1963.

Ewald, William Bragg, Jr. *Eisenhower The President: Crucial Days, 1951-1960.* Englewood Cliffs, NJ: Prentice-Hall, Inc., 1981.

Fearey, Robert A. *The Occupation of Japan Second Phase: 1948-50.* New York: The Macmillan Company, 1950.

Feis, Herbert. *The China Tangle: The American effort in China from Pearl Harbor to the Marshall Mission.* Princeton: Princeton University Press, 1953.

Ferrell, Robert H. ed. *America in A Divided World 1945-1972.* Columbia, SC: University of South Carolina Press, 1975.

Ferrell, Robert H. ed. *The Eisenhower Diaries.* New York: W. W. Norton & Company, 1981.

Ferrell, Robert H. ed. *The Diary of James C. Hagerty: Eisenhower in Mid-Course 1954-1955.* Bloomington: Indiana University Press, 1983.

Fifield, Russell H. *Southeast Asia in United States Policy.* New York: Frederick A. Praeger, Publisher, 1963.

Fifield, Russell. *Americans in Southeast Asia: The Roots of Commitment.* New York: Crowell, 1973.

Finn, Richard. *Winners in Peace: MacArthur, Yoshida, and Postwar Japan.* Berkeley: University of California Press, 1992.

Fleisher, Wilfrid. *What to do with Japan.* New York: Doubleday, Doran and Co., Inc., 1945.

Foot, Rosemary. *The Wrong War: American Policy and the Dimensions of the Korean Conflict, 1950-53.* Ithaca: Cornell University Press, 1985.

Forsberg, Aaron. *America and the Japanese miracle : the Cold War context of Japan's postwar economic revival, 1950-1960.* Chapel Hill: University of North Carolina Press, 2000.

Friedman, David. *The Misunderstood Miracle: Industrial Development and Political Change in Japan.* Ithaca and London: Cornell University Press, 1988.

Friedman, Edward & Mark Selden. *America's Asia: Dissenting Essays on Asian-American Relations.* New York: Pantheon Books, 1971.

Funigiello, Philip J. *American-Soviet Trade in the Cold War.* Chapel Hill: The University of North Carolina Press, 1988.

Gaddis, John Lewis. *The United States and the Origins of the Cold War 1941-1947.* New York: Columbia University Press, 1972.

Gaddis, John Lewis. *Strategies of Containment: A Critical Appraisal of Postwar American National Security Policy.* Oxford: Oxford University Press, 1982.

Gaddis, John Lewis. *The Long Peace: Inquiries into the History of the Cold War.* New York: Oxford University Press, 1987.

Gallicchio, Marc S. *The Cold War Begins in Asia: American East Asian Policy and the Fall of the Japanese Empire.* New York: Columbia University Press, 1988.

Gardner, Lloyd, Walter LaFeber, and Thomas McCormick. *Creation of the American Empire: U.S. Diplomatic History.* Chicago: Rand McNally & Company, 1973.

Gayn, Mark. *Japan Diary.* New York: W. Sloane Associates, 1948.

General Headquarters Supreme Commander for the Allied Powers. *History of the Nonmilitary Activities of the Occupation of Japan.* 1945 through 1951.

Gibney, Frank. *Miracle By Design: The Real Reasons Behind Japan's Economic Success.* New York: Times Books, 1982.

Gittings, John. *The World and China, 1922-1972.* London: Eyre Methuen, 1974.

Gluck, Carol and Stephen R. Graubard eds. *Showa: The Japan of Hirohito.* New York: W.W. Norton Company, 1992.

Goldman, Eric. *The Crucial Decade: America, 1945-1955.* New York: Alfred A. Knopf, 1956.

Goncharov, Sergei, John Lewis, and Xue Litai. *Uncertain Partners: Stalin, Mao, and the Korean War.* Stanford: Stanford University Press, 1993.

Goodman, Grant K. comp. *The American Occupation of Japan: A Retrospective View.* New York: Paragon Book Gallery, Ltd., 1968.

Gordon, Andrew ed. *Postwar Japan as History.* Berkeley: University of California Press, 1993.

Grasso, June. *Truman's Two-China Policy 1948-1950.* New York: M.E. Sharpe, Inc., 1987.

Gray, Gordon, et al. *Report to the President on Foreign Economic Policy.* Washington, D.C.: Government Printing Office, 1950.

Greenstein, Fred I. *The Hidden-Hand Presidency: Eisenhower as Leader.* New York: Basic Books, Inc., Publishers, 1982.

Gross, Ernest A. *Japan Between East and West.* New York: Harper and Brothers, 1957.

Guhin, Michael A. *John Foster Dulles: A Statesman and His Times.* New York: Columbia University Press, 1972.

Hadley, Eleanor. *Antitrust in Japan.* Princeton: Princeton University Press, 1970.

Halle, Louis. *The Cold War As History.* New York: Harper & Row, 1967.

Halliday, Jon. *A Political History of Japanese Capitalism.* New York: Pantheon Books, 1975.

Harding, Harry and Yuan Ming eds. *Sino-American Relations, 1945-1955: A Joint Reassessment of a Critical Decade.* Wilmington: Scholarly Resources, 1989.

Harries, Meirion and Susie. *Sheathing the Sword: The Demilitarisation of Japan.* London: Hamish Hamilton, 1987.

Hayes, Samuel P. *The Beginning of American Aid to Southeast Asia: The Griffin Mission of 1950.* Lexington: Heath Lexington Books, 1971.

Hersh, Jacques. *The USA and the Rise of East Asia since 1945: Dilemmas of the Postwar International Political Economy.* New York: St. Martin's Press, 1993.

Hess, Gary R. *The United States' Emergence as a Southeast Asian Power, 1940-1950.* New York: Columbia University Press, 1987.

Hollerman, Leon. *Japan's Dependence on the World Economy: The Approach toward Economic Liberalization.* Princeton: Princeton University Press, 1967.

Hollerman, Leon, ed. *Japan and the United States: Economic and Political Adversaries.* Boulder: Westview Press, 1980.

Hunsberger, Warren S. *Japan and the United States in World Trade.* New York: Harper & Row, Publishers, 1964.

Hunt, Michael. *The Genesis of Chinese Communist Foreign Policy.* New York: Columbia University Press, 1996.

Immerman, Richard H. ed. *John Foster Dulles and the Diplomacy of the Cold War.* Princeton: Princeton University Press, 1990.

Institute of World Economy. *Recent Trend of Japan's Economy.* Tokyo: Institute of World Economy, 1951.

Iriye, Akira. *Across the Pacific: An Inner History of American-East Asian Relations.* New York: Harcourt, Brace & World, Inc., 1967.

Iriye, Akira. *The Cold War in Asia: A Historical Introduction.* Englewood Cliffs: Prentice-Hall, 1974.

Iriye, Akira. *After Imperialism: The Search for a New Order in the Far East 1921-1931.* New York: Atheneum, 1978.

Iriye, Akira. *Power and Culture: The Japanese-American War, 1941-45.* Cambridge: Harvard University Press, 1981.

Iriye, Akira and Warren I. Cohen eds. *The United States and Japan in the Postwar World.* Lexington: The University Press of Kentucky, 1989.

Iriye, Akira and Warren Cohen eds. *American, Chinese, and Japanese Perspectives on Wartime Asia 1931-1949.* Wilmington: Scholarly Resources Inc., 1990.

Isenberg, Irwin ed. *Japan Asian Power.* New York: The H. Wilson Company, 1971.

Jain, R. K. *China and Japan 1949-1980.* Oxford: Martin Robertson & Co. Ltd., 1981.

Jain, Rajendra Kuman. *The USSR and Japan 1945-1980.* New Delhi: Radiant Publishers, 1981.

James, D. Clayton. *The Years of MacArthur Volume III Triumph and Disaster 1945-1964.* Boston: Houghton Mifflin Company, 1985.

Johnson, Chalmers. *MITI and the Japanese Miracle: The Growth of Industrial Policy, 1925-1975.* Stanford: Stanford University Press, 1982.

Jurika, Stephen, Jr. ed. *From Pearl Harbor to Vietnam: The Memoirs of Admiral Arthur W. Redford.* Stanford: Hoover Institution Press, 1980.

Kataoka, Tetsuya and Ramon H. Myers. *Defending an Economic Superpower: Reassessing the U.S.-Japan Security Alliance.* Boulder, Colorado: Westview Press, 1989.

Kattenburg, Paul M. *The Vietnam Trauma in American Foreign Policy, 1945-75.* New Brunswick: Transaction Books, 1980.

Kawai, Kazuo. *Japan's American Interlude.* Chicago: The University of Chicago Press, 1960.

Kesavan, K.V. *Japan's Relations with Southeast Asia: 1952-60: With Particular Reference to the Philippines and Indonesia.* Bombay: Somaiya Publications PVT LTD, 1972.

Kennan, George. *Memoirs, 1925-50.* Boston: Little Brown, 1967.

Kofsky, Frank *Harry S. Truman and the War Scare of 1948: A Successful Campaign to Deceive the Nation* New York: St. Martin's Press, 1995.

Kolko, Gabriel. *Confronting the Third World: United States Foreign Policy 1945-1980.* New York: Pantheon Books, 1988.

Kolko, Joyce, and Gabriel Kolko. *The Limits of Power.* New York: Vantage, 1973.

LaFeber, Walter. *The American Age: United States Foreign Policy at Home and Abroad since 1750.* New York: W. W. Norton & Company, 1989.

Lattimore, Owen. *Solution in Asia.* Boston: Little Brown, 1945.

Lee, Chae-Jin and Hideo Sato. *U.S. Policy Toward Japan and Korea: A Changing Influence Relationship.* New York: Praeger Publishers, 1982.

Lee, Chung H. and Ippei Yamazawa, eds. *The Economic Development of Japan and Korea: A Parallel with Lessons.* New York: Praeger, 1990.

Leffler, Melvyn. *A Preponderance of Power: National Security, the Truman Administration, and the Cold War.* Stanford: Stanford University Press, 1992.

Leffler, Melvyn. *The Specter of Communism The United States and the Origins of the Cold War, 1917-1953.* New York: Hill and Wang, 1994.

Leffler, Melvyn and David Painter. *Origins of the Cold War: An International History.* New York: Routledge, 1995.

Levantrosser, William F. *Harry S. Truman, the man from Independence.* New York: Greenwood Press, 1986.

Liu, Xiaoyuan. *A Partnership for Disorder: China, the United States, and Their Policies for the Postwar Disposition of the Japanese Empire, 1941-1945.* New York: Cambridge University Press, 1996.

Louis, William R. *Imperialism at Bay.* New York: Oxford University Press, 1978.

MacArthur, Douglas. *Reminiscences.* New York: McGraw-Hill, 1964.

McCormick, Thomas. *America's Half-Century: United States Foreign Policy in the Cold War.* Baltimore: Johns Hopkins University Press, 1995.

Maddison, Angus. *Economic Growth in JAPAN and the USSR.* New York: W.W. Norton & Company, 1969.

Manchester, William. *American Caesar: Douglas MacArthur, 1880-1964.* New York: Dell Publishing Co., 1978.

Martin, Edwin. *The Allied Occupation of Japan.* New York: American Institute of Pacific Relations, 1948.

Martin, Edwin W. *Divided Counsel: The Anglo-American Response to Communist Victory in China.* Lexington: The University Press of Kentucky, 1986.

Masuhara, Keikichi. *A Review of Japan's Defense Strength.* Tokyo: Public Information and Cultural Affairs Bureau, Ministry of Foreign Affairs, 1956.

Masumi, Junnosuke. *Postwar Politics in Japan, 1945-1955.* Berkeley: Institute of East Asian Studies, University of California, Berkeley, 1985.

Mayers, David. *Cracking the Monolith: U.S. Policy Against the Sino-Soviet Alliance, 1949-1955.* Baton Rouge: Louisiana State University Press, 1986.

Mayers, David. *George Kennan and the Dilemmas of US Foreign Policy.* Oxford: Oxford University Press, 1988.

McGlothlen, Ronald. *Controlling the Waves: Dean Acheson and U.S. Foreign Policy in Asia.* New York: W.W. Norton & Company, 1993.

Melanson, Richard A. and David Mayers eds. *Reevaluating Eisenhower: American Foreign Policy in the 1950s.* Urbana: University of Illinois Press, 1987.

Merrill, Dennis ed. *Documentary History of the Truman Presidency Volume 5: Creating a Pluralistic Democracy in Japan: The Occupation Government, 1945-1952.* Bethesda: University Publications of America, 1995.

Miller, Francis. *General Douglas MacArthur Soldier-Statesman.* Philadelphia: The John C. Winston Company, 1951.

Millis, Walter ed. *The Forrestal Diaries.* New York: The Viking Press, 1951.

Minobe, Ryokichi. *Japan's Foreign Trade.* Tokyo: Public Information and Cultural Affairs Bureau, Ministry of Foreign Affairs, 1956.

Miscamble, Wilson D. *George F. Kennan and the Making of American Foreign Policy, 1947-1950.* Princeton: Princeton University Press, 1992.

Mitsubishi Economic Research Institute. *Mitsui-Mitsubishi-Sumitomo: Present Status of the Former Zaibatsu Enterprises.* Tokyo: Mitsubishi Economic Research Institute, 1955.

Montgomery, John D. *Forced To Be Free: The Artificial Revolution in Germany and Japan.* Chicago: The University of Chicago Press, 1957.

Moore, Joe. *Japanese Workers and the Struggle for Power.* Madison: University of Wisconsin Press, 1983.

Morishima, Michio. *Why haa Japan 'succeeded'?: Western technology and the Japanese ethos.* Cambridge: Cambridge University Press, 1983.

Morly, James W. *Japan and Korea: America's Allies in the Pacific.* Westport: Greenwood Press, 1965.

Morris, Ivan I. *Nationalism and the Right Wing in Japan: A Study of post-war trends.* London: Oxford University Press, 1960.

Morris-Suzuki, T. and T. Seiyama, eds. *Japanese Capitalism since 1945: Critical Perspectives.* London: M. E. Sharpe, Inc., 1989.

Nagai, Yonosuke and Iriye, Akira. *The Origins of the Cold War in Asia.* Tokyo: University of Tokyo Press, 1977.

Nakamura, Takafusa. *The Postwar Japanese Economy: Its Development and Structure.* Tokyo University of Tokyo Press, 1983.

Neary, Ian ed. *War Revolution & Japan.* Kent: Japan Library, 1993.

Nester, William R. *Japan's Growing Power over East Asia and the World Economy: Ends and Means.* London: The Macmillan Press, 1990.

Neumann, William. *America Encounters Japan: From Perry to MacArthur.* Baltimore: The Johns Hopkins Press, 1963.

Nish, Ian ed. *Anglo-Japanese Alienation 1919-1952: Papers of the Anglo-Japanese Conference on the History of the Second World War.* Cambridge: Cambridge University Press, 1982.

Nish, Ian ed. *The East Asian Crisis, 1945-1951 The Problem of China, Korea and Japan.* International Centre for Economics and Related Disciplines, London School of Economics, International Studies 1982/1 (1982).

Nish, Ian ed. *The British Commonwealth and the Occupation of Japan.* International Centre for Economics and Related Disciplines, London School of Economics, International Studies 1983/1 (1983).

Nish, Ian ed. *Aspects of the Allied Occupation of Japan.* Suntory Toyota International Centre for Economics and Related Disciplines, London School of Economics and Political Science, International Studies 1986/4 (1986).

Nish, Ian ed. *The Occupation of Japan 1945-52.* Suntory-Toyota International Centre for Economics and Related Disciplines, London School of Economics and Political Science, International Studies IS/91/224 (1990/III).

Nish, Ian ed. *Aspects of the Allied Occupation of Japan Part II.* Suntory-Toyota International Centre for Economics and Related Disciplines, London School of Economics and Political Science, International Studies IS/91/229, 1991/IV (1991).

Ohkawa, Kazushi & Henry Rosovsky. *Japanese Economic Growth: Trend Acceleration in the Twentieth Century.* Stanford: Stanford University Press, 1973.

Ohno, Takushi. *War Reparations and Peace Settlement: Philippines-Japan Relations 1945-1956.* Manila: Solidaridad Publishing House, 1986.

Okita, Saburo. *The Rehabilitation of Japan's Economy and Asia.* Tokyo: Public Information and Cultural Affairs Bureau, Ministry of Foreign Affairs, 1956.

Okuda, Yoshio. *Japan's Postwar Industry.* Tokyo: The International Society for Educational Information, Inc., 1976.

Overseas Consultants, Inc. *Report on Industrial Reparations Survey of Japan to the United States of America.* New York: 1948.

Ozawa, Terutomo. *Japan's Technological Challenge to the West, 1950-1974: Motivation and Accomplishment.* Cambridge: The MIT Press, 1974.

Passin, Herbert ed. *The United States and Japan.* Englewood Cliffs: Prentice-Hall, 1966.

Passin, Herbert. *The Legacy of the Occupation - Japan.* New York: The East Asian Institute, Columbia University, 1968.

Patrick, Hugh and Henry Rosovsky eds. *Asia's New Giant: How the Japanese Economy Works.* Washington, D.C.: The Brookings Institution, 1976.

Pempel, T. J. *Policy and Politics in Japan: Creative Conservative.* Philadelphia: Temple University Press, 1982.

Pollard, Robert A. *Economic Security and the Origins of the Cold War, 1945-1950.* New York: Columbia University Press, 1985.

Porter, Brian. *Britain and the Rise of Communist China: A Study of British Attitudes 1945-1954.* London: Oxford University Press, 1967.

Prichard, John R. ed. *An Overview of the Historical Importance of the Tokyo War Trial.* Nissan Occasional Paper Series No. 5, London: School of Oriental and African Studies, University of London, 1987.

Randall, Clarence B. *A Foreign Economic Policy for the United States.* Chicago: The University of Chicago Press, 1954.

Redford, Lawrence H. *The Occupation of Japan: Economic Policy and Reform.* Norfolk: The MacArthur Memorial, 1980.

Reischauer, Edwin and others. *Japan and America Today.* Stanford: Stanford University Press, 1953.

Reischauer, Edwin. *The United States and Japan,* 3rd rev. ed. Cambridge: Harvard University Press, 1965.

Rose, Lisle. *Roots of Tragedy: The United States and the Struggle for Asia, 1945-1953.* Westport, Connecticut: Greenwood Press, 1976.

Rotter, Andrew J. *The Path to Vietnam: Origins of the American Commitment to Southeast Asia.* Ithaca and London: Cornell University Press, 1987.

Roxas, Manuel. *Speeches Messages and Other Pronouncements of president Manuel Roxas.* Manila: Bureau of Printing, 28 May 1947.

Samuels, Richard J. *"Rich Nation, Strong Army": National Security and the Technological Transformation of Japan.* Ithaca: Cornell University Press, 1994.

Sansom, Katharine. *Sir George Sansom and Japan A Memoir.* Tallahassee, Florida: The Diplomatic Press, Inc., 1972.

Scalapino, Robert. *The Japanese Communist Movement, 1920-1966.* Berkeley: University of California Press, 1967.

Scalapino, Robert A. ed. *The Foreign Policy of Modern Japan.* Berkeley: University of California Press, 1977.

Scalapino, Robert A., Seizaburo Sato, and Jusuf Wanandi eds. *Asian Economic Development–Present and Future.* Berkeley: Institute of East Asian Studies, 1985.

Schaller, Michael. *The U.S. Crusade in China, 1938-1945.* New York: Columbia University Press, 1979.

Schaller, Michael. *The American Occupation of Japan: The Origins of the Cold War in Asia.* New York: Oxford University Press, 1985.

Schaller, Michael. *Douglas MacArthur: The Far Eastern General.* New York: Oxford University Press, 1989.

Schaller, Michael. *Altered States The United States and Japan Since the Occupation.* New York: Oxford University Press, 1997.

Schonberger, Howard B. *Aftermath of War: Americans and the Remaking of Japan, 1945-1952.* Kent: The Kent State University Press, 1989.

Sebald, William. *With MacArthur in Japan.* New York: W. W. Norton, 1965.

Sebald, William J. and C. Nelson Spinks. *Japan: Prospects, Options, and Opportunities.* Washington, D. C.: American Enterprise Institute for Public Policy Research, 1967.

Shimizu, Sayuri. *Creating People of Plenty : The United States and Japan's Economic Alternatives, 1950-1960.* Kent: Kent State University Press, 2001.

Shiomi, Saburo. *Japan's Finance and Taxation 1940-1956.* New York: Columbia University Press, 1957.

Simmons, Robert. *The Strained Alliance: Peking, P'yongyang, Moscow, and the Politics of the Korean Civil War.* New York: Free Press, 1975.

Stockwin, J.A.A. *Japan: Divided Politics in a Growth Economy.* New York: W.W. Norton & Company, 1982.

Stone, I. F. *The hidden history of the Korean War.* New York: Monthly Review Press, 1952.

Stueck, William, Jr. *The Road to Confrontation: American Policy toward China and Korea, 1947-1950.* Chapel Hill: The University of North Carolina Press, 1981.

Swearingen, Rodger. *The Soviet Union and Postwar Japan: Escalating Challenge and Response.* Stanford: Hoover Institute Press, 1978.

Symonds, Craig ed. *New Aspects of Naval History.* Annapolis: Naval Institute Press, 1981.

The Economist. *Consider Japan.* London: Gerald Duckworth & Co. Ltd., 1962.

Thomas, Burkman, ed. *Proceedings of a Symposium by the MacArthur Memorial.* Norfolk: The MacArthur Memorial, 1978.

Thorne, Christopher. *Allies of a Kind: The United States, Great Britain and the War Against Japan, 1941-45.* New York: Oxford University Press, 1978.

Thorne, Christopher. *Racial Aspects of the Far Eastern War of 1941-1945.* New York: Oxford University Press, 1982.

Thorne, Christopher. *The Issue of War.* New York: Oxford University Press, 1985.

Thorpe, James A. *Pentagon Papers Perspective: Indo-China and the Roosevelt Years, 1937-1945.* Superior, Wisconsin: Superior Publications, 1972.

Truman, Harry S. *Memoirs.* 2 Vols. Garden City: Doubleday, 1955-56.

Tsou, Tang. *America's Failure in China, 1941-50.* Chicago: University of Chicago Press, 1963.

Tsuru, Shigeto. *Essays on Japanese Economy.* Economic Research Series 2, The Institute of Economic Research, Hitotsubashi University, Tokyo: Kinokuniya Bookstore Co., Ltd., 1958.

Tucker, Nancy. *Patterns in the Dust: Chinese-American Relations and the Recognition Controversy, 1949-50.* New York: Columbia University Press, 1983.

Van Slyke, Lyman. *The China White Paper.* Stanford: Stanford University Press, 1967.

Varg, Paul. *The Closing of the Door: Sino-American Relations 1936-1946.* East Lansing: Michigan State University Press, 1973.

Vinacke, Harold. *The United States and the Far East 1945-1951.* Stanford: Stanford University Press, 1952.

Wallerstein, Immanuel. *The Politics of the World-Economy: The States, the Movements, and the Civilization.* Cambridge: Cambridge University Press, 1984.

Ward, Robert ed. *Political Development in Modern Japan.* Princeton: Princeton University Press, 1968.

Ward, Robert and Frank J. Shulman. *Bibliography of the Occupation of Japan.* Chicago: American Library Association, 1974.

Ward, Robert and Yoshikazu Sakamoto eds., *Democratizing Japan: The Allied Occupation.* Honolulu: University of Hawaii Press, 1987.

Weinstein, Martin. *Japan's Postwar Defense Policy, 1947-1968.* New York: Columbia University Press, 1971.

Welfield, John. *An Empire in Eclipse: Japan in the Postwar American Alliance System, A Study in the Interaction of Domestic Politics and Foreign Policy.* London: The Athlone Press, 1988.

Whiting, Allen S. *China Crosses the Yalu: The Decision to Enter the Korean War.* Stanford: Stanford University Press, 1960.

Whitney, Courtney. *MacArthur: His Rendezvous with History.* New York: Knopf, 1956.

Wilhelm, John and Gerry Feinstein eds. *U.S. Foreign Assistance Investment or Folly?* New York: Praeger Publishers, 1984.

Williams, Justin, Sr. *Japan's Political Revolution under MacArthur: A Participant's Account.* Athens: University of Georgia Press, 1979.

Williams, William A. *The Contours of American History.* Chicago: Quadrangle Books, 1966.

Williams, William, Thomas McCormick, Lloyd Gardner and Walter LaFeber eds. *America in Vietnam A Documentary History.* New York: Anchor Press, 1985.

Willoughby, Charles A. and Chamberlain, John. *MacArthur, 1941-51.* New York: McGraw-Hill 1954.

Wolfe, Robert ed. *Americans as Proconsuls: United States Military Government in Germany and Japan, 1944-1952.* Carbondale and Edwardsville: Southern Illinois University Press, 1984.

Wood, Gordon. *The Creation of the American Republic, 1776-1787.* New York: W. W. Norton, 1969.

Yamamura, Kozo. *Economic Policy in Postwar Japan: Growth Versus Economic Democracy.* Berkeley: University of California Press, 1967.

Yanaga, Chitoshi. *Big Business in Japanese Politics.* New Haven: Yale University Press, 1968.

Yergin, Daniel. *Shattered Peace: The Origins of the Cold War.* New York: Penguin Books, 1990.

Yoshitsu, Michael M. *Japan and the San Francisco Peace Settlement.* New York: Columbia University Press, 1983.

Yoshida Shigeru. *The Yoshida Memoirs.* London: Heinemann, 1961.

Zubok, Vladislav and Constantine Pleshakov. *Inside the Kremlin's Cold War.* Cambridge: Harvard University Press, 1996.

SELECTED SECONDARY SOURCES: PERIODICALS

Abegg, Lily. "Japan Reconsiders," *Foreign Affairs,* Vol. 33 #3 (April 1955).

Allen, G.C. "Britain's Perception of Japan's Post-War Economic Prospects," *Proceedings of the British Association for Japanese Studies,* Vol. 11 (1977).

The Annals of the American Academy of Political and Social Science. Vol. 308 (November 1956).

Aruga, Tadashi. "The Problem of Security Treaty Revision in Japan's Relations with the United States: 1951-1960," *Hitotsubashi Journal of Law & Politics* Vol. 13 (February 1985).

Aruga, Tadashi. "Reflections on the Impact of the Pacific War on Japanese-American Relations," *Japan Forum* Vol. 4, No. 1 (April 1992).

Asada, Sadao. "Recent Works on the American Occupation of Japan: The State of the Art," *The Japanese Journal of American Studies,* No. 1 (1981).

Ayusawa, Iwao. "Developments in Organized Labor," *Contemporary Japan* Vol. 21 (1952).

Baba, Tsunego. "Japanese Response to Peace Treaty," *Contemporary Japan* Vol. 20 (1951).

Bennett, Martin. "Japanese Reparations: Fact or Fantasy?" *Pacific Affairs,* Vol. XXI No. 2 (June 1948).

Bernstein, Barton J. "New Light on the Korean War," *The International History Review,* Vol. III (1981).

Bisson, T.A. "Reparations and Reform in Japan," *Far Eastern Survey* (17 December 1947).

Bix, Herbert. "The Showa Emperor's "Monologue" and the Problem of War Responsibility," *Journal of Japanese Studies* 18 -2 (1992).

Brands, H.W., Jr. "The United States and the Reemergence of Independent Japan," *Pacific Affairs,* Vol. 59, No. 3 (Fall 1986).

Bridgham, Philip, Arthur Cohen, and Leonard Jaffe. "Mao's Road and Sino-Soviet Relations: A View from Washington, 1953," *The China Quarterly,* #52 (Oct./Dec 1972).

Bronfendbrenner, Martin. "Monopoly and Inflation in Contemporary Japan," *Osaka Economic Papers.* III, 2 (March 1955).

Bryn-Jones, David. "Japan's General Election 1952: An Interpretation," *Contemporary Japan* Vol. 21 (1952).

Buck, David. "Themes in the Socioeconomic History of China, 1840-1949 - A Review Article," *Journal of Asian Studies* Vol. XLIII No. 3 (May 1984).

Buckley, Roger. "Britain and the Emperor: The Foreign Office and Constitutional Reform in Japan, 1945-46," *Modern Asian Studies,* 12, 4 (1978).

Buckley, Roger. "The British Model: Institutional Reform and Occupied Japan," *Modern Asian Studies,* 16, 2 (1982).

Buckley, Roger. "Joining the Club: The Japanese Question and Anglo-American Peace Diplomacy," *Modern Asian Studies* Vol. 19 No. 2 (1985).

Buhite, Russell D. "'Major Interests': American Policy toward China, Taiwan, and Korea, 1945-1950," *Pacific Historical Review,* Vol. XLVII, No. 3 (August 1978).

Buss, Claude. "US Policy on the Japan Treaty," *Far Eastern Survey* (13 June 1951).

Castle, Alfred. "William R. Castle and the Postwar Transformation of Japan, 1945-1955," *Wisconsin Magazine of History* Vol. 74 No. 2 (Winter 1990-1991).

Chern, Kenneth S. "Politics of American China Policy, 1945: Roots of the Cold War in Asia," *Political Science Quarterly,* Vol. 91, No. 4 (Winter 1976-77).

Chun, Chang. "Sino-Japanese Relations," *Contemporary Japan* Vol. 21 (1952).

Cohen, Jerome B. "Japan: Reform VS. Recovery," *Far Eastern Survey* (23 June 1948).

Cohen, Jerome B. "Japan's Foreign Trade Problems," *Far Eastern Survey* (19 November 1952).

Cohen, Warren I. "Conversations with Chinese Friends: Zhou Enlai's Associates Reflect on Chinese-American Relations in the 1940s and the Korean War," *Diplomatic History,* Vol. 11, No. 3 (Summer 1987).

Danno, Nobuo. "Japanese Agriculture after the Postwar Land Reform," *Japan Quarterly,* Vol. II, No. 1 (Jan.-Mar. 1955).

Dingman, Roger. "Reconsiderations of the U.S.-Japan Security Treaty," *Pacific Community,* 7 (July 1976).

Dingman, Roger. "Straategic Planning and the Policy Process: America Plans for War in East Asia, 1945-1950," *Naval War College Review* (Nov.-Dec. 1979).

Dingman, Roger. "Atomic Diplomacy During the Korean War," *International Security,* Vol. 13, No. 3 (Winter 1988/89).

Dingman, Roger. "Korea at Forty-plus: The Origins of the Korean War Reconsidered," *The Journal of American-East Asian Relations* (Spring 1992).

Dooman, Eugene H. "A Letter to My Japanese Friends," *Contemporary Japan* Vol. XIX, Nos. 1-3 (Jua.- Mar. 1950).

Dower, John. "Occupied Japan as History and Occupation Hisstory As Politics," *Journal of Asian Studies* Vol. XXXIV, No. 2 (February 1975).

Dower, John. "Rethinking World War II in Asia," *Reviews in American History* (June 1984).

Dower, John. "The Useful War," *Daedalus* Vol. 119 No. 3 (Summer 1990).

Dulles, John Foster. "Peace with Justice and Freedom," *Contemporary Japan* Vol. XX Nos. 10-12 (Oct.-Dec. 1951).

Dulles, John Foster. "Security in the Pacific," *Foreign Affairs,* Vol. 30, No. 2 (January 1952).

Economic Planning Board. "Annual Economic Survey of Japan 1956," *Asian Affairs,* Vol. I, No. 3, (September 1956).

Edwards, Corwin D. "The Dissolution of the Japanese Combines," *Pacific Affairs,* XIX No. 3 (September 1946).

Falk, Stanley. "The National Security Council Under Truman, Eisenhower, and Kennedy," *Political Science Quarterly* 79 (1964).

Farley, Miriam. "San Francisco and After," *Far Eastern Survey* (26 September 1951).

Farley, Miriam. "Japan and US: Post-Treaty Problems" *Far Eastern Survey* (27 February 1952).

Fifield, Russell H. "Philippine Foreign Policy," *Far Eastern Survey* (21 February 1952).

Fine, Sherwood. "Japan's Postwar Industrial Recovery," *Contemporary Japan* Vol. XXI, Nos. 4-6 (1952).

The Fuji Bank. "Banking in Modern Japan," *Fuji Bank Bulletin* Vol. XI No. 4 (1961).

Fujiyama, Aichiro. "United States-Japan Economic Relation," *Contemporary Japan* Vol.

XXII Nos. 1-3 (1953).

Fujiyama, Aiichiro. "Southeast Asia and Japanese Economic Diplomacy," *Contemporary Japan* Vol. XXV No. 2 (April 1958).

Fukui, Haruhiro. "Economic Planning in Postwar Japan: A Case Study in Policy Making," *Asian Survey,* Vol. XII #4 (April 1972).

Gaddis, John Lewis. "Was The Truman Doctrine A Real Turning Point?" *Foreign Affairs* 52 (January 1974).

Gaddis, John Lewis. "Containment: A Reassessment," *Foreign Affairs* Vol. 55, No. 4 (July 1977).

Gaddis, John Lewis. "The Emerging Post-Revisionist Synthesis on the Origins of the Cold War," *Diplomatic History,* Vol. 7, No. 3 (Summer 1983).

Gaddis, John Lewis. "The Cold War, the Long Peace, and the Future," *Diplomatic History,* Vol. 16, No. 2 (Spring 1992).

Gaddis, John Lewis and Paul Nitze. "NSC 68 and the Soviet Threat Reconsidered," *International Security,* Vol. 4 #4 (Spring 1980).

Gargon, Sheldon. "The Imperial Bureaucracy and Labor Policy in Postwar Japan," *Journal of Asian Studies* Vol. XLIII NO. 3 (May 1984).

Garthoff, Raymond L. "Why Did the Cold War Arise, and Why Did It End?" *Diplomatic History,* Vol. 16, No. 2 (Spring 1992).

Gilmartin, William M. And W. I. Ladejinsky. "The Promise of Agrarian Reform in Japan," *Foreign Affairs* Vol. 26, #2 (Jan. 1948).

Guhin, Michael A. "The United States and the Chinese People's Republic," *International Affairs,* Vol. 45, No. 1 (January 1969).

Guhin, Michael A. "Dulles' Thoughts on International Politics: Myth and Reality," *Orbis,* Vol. XIII #3(Fall 1969).

Hadley, Eleanor M. "Trust Busting in Japan," *Harvard Business Review,* Vol. XXVI, #4 (July 1948).

Hara, Yoshihisa. "The Significance of the U.S.-Japan Security System to Japan: The Historical Background," *Peace and Change* Vol. 12 #3/4 (1987).

Hata, Ikuhiko. "Japan Under the Occupation," *The Japan Interpreter,* Vol. 10, Nos. 3-4 (winter 1976).

Hatano, Ken-ichi. "Japan's Choice: Taipei or Peking," *Contemporary Japan* Vol. 20 (1951).

Hayashi, Yujiro. "The Relations between Reparations and Foreign Trade," *Asian Affairs,* Vol. I, No. 3 (September 1956).

Hein, Laura E. "In Search of Peace and Democracy: Japanese Economic Debate in Political Context," *The Journal of Asian Studies* 53, No. 3 (August 1994).

Hodgson, Lt.-Colonel W. R. "Rehabilitation for Peace," *Contemporary Japan,* 21 (1952).

Holland, William L. "Japan and the New Balance of Power in the Far East," *International Affairs,*Vol. XXVIII, No. 3 (July 1952).

Hollerman, Leon. "International Economic Controls in Occupied Japan," *Journal of Asian Studies,* Vol. XXXVIII, No. 4 (August 1979).

Holsti, Ole. "The 'Operational Code' Approach to the Study of Political Leaders: John Foster Dulles' Philosophical and Instrumental Beliefs," *Canadian Journal of Political Science* Vol. III #1 (March 1970).

Hosoya, Chihiro. "Japan's Response to U.S. Policy on the Japanese Peace Treaty: The Dulles-Yoshida Talks," *Hitotsubashi Journal of Law and Politics* 10 (December 1981).

Hosoya, Masahiro. "Economic Democratization and the 'Reverse Course' during the Allied Occupation of Japan, 1945-1952," *Kokusaigaku Ronshu,* Vol. 11 (July 1983).

Hoynden, Yoshio. "Economic Cooperation–It's Nature and Problems," *Asian Affairs,* Vol. I, No. 3, (September 1956).

Hudson, G. F. "Will Britain and America Split in Asia?" *Foreign Affairs* Vol. 31, No. 3 (April 1953).

Hulse, Frederick. "Some Effects of the War Upon Japanese Society," *The Far Eastern Quarterly,* Vol. VII, Number 1 (November 1947).

Iokibe, Makoto. "Japan Meets the United States for the Second Time," *Daedalus* Vol. 119, No. 3 (Summer 1990).

Iriye, Akira. "Chinese-Japanese Relations, 1945-90," *The China Quarterly* No. 124 (December 1990).

Ishibashi, Tanzan. "Current Thoughts on Economic Reform," *Contemporary Japan* Vol. XXI, Nos. 4-6, (1952).

Ishida, Takeshi. "Changes in Japanese Perceptions of the Occupation," *Asian and African Studies* 18 (1984).

Itagaki, Yoichi. "Reparations and Southeast Asia," *Japan Quarterly,* Vol. VI, #4 (Oct.-Dec. 1959).

Jansen, Marius. "From Hatoyama to Hatoyama," *The Far Eastern Quarterly,* Vol. XIV, Number 1 (November 1954).

Jansen, Marius. "Japan Since the Occupation," *Asian and African Studies* 18 (1984).

Jenkins, Shirley. "Philippine White Paper," *Far Eastern Survey* (10 January 1951).

Jervis, Robert. "The Impact of the Korean War on the Cold War," *The Journal of Conflict Resolution,* Vol. 24, No. 4 (December 1980).

Kades, Charles. "The American Role in Revising Japan's Imperial Constitution," *Political Science Quarterly,* Vol. 104 Number 2 (1989).

Kan, Hideki. "The Significance of the U.S.-Japan Security System to the United Staes: A Japanese Perspective," *Peace and Change* Vol. XII Number 3/4 (1987).

Kase, Toshikazu. "Japan's New Role in East Asia," *Foreign Affairs,* Vol. 34 #1 (Oct. 1955).

Kato, Fusajiro. "Road To Reconstruction," *Contemporary Japan* 21 (1952).

Kawai, Kazuo. "Sovereignty and Democracy in the Japanese Constitution," *American Political Science Review* Vol. XLIX No. 3 (September 1955).

Kennan, George. "Japanese Security and American Policy," *Foreign Affairs*, Vol. 43 No. 1 (October 1964).

Kimura, Kihachiro. "International Development and Japanese Economy," *Contemporary Japan* Vol. 23 (1955).

Kishida, Junnosuke. "Marketable Technology, Key to Postwar Success," *Japan Quarterly* Vol. 34 No. 3 (Jul-Sep 1987).

Koizumi, Shinzo. "Security for Tomorrow's Japan," *Contemporary Japan* Vol. XX Nos. 10-12 (Oct.-Dec. 1951).

Kurata, Chikara. "Machine Industry of Japan and Southeast Asia," *Contemporary Japan* Vol. 23 (1955).

Kurihara, Kenneth. "Post-War Inflation and Fiscal-Monetary Policy in Japan," *American Economic Review* 36 (1946).

Leffler, Melvyn. "The American Conception of National Security and the Beginning of the Cold War, 1945-48," *American Historical Review* Vol. 89 No. 2 (April 1984).

Lewis, John Wilson. "Quemoy and American China Policy," *Asian Survey*, Vol. II #1 (March 1962).

Luttwak, Edward. "The Strange Case of George F. Kennan: From Containment to Isolationism," *Commentary*, Vol. 64, Number 5 (November 1977).

McDiarmid, Orville. "The Japanese Exchange Rate," *Far Eastern Survey* (15 June 1949).

McLean, David. "American Nationalism, the China Myth, and the Truman Doctrine: The Question of Accommodation with Peking, 1949-50," *Diplomatic History*, Vol. 10, No. 1 (Winter 1986).

McLellan, David. "Dean Acheson and the Korean War," *Political Science Quarterly* Vol. 83 No. 1 (March 1968).

Miyata, Kiyozo. "Reparations and Japan's Economy," *Asian Affairs*, Vol. I, No. 3, (September 1956).

Mesaki, Kenji. "Anti-Monopoly Law and Elimination of Excessive Concentration of Economic Power Law in Japan," *Osaka Economic Papers* II 2 (March 1954).

Moore, Ray A. "Reflections on the Occupation of Japan," *Journal of Asian Studies*, Vol. XXXVIII, No. 4 (August 1979).

Moore, Ray A. "The Occupation of Japan as History Some Recent Research," *Monumenta Nipponica*, Vol. XXXVI, No. 3.

Morley, James. "Presidential Address: Japan and America - The Dynamics of Partnership," *Journal of Asian Studies* Vol. XLV, No. 1 (November 1985).

Nagai, Michio. "Educational Reform: Development in the Postwar Years," *Japan Quarterly* Vol. 32 No. 1 (Jan.-March 1985).

Nagao, Ryuichi. "MacArthur and Postwar Democracy in Japan," *Japan Echo*, Vol. 1, No.

2 (1974).

Nelson, Anna Kasten. "President Truman and the Evolution of the National Security Council," *The Journal of American History*, Vol. 72, No. 2 (September 1985).

Nomura, Kichisaburo. "A Peace Treaty and Japan's Security," *Contemporary Japan* (July-September 1950).

Nomura, Kichisaburo. "Prospects after Peace," *Contemporary Japan*, 21 (1952).

Ohkawa, Kazushi and Henry Rosovsky. "Japanese Economic Development: Recent Japanese Growth in Historical Perspective," *American Economic Review* Vol. LIII #2 (May 1963).

Okamoto, Tadashi. "Economic Independence, And the Future of Foreign Trade," *Contemporary Japan* (October-December 1950).

Okita, Saburo. "South & Southeast Asia and Japanese Economy," *Japan Quarterly*, Vol. 1, No. 1 (Oct.-Dec. 1954).

Okita, Saburo. "A Reappraisal of Japan's Economy," *Japan Quarterly*, Vol. VI #3 (Jul.-Sep. 1959).

Oshima, Harry. "Reinterpreting Japan's Postwar Growth," *Economic Development and Cultural Change*, Vol. 31, Number 1 (October 1982).

Ovendale, R. "Britain, The United States, and the Recognition of Communist China," *The Historical Journal*, Vol. 26, 1 (March 1983).

Ozawa, Takeo. "Japanese Foreign Debts and Reparation Problem," *Asian Affairs*, Vol. I, No. 3, (September 1956).

Passin, Herbert. "The Occupation–Some Reflections," *Daedalus* Vol. 119, No. 3 (Summer 1990).

Pempel, T. J. "The Bureaucratization of Policymaking in Postwar Japan," *American Journal of Political Science* 18 (1974).

Pritchard, R. John. "An Overview of the Historical Importance of the Tokyo War Trial," *Nissan Occasional Paper*, Series No. 5 (1987).

Reday, Joseph. "Reparations from Japan," *Far Eastern Survey* (29 June 1949).

Reynolds, David. "Beyond Bipolarity in Space and Time," *Diplomatic History*, Vol. 16, No. 2 (Spring 1992).

Roberts, John G. "The 'Japan Crowd' and the Zaibatsu Restoration," *The Japan Interpreter*, Vol. 12, #3-4 (Summer 1979).

Rockefeller, John D. "Japan Tackles Her Problems," *Foreign Affairs* Vol. 32 No. 4 (July 1954).

Roskin, Michael. "From Pearl Harbor to Vietnam: Shifting Generational Paradigms and Foreign Policy," *Political Science Quarterly* Vol. 89, No. 3 (Fall 1974).

Rotwein, Eugene. "Economic Concentration and Monopoly in Japan," *The Journal of Political Economy*, Vol. LXXII #3 (June 1964).

Ryu, Shintaro. "The Timing of Japan's Peace Treaty," *Far Eastern Survey* (26 September 1951).

Saito, Makoto. "What Effect Has the Occupation Had on Japan-U.S. Relations?" *Japan Quarterly* Vol. 28 No. 4 (Oct.-Dec. 1981).

Samuels, Richard J. "Reinventing Security: Japan Since Meiji," *Daedalus* Special Issue (1991).

Sansom, George. "Conflicting Purposes in Japan," *Foreign Affairs,* Vol. 26 #2 (Jan. 1948).

Sato, Naotake. "Peace Treaty and Japan's Future," *Contemporary Japan* Vol. XX Nos. 4-6 (April-June 1951).

Sato, Tatsuo. "The Origin and Development of the Draft Constitution of Japan," *Contemporary Japan* Vol. XXIV Nos. 4-6 & 7-9 (1956).

Scalapino, Robert. "The American Occupation of Japan: Perspectives after Three Decades," *Annals of the American Academy of Political and Social Science,* 428 (November 1976).

Schaller, Michael. "MacArthur's Japan: The View from Washington," *Diplomatic History,* Vol. 10, No. 1 (Winter 1986).

Schneiber, Harry & Akio Watanabe. "Occupation Policy and Economic Planning in Postwar Japan," *Studies in Social and Economic History,* Vol. 7 (1990).

Schonberger, Howard. "Zaibatsu Dissolution and the American Restoration of Japan," *Bulletin of Concerned Asian Scholars,* Vol. 5 No. 2 (September 1973).

Schonberger, Howard. "The General and the Presidency: Douglas MacArthur and the Election of 1948," *Wisconsin Magazine of History* 57 (Spring 1974).

Schonberger, Howard. "The Japan Lobby in American Diplomacy, 1947-1952," *Pacific Historical Review* 46 (1977).

Schonberger, Howard. "American Labor's Cold War in Occupied Japan," *Diplomatic History* 3 (Summer 1979).

Schonberger, Howard. "U.S. Policy in Post-War Japan: The Retreat from Liberalism," *Science & Society* Vol. XLVI, No. 1 (Spring 1982).

Schonberger, Howard. "Peacemaking in Asia: The United States, Great Britain, and the Japanese Decision to Recognize Nationalist China, 1951-52," *Diplomatic History,* Vol. 10, No. 1 (Winter 1986).

Shalhope, Robert E. "Toward a Republican Synthesis: The Emergence of an Understanding of Republicanism in American Historiography," *William and Mary Quarterly,* 3rd Series, 1972.

Simmons, Robert R. "China's Cautious Relations with North Korea and Indochina," *Asian Survey,* Vol. XI #7 (July 1971).

Sissons, D.C.S. "The Pacifist Clause of the Japanese Constitution," *International Affairs,* Vol. 37 #1 (Jan. 1961).

Snidal, Duncan. "The Limits of Hegemonic Stability Theory," *International Organization* Vol. 39, No. 4 (Autumn, 1985).

Snyder, William. "Dean Rusk to John Foster Dulles, May-June 1953: The Office, the First 100 Days, and Red China," *Diplomatic History,* Vol. 7, No. 1 (Winter

1983).

Spinks, Charles Nelson. "Postwar Political Parties in Japan," *Pacific Affairs,* XIX No. 3 (September 1946).

Steel, Ronald. "The End and the Beginning," *Diplomatic History,* Vol. 16, No. 2 (Spring 1992).

Stein, Arthur. "The Hegemon's Dilemma: Great Britain, the United States, and the International Economic Order," *International Organization* Vol. 38, No. 2 (Spring 1984).

Stockwin, J. A. A. "The Occupation: Continuity or Change?" *Asian and African Studies* 18 (1984).

Suga, Kenji. "Industrial and Economic Recovery of Japan," *Contemporary Japan* Vol. 23 (1955).

Sugimoto, Yoshio. "Labor Reform and Industrial Turbulence: The Case of the American Occupation of Japan," *Pacific Sociological Review* Vol. 20, No. 4 (October 1977).

Takahashi, Kamekichi. "Problems of Post-Treaty Economy," *Contemporary Japan* Vol. 20 (1951).

Takami, Shigeyoshi. "Prospect of Foreign Trade," *Contemporary Japan* Vol. 20 (1951).

Tanaka, Mitsuo. "Postwar Foreign Relations," *Contemporary Japan* Vol. 23 (1955).

Tiltman, Hessell. "Japan and the Korean War," *Contemporary Japan,* Vol. XIX Nos. 7-9 (July-Sept. 1950).

Tominomori, Kenji. "Big Business Groups and Financial Capital in Postwar Japan," *Hokkaido Economic Papers* IX (1979-80).

Trezise, Philip. "The Place of Japan in the Network of World Trade," *American Economic Review* Vol. LIII #2 (May 1963).

Tsuru, Shigeto. "Growth and Stability of the Postwar Japanese Economy," *American Economic Review* Vol. LI #2 (May 1961).

Tsuru, Shigeto. "Survey of Economic Research in Postwar Japan," *American Economic Review* Supplement (June 1964).

Tucker, Nancy Bernkopf. "American Policy Toward Sino-Japanese Trade in the Postwar Years: Politics and Prosperity," *Diplomatic History,* Vol. 8, No. 3 (Summer 1984).

Wada, Teiichi. "Zaibatsu Dissolution and Business Groupings," *Waseda Journal of Asian Studies* Vol. 2 (1980).

Weste, John. "Salvation from Without: Mutual Security Assistance and the Military-Industry Lobby in Post-War Japan," *Japan Forum* Vol. 4, No. 2, October 1992.

Wilkins, Mira. "American-Japanese Direct Foreign Investment Relationships, 1930-1952," *Business History Review* Vol. LVI No. 4 (Winter 1982).

Williams, Justin. "Making the Japanese Constitution: A Further Look," *American Political Science Review* Vol. LIX No. 3 (September 1965).

Williams, Justin, John Dower, and Howard Schonberger. "Forum: American Democratization Policy for Occupied Japan: Correcting the Revisionist Version," *Pacific Historical Review* (1988).

Wittner, Lawrence. "Forum: Japanese-American Military Relations in the Postwar Era," *Peace and Change*, Vol. IV, Number 1 (Fall 1976).

Wolf, David C. "'To Secure a Convenience': Britain Recognizes China - 1950," *Journal of Contemporary History* Vol. 18 (1983).

Yamamoto, Noboru. "Reparation and Economic Cooperation," *Asian Affairs*, Vol. I, No. 3, (September 1956).

Yamamura, Kozo. "Zaibatsu, Prewar and Zaibatsu, Postwar," *JAS* XXIII No. 4 (August 1964).

Yasuhara, Yoko. "Japan, Communist China, and Export Controls in Asia, 1948-52," *Diplomatic History*, Vol. 10, No. 1 (Winter 1986).

Yoshida, Shigeru. "Japan and the Crisis in Asia," *Foreign Affairs*, Vol. 29 No. 2 (January 1951).

UNPUBLISHED SECONDARY SOURCES

Edwards, Catherine Rita. "U.S. Policy Towards Japan, 1945-1951: Rejection of Revolution." Ph. D. dissertation, University of California, Los Angeles, 1977.

Foltos, Lester J. "The Bulwark of Freedom: American Security Policy for East Asia, 1945-1950." Ph. D. dissertation, University of Illinois, 1980.

Guttman, William L. "Miracles of Power: America and the Making of East Asian Economic Growth." D. Phil. Dissertation, University of Oxford, 1989.

Kelley, Richard Brian. "America's Defense of Japan 1945-1990." Ph.D. dissertation, Georgetown University, 1991.

Kil, Soong Hoom. "The Dodge Line and the Japanese Conservative Party." Ph. D. dissertation, The University of Michigan, 1977.

Krishnaswami, Sridhar. "A Study of Alliance Politics: The Impact of the Vietnam War on American-Japanese Relations." Ph. D. dissertation, Miami University, 1983.

Nanto, Dick K. "The United States' Role in the Postwar Economic Recovery of Japan." Ph. D. dissertation, Harvard University, 1976.

Shimizu, Sayuri. "Creating People of Plenty: The United States and Japan's Economic Alternatives, 1953-1958." Ph. D. dissertation, Cornell University, 1991.

BIBLIOGRAPHY
(JAPANESE LANGUAGE SOURCES)

BOOKS AND DOCUMENTS

Abe Koji. *Ichimada Naoto Den.* Tokyo: Toyo Shokan, 1955.

Akazawa Shiro, et. al. eds. *Nempo Nihon Gendaishi Vol. 2.* Tokyo: Higashi Shuppan, 1996.

Amakawa Akira and Igarashi Takeshi eds. *Sengo Nihonshi to Gendai no Kadai.* Tokyo: Tsukiji Shokan, 1996.

Ando Yoshio ed. *Showa Keizaishi Heno Shogen.* Tokyo: Mainichi Shimbun, 1966.

Ara Takashi ed. *Nihon Senryo: Gaiko Kankei Shiryoshu.* Tokyo: Kashiwa Shobo, 1991.

Ara Takashi. *Nihon Senryoshi Kenkyu Josetsu.* Tokyo: Kashiwa Shobo, 1994.

Arai Shinichi. *Senso Sekininron.* Tokyo: Iwanami Shoten, 1995.

Arisawa Hiromi. *Infureshon to Shakaika.* Tokyo: Nihon Hyoronsha, 1948.

Arisawa Hiromi. *Saigunbi no Keizaigaku.* Tokyo: Tokyo Daigaku Shuppankai, 1953.

Arisawa Hiromi ed. *Nihon Keizai.* Tokyo: Kawaide Shobo, 1953.

Arisawa Hiromi. *Sengo Keizai wo Kataru.* Tokyo: Tokyo Daigaku Shuppankai, 1989.

Asahi Journal ed. *Sekai Keizai Sangokushi.* Tokyo: Asahi Shimbun, 1989.

Asahi Shimbun Seron Chosashitsu ed. *Nihon no Seiji Ishiki.* Tokyo: Asahi Shimbun, 1976.

Asakai Koichiro. *Shoki Tainichi Senryo Seisaku.* Tokyo: Mainichi Shimbun, 1978.

Ashida Hitoshi. *Ashida Hitoshi Nikki.* Tokyo: Iwanami Shoten, 1986.

Awatoku Saburo, et. al. *Daresu Soan ni Kotaeru.* Tokyo: Jiyu no Koe Sha, 1951.

Awaya Kentaro. *Tokyo Saiban Heno Michi.* Tokyo: NHK Shuppan, 1994.

Cohen, Theodore. *Nihon Senryo Kakumei.* Tokyo: TBS Buritanika, 1983.

Dodge, Joseph. *Jigyo Keieisha no Michi.* Tokyo: Teikoku Ginko Chosabu, 1950.

Fujiwara Akira ed. *Taikei Nihon Gendaishi Vol. 6.* Tokyo: Nihon Hyoronsha, 1979.

Fujiwara Akira and Imai Seiichi eds. *Jugonen Sensoshi Vol. 4.* Tokyo: Aoki Shoten, 1989.

Furukawa Mantaro. *Nicchu Sengo Kankeishi.* Tokyo: Hara Shobo, 1988.

Gaimusho Johobu. *Nihonkoku tono Heiwa Joyaku Soan no Kaisetsu.* Gaimusho, 1946.

Hanai Hitoshi. *Sengo Nihon wo Kizuita Saishotachi.* Tokyo: Bungei Shunju, 1996.

Hara Yoshihisa. *Sengo Nihon to Kokusai Seiji.* Tokyo: Chuo Koron, 1988.

Hasegawa Masayasu. *Showa Kemposhi.* Tokyo: Iwanami Shoten, 1971.

Hasegawa Masayasu. *Kempo Gendaishi.* Tokyo: Nihon Hyoronsha, 1981.

Hata Ikuhiko. *Shiroku Nihon Saigunbi.* Tokyo: Bungei Shunju, 1976.

Hata Ikuhiko and Sodei Rinjiro. *Nihon Senryo Hishi.* Tokyo: Asahi Shimbun, 1977.

Hatoyama Ichiro. *Hatoyama Ichiro Kaikoroku.* Tokyo: Bungei Shunjushinsha, 1957.

Hayashi Shigeru and Tsuji Kiyoaki eds. *Nihon Naikaku Shiroku Vol. 5.* Tokyo: Daiichi Hoki Shuppan, 1981.

Higuchi Hiroshi. *Zaibatsu no Fukkatsu.* Tokyo: Naigai Keizaisha, 1953.

Hiwatari Nobuhiro. *Sengo Nihon no Shijo to Seiji.* Tokyo: Tokyo Daigaku Shuppankai, 1991.

Hiwatari Yumi. *Sengo Seiji to Nichibei Kankei.* Tokyo: Tokyo Daigaku Shuppankai, 1990.

Hosei Daigaku Sangyo Joho Center, et. al. eds. *Nihon Keizai no Hatten to Kigyo Shudan* Tokyo: Tokyo Daigaku Shuppankai, 1993.

Hosoya Chihiro. *Nihon Gaiko no Zahyo.* Tokyo: Chuo Koron, 1979.

Hosoya Chihiro. *San Francisco Kowa heno Michi.* Tokyo: Chuo Koron, 1984.

Ichiki Yutaka. *Zosho: Jidai to Ketsudan.* Tokyo: Nihon Keizai Shimbun, 1984.

Ichimada Naoto. *Kyu Gensoku to Keizai Antei.* Tokyo: Rodo Bunkasha, 1949.

Ichimada Naoto. *Genka no Keizai Kinyu Mondai ni tsuite.* Kobe Shoko Kaigisho, 1950.

Ichimada Naoto Denki Tsuitoroku Kankokai ed. *Ichimada Naoto Denki Tsuitoroku.* Tokyo: Tokuma Shoten, 1986.

Igarashi Takeshi. *Tainichi Kowa to Reisen.* Tokyo: Tokyo Daigaku Shuppankai, 1986.

Iida Tsuneo, et. al. *Gendai Nihon Keizaishi.* Tokyo: Chikuma Shobo, 1976.

Ikeda Hayato. *Kinko Zaisei.* Tokyo: Jitsugyo no Nihonsha, 1952.

Inaba Shuzo. *Gekido 30nen no Nihon Keizai.* Tokyo: Jitsugyo no Nihonsha, 1965.

Inoki Masamichi. *Hyoden Yoshida Shigeru.* Tokyo: Yomiuri Shimbun, 1981.

Iokibe Makoto. *Beikoku no Nihon Senryo Seisaku.* Tokyo: Chuo Koron, 1985.

Iokibe Makoto. *Nichibei Senso to Sengo Nihon.* Osaka: Osaka Shoseki, 1989.

Iriye Akira. *Beichu Kankeishi.* Tokyo: Simul Shuppankai, 1971.

Iriye Akira. *Nichibei Senso.* Tokyo: Chuo Koron, 1978.

Iriye Toshiro. *Kempo Seiritsu no Keii to Kempojo no Shomondai.* Tokyo: Daiichi Hoki Shuppan, 1976.

Ishida Keisuke. *Sengo Tennoron no Kiseki.* Tokyo: Nihon Kyobunsha, 1989.

Ishida Masaharu. *Reisen Kokka no Keisei.* Tokyo: Sanichi Shobo, 1993.

Ishii Akira. *Chuso Kankeishi no Kenkyu 1945-1950.* Tokyo: Tokyo Daigaku Shuppankai, 1990.

Ishii Osamu. *Reisen to Nichibei Kankei.* Tokyo: Japan Times, 1989.

Ishikawa Masumi. *Data Sengo Seiji.* Tokyo: Iwanami Shoten, 1984.

Ishimaru Kazuto. *Sengo Nihon Gaikoshi.* Tokyo: Sanseido, 1983.

Ito Masaya. *Ikeda Hayato.* Tokyo: Jiji Tsushinsha, 1985.

Iwanaga Kenkichiro. *Sengo Nihon no Seito to Gaiko.* Tokyo: Tokyo Daigaku Shuppankai, 1985.

Jochi Daigaku America/Canada Kenkyujo ed. *Amerika to Nihon.* Tokyo: Sairyusha, 1993.

Kamiya Fuji. *Nihon to Amerika.* Tokyo: Nihon Keizai Shimbun, 1973.

Kamiya Fuji. *Sengoshi no Naka no Nichibei Kankei.* Tokyo: Shinchosha, 1989.

Kan Hideki. *Beiso Reisen to Amerika no Ajia Seisaku.* Kyoto: Mineruva Shobo, 1992.

Kanda Fuhito ed. *Taikei Nihon Gendaishi Vol. 5.* Tokyo: Nihon Hyoronsha, 1979.

Kashima Heiwa Kenkyujo ed. *Nihon Gaikoshi Vol. 26.* Tokyo: Kashima Kenkyujo Shuppankai, 1973.

Kase Toshikazu. *Kase Toshikazu Kaisoroku.* Tokyo: Yamanote Shobo, 1986.

Kase Toshikazu. *Yoshida Shigeru no Yuigon.* Tokyo: Nihon Bungeisha, 1993.

Kasuya Susumu. *Sengo Nihon no Anzen Hosho Rongi.* Tokyo: Shinzansha, 1992.

Keizai Antei Hombu. *Fukkoku Keizai Hakusho Vol. 2.* Tokyo: Nihon Keizai Hyoronsha, 1975.

Keizai Antei Hombu. *Fukkoku Keizai Hakusho, Showa 22nen - Showa 25nen.* Tokyo: Nihon Keizai Hyoronsha, 1987.

Keizai Antei Hombu Keizai Fukko Keikaku Iinkai ed. *Nihon Keizai Fukko Keikaku.* Tokyo: Kokumin Keizai Kenkyu Kyokai, 1949.

Keizai Doyukai ed. *Keizai Doyukai Junenshi.* Tokyo: Keizai Doyukai, 1956.

Keizai Kikakucho ed. *Sengo Keizaishi.* Tokyo: Hara Shobo, 1992.

Keizai Kikakucho ed. *Sengo Nihon Keizai no Kiseki.* Keizai Kikakucho, 1997.

Keizai Saiken Kenkyukai ed. *Pore kara Daresu He.* Tokyo: Diamondsha, 1952.

Kikuchi Hisashi. *Showa Tenno to Makkasa.* Tokyo: Sairyusha, 1989.

Kindai Nihon Kenkyukai ed. *Nempo Kindai Nihon Kenkyu Vol. 16.* Tokyo: Yamakawa Shuppan, 1994.

Kojima Noboru. *Nihon Senryo.* Tokyo: Bungei Shunju, 1978.

Kojima Noboru. *Kowa Joyaku.* Tokyo: Shinchosha, 1996.

Kono Ichiro. *Ima dakara Hanaso.* Tokyo: Bungei Shunjushinsha, 1958.

Kosai Yutaka and Teranishi Jurou eds. *Sengo Nihon no Keizai Kaikaku.* Tokyo: Tokyo Daigaku Shuppankai, 1993.

Kosaka Masataka. *Saisho Yoshida Shigeru.* Tokyo: Chuo Koron, 1968.

Kowalski Frank. *Nihon Saigunbi.* Tokyo: Simul Shuppankai, 1969.

Kyutei Kishadan. *Kunaicho.* Tokyo: Hobunsha, 1957.

Makino Hiroshi. *Reisen no Kigen to Amerika no Haken.* Tokyo: Ochanomizu Shobo, 1993.

Masamura Kimihiro. *Sengoshi.* Tokyo: Chikuma Shobo, 1985.

Masuda Hiroshi. *Ishibashi Tanzan.* Tokyo: Soshisha, 1988.

Masumi Junnosuke. *Sengo Seiji.* Tokyo: Tokyo Daigaku Shuppankai, 1988.

Masumi Junnosuke. *Nihon Seijishi Vol. 4.* Tokyo: Tokyo Daigaku Shuppankai, 1992.

Miura Yoichi. *Yoshida Shigeru to San Francisco Kowa.* Tokyo: Ohtsuki Shoten, 1996.

Miyake Masaki, et. al. eds. *Showashi no Gunbu to Seiji Vol. 5.* Tokyo: Daiichi Hoki Shuppan, 1983.

Miyazaki Giichi. *Nihon Keizai no Kozo to Kodo.* Tokyo: Chikuma Shobo, 1985.

Miyazawa Kiichi. *Tokyo-Washington no Mitsudan.* Tokyo: Jitsugyo no Nihonsha, 1956.

Moore, Ray. *Tenno ga Baiburu wo Yonda Hi.* Tokyo: Kodansha, 1982.

Morikawa Hidemasa. *Sengo Keieishi Nyumon.* Tokyo: Nihon Keizai Shimbun, 1992.

Murakawa Ichiro. *Daresu to Yoshida Shigeru.* Tokyo: Kokusho Kankokai, 1991.

Muroyama Yoshimasa. *Nichibei Ampo Taisei.* Tokyo: Yuhikaku, 1992.

Nagai Yonosuke. *Reisen no Kigen.* Tokyo: Chuo Koron, 1978.

Nagaoka Shinkichi and Nishikawa Hiroshi eds. *Nihon Keizai to Higashi Ajia.* Kyoto: Mineruva, 1995.

Naikaku Hoseikyoku Hyakunennshi Henshu Iinkai ed. *Shogen Kindai Hosei no Kiseki.* Tokyo: Gyosei, 1985.

Naiseishi Kenkyukai. *Suzuki Tadakatsushi Danwa Sokkiroku.* Tokyo: Mizutani, 1974.

Nakajima Mineo. *Chuso Tairitsu to Gendai.* Tokyo: Chuo Koron, 1978.

Nakamura Akira. *Sengo Seiji ni Yureta Kempo Kyujo.* Tokyo: Chuo Keizaisha, 1996.

Nakamura Masanori ed. *Kindai Nihon no Kiseki Vol. 6.* Tokyo: Yoshikawa Kobunkan, 1994.

Nakamura Masanori, et. al. *Sengo Nihon 6 vols.* Tokyo: Iwanami Shoten, 1995.

Nakamura Masanori. *Gendaishi wo Manabu.* Tokyo: Yoshikawa Kobunkan, 1997.

Nakamura Takafusa ed. *Nihon Keizaishi Vol. 7.* Tokyo: Iwanami Shoten, 1989.

Nakamura Takafusa ed. *Shiryo Sengo Nihon no Keizai Seisaku Koso.* Tokyo: Tokyo Daigaku Shuppankai, 1990.

Nakamura Takafusa. *Nihon Keizai.* Tokyo: Tokyo Daigaku Shuppankai, 1993.

Nakamura Takafusa. *Showashi.* Tokyo: Toyo Keizai Shimposha, 1993.

Nakaoka Saneki ed. *Sengo Nihon no Tai Ajia Keizai Seisakushi.* Tokyo: Ajia Keizai Kenkyujo, 1981.

Nakayama Shigeru and Yoshioka Hitoshi eds. *Sengo Kagaku Gijutsu no Shakaishi.* Tokyo: Asahi Shimbun, 1994.

Nihon Gaimusho. *Nihon Gaiko Monjo.* Tokyo: Gaiko Shiryokan.

Nihon Gaimusho Kokusai Shiryobu Shiryoka. *Sengo no Chuso Kankei.* August 1963.

Nihon Gaimusho Sengo Gaikoshi Kenkyukai ed. *Nihon Gaikoshi 30nen.* Tokyo: Sekai no Ugokisha, 1982.

Nihon Gendaishi Kenkyukai ed. *Sengo Taisei no Keisei.* Tokyo: Ohtsuki Shoten, 1988.

Nihon Ginko Chosakyoku. *Genka Infureshon no Shomondai.* January 1948.

Nishi Toshio. *Makkasa no 'Hanzai'.* Tokyo: Nihon Kogyo Shimbun, 1983.

Nishimura Kumao. *Kaitei Shinpan Anzen Hosho Joyakuron.* Tokyo: Jijitsushinsha, 1960.

Nishimura Kumao. *Nihon Gaikoshi Vol. 27.* Tokyo: Kajima Kenkyujo Shuppankai, 1971.

Ohkurasho Zaiseishishitsu ed. *Showa Zaiseishi, Vols. 1-20.* Tokyo: Toyo Keizai Shimposha, 1976-84.

Ohkurasho Zaiseishishitsu ed. *Watanabe Takeshi Nikki.* Tokyo: Toyo Keizai Shimposha, 1983.

Ohtake Hideo. *Nihon Seiji no Soten.* Tokyo: Sanichi Shobo, 1984.

Ohtake Hideo. *Adenauer to Yoshida Shigeru.* Tokyo: Chuo Koron, 1986.

Ohtake Hideo. *Saigunbi to Nationalism.* Tokyo: Chuo Koron, 1988.

Ohtake Hideo. *Futatsu no Sengo.* Tokyo: Nihon Hoso Kyokai, 1992.

Ohtake Hideo. *Sengo Nihon no Ideology Tairitsu.* Tokyo: Sanichi Shobo, 1996.

Ohtake Hideo ed. *Sengo Nihon Boei Mondai Shiryoshu.* Tokyo: Sanichi Shobo, 1991-93.

Ohtsuka Takamasa. *Gaiko to Nihonkoku Kempo.* Tokyo: Bunshindo, 1992.

Okazaki Tetsuji and Okuno Masahiro eds. *Gendai Nihon Keizai Shisutemu no Genryu.* Tokyo: Nihon Keizai Shimbun, 1993.

Okazaki Tetsuji et. al. *Sengo Nihon Keizai to Keizai Doyukai.* Tokyo: Iwamani Shoten, 1996.

Okonogi Masao. *Chosen Senso.* Tokyo: Chuo Koron, 1986.

Okonogi Masao and Akagi Kanji eds. *Reisenki no Kokusai Seiji.* Tokyo: Keio Tsushin, 1987.

Rekishigaku Kenkyukai ed. *Sengo Nihonshi.* Tokyo: Aoki Shoten, 1964.

Rekishigaku Kenkyukai ed. *Nihon Dojidaishi.* Tokyo: Aoki Shoten, 1990.

Rekishigaku Kenkyukai Nihonshi Kenkyukai ed. *Koza Nihon Rekishi Vol. 8.* Tokyo: Tokyo Daigaku Shuppankai, 1971.

Rekishigaku Kenkyukai Nihonshi Kenkyukai ed. *Koza Nihon Rekishi Vol. 11* Tokyo: Tokyo Daigaku Shuppankai, 1985.

Saito Eizaburo. *Senryoka no Nihon.* Tokyo: Gennando Shoten, 1966.

Sakai Saburo. *Showa Kenkyukai.* Tokyo: TBS Buritanika, 1979.

Sakamoto Kazuya. *Nichibei Domei no Kizuna.* Tokyo: Yuhikaku, 2000.

Sakamoto Yoshikazu and R. E. Ward eds. *Nihon Senryo no Kenkyu.* Tokyo: Tokyo Daigaku Shuppankai, 1987.

Sasaki Ryuji ed. *Taikei Nihon Gendaishi Vol. 7.* Tokyo: Nihon Hyoronsha, 1979.

Sasaki Ryuji *Sekaishi no Naka no Ajia to Nihon.* Tokyo: Ochanomizu Shobo, 1988.

Sasaki Takuya. *Fujikome no Keisei to Henyo.* Tokyo: Sanrei Shobo, 1993.

Sato Tatsuo. *Nihonkoku Kempo Seiritsushi.* Tokyo: Yuhikaku, 1964.

Shimizu Shinzo. *Sengo Kakushin Seiryoku.* Tokyo: Aoki Shoten, 1966.

Shimoda Takezo. *Sengo Nihon Gaiko no Shogen.* Tokyo: Gyosei Mondai Kenkyujo, 1984.

Shiraishi Takashi. *Sengo Nihon Tsusho Seisakushi.* Tokyo: Zeimu Keiri Kyokai, 1983.

Shiratori Rei ed. *Nihon no Naikaku.* Tokyo: Shin Hyoron, 1981.

Shiso no Kagaku Kenkyukai ed. *Nihon Senryo.* Tokyo: Tokuma Shoten, 1972.

Shiso no Kagaku Kenkyukai ed. *Nihon Senryo Kenkyu Jiten.* Tokyo: Tokuma Shoten, 1978.

Shiso no Kagaku Kenkyukai ed. *Nihon Senryogun.* Tokyo: Tokuma Shoten, 1978.

Sodei Rinjiro. *Makkasa no Nisennichi.* Tokyo: Chuo Koron, 1975.

Sodei Rinjiro. *Sekaishi no Naka no Nihon Senryo.* Tokyo: Nihon Hyoronsha, 1985.

Sodei Rinjiro and Takemae Eiji eds. *Sengo Nihon no Genten.* Tokyo: Shushisha, 1992.

Suekawa Hiroshi and Iyenaga Saburo eds. *Nihon Gendaishi Shiryo.* Tokyo: Sanseido, 1971.

Sumitomo Toshio. *Senryo Hishi.* Tokyo: Mainichi Shimbun, 1965.

Suzuki Akinori. *Nihonkoku Kempo wo Unda Misshitsu no Kokonokakan.* Tokyo: Sogensha, 1995.

Suzuki Takeo. *Dodge Line.* Tokyo: Jiji Tsushinsha, 1950.

Suzuki Takeo Sensei Kanreki Kinen Ronshu Henshu Iinkai ed. *Keizai Seicho to Zaisei Kinyu.* Tokyo: Shiseido, 1962.

Suzuki Yasuzo. *Kempo Seitei Zengo.* Tokyo: Aoki Shoten, 1977.

Takayanagi Kenzo, Ohtomo Ichiro, and Tanaka Hideo eds. *Nihonkoku Kempo Seitei no Katei.* Tokyo: Yuhikaku, 1978.

Takeda Takao ed. *Gendai Nihon Shihon Shugi Taikei.* Tokyo: Kobundo, 1958.

Takemae Eiji. *Amerika Tainichi Rodo Seisaku no Kenkyu.* Tokyo: Nihon Hyoronsha, 1970.

Takemae Eiji. *Sengo Rodo Kaikaku.* Tokyo: Tokyo Daigaku Shuppankai, 1982.

Takemae Eiji. *Senryo Sengoshi.* Tokyo: Iwanami Shoten, 1992.

Tanaka Nobumasa. *Document Showa Tenno Vol. 6.* Tokyo: Ryokufu Shuppan, 1990.

Tokyo Daigaku Shakai Kagaku Kenkyujo ed. *Sengo Kaikaku 8 Vols.* Tokyo: Tokyo

Daigaku Shuppankai, 1974-75.

Tokyo Rekishi Kagaku Kenkyukai Gendaishi Bukai ed. *Nihon Gendaishi no Shuppatsu.* Tokyo: Aoki Shoten, 1978.

Toyoshita Narahiko. *Nihon Senryo Kari Taisei no Seiritsu.* Tokyo: Iwanami Shoten, 1992.

Toyoshita Narahiko. *Ampo Joyaku no Seiritsu.* Tokyo: Iwanami Shoten, 1997.

Tsugita Daisaburo. *Tsugita Daisaburo Nikki.* Okayama: Sanyo Shimbun, 1991.

Tsuru Shigeto. *Antei to Jiritsu no Tame ni.* Nagoya: Reimei Shobo, 1949.

Tsusho Sangyo Seisakushi Hensan Iinkai ed. *Tsusho Sangyo Seisakushi Vol. 4.* Tokyo: Tsusho Sangyo Chosakai, 1991.

Uchida Kenzo. *Sengo Saishoron.* Tokyo: Bungei Shunju, 1994.

Uemura Hideki. *Saigunbi to 55nen Taisei.* Tokyo: Bokutakusha, 1995.

Umegaki Michio. *Sengo Nichibei Kankei wo Yomu.* Tokyo: Chuo Koron, 1993.

Wada Haruki. *Chosen Senso.* Tokyo: Iwanami Shoten, 1994.

Watanabe Akio ed. *Sengo Nihon no Taigai Seisaku.* Tokyo: Yuhikaku, 1985.

Watanabe Akio and Miyazato Seigen eds. *San Francisco Kowa.* Tokyo: Tokyo Daigaku Shuppankai, 1986.

Watanabe Akio. *Sengo Nihon no Saisho tachi.* Tokyo: Chuo Koron, 1995.

Watanabe Takeshi. *Senryoka no Nihon Zaisei Oboegaki.* Tokyo: Nihon Keizai Shimbun, 1966.

Yamagiwa Akira and Nakamura Masanori eds. *Shiryo Nihon Senryo Vol. I.* Tokyo: Ohtsuki Shoten, 1990.

Yamagiwa Akira ed. *Higashi Ajia to Reisen.* Tokyo: Sanrei Shobo, 1994.

Yamazawa Ippei. *Nihon no Keizai Hatten to Kokusai Bungyo.* Tokyo: Toyo Keizai Shimposha, 1988.

Yomiuri Shimbun Sengoshihan ed. *Showa Sengoshi 'Saigunbi' no Kiseki.* Tokyo: Yomiuri Shimbun, 1981.

Yonekawa Shinichi, et. al. eds. *Sengo Nihon Keieishi.* Tokyo: Toyo Keizai Shimposha, 1990-91.

Yoshida Hiroshi. *Gendai Rekishigaku to Senso Sekinin.* Tokyo: Aoki Shoten, 1997.

Yoshida Kazuo. *Kempo Kaiseiron.* Tokyo: PHP Kenkyujo, 1996.

Yoshida Naikaku Kankokai ed. *Yoshida Naikaku.* Tokyo: Yoshida Naikaku Kankokai, 1954.

Yoshida Shigeru, Koizumi Shinzo, and Tatsuno Takashi. *Kuni to Boei.* Tokyo: Asakumo Shimbun, 1963.

Yoshida Shigeru. *Nihon wo Kettei shita Hyakunen.* Tokyo: Nihon Keizai Shimbun, 1967.

Yoshida Shigeru. *Kaiso Junen.* Tokyo: Tokyo Shirakawa Shoin, 1982-83.

Yoshida Shigeru. *Sekai to Nihon.* Tokyo: Chuo Koron, 1991.

Yoshida Shigeru. *Ohiso Zuiso.* Tokyo: Chuo Koron, 1991.

Yoshida Shigeru Kinen Jigyo Zaidan ed. *Ningen Yoshida Shigeru.* Tokyo: Chuo Koron, 1991.

Yoshida Shigeru Kinen Jigyo Zaidan ed. *Yoshida Shigeru Shokan.* Tokyo: Chuo Koron, 1994.

Yoshikawa Yoko. *Nippi Baisho Gaiko Kosho no Kenkyu 1949-1956.* Tokyo: Keiso Shobo, 1991.

Yoshino Toshihiko. *Kyu Gensoku to Keizai Antei.* Tokyo: Rodo Bunkasha, 1949.

Yui Daizaburo. *Mikan no Senryo Kaikaku.* Tokyo: Tokyo Daigaku Shuppankai, 1989.

Yui Daizaburo. *Nichibei Sensokan no Sokoku.* Tokyo: Iwanami Shoten, 1995.

Yui Daizaburo, Nakamura Masanori, and Toyoshita Narahiko eds. *Senryo Kaikaku no Kokusai Hikaku.* Tokyo: Sanseido, 1994.

Zenkoku Kempo Kenkyukai ed. *Kempo Mondai Vol. 8.* Tokyo: Saiseido, 1997.

PERIODICALS

Amakawa Akira. "Nihon ni okeru Senryo," *Economiya* 87 (December 1985).

Asakai Koichiro, et. al. "'Nihon Senryo' ga Nokoshita mono," *Bungei Shunju* 61-4 (April 1983).

Aso Taro. "Mago ga Mita Tai Bei Kowa Zenya no Yoshida Shigeru," *Bungei Shunju* 74-10 (October 1996).

Chuma Kiyofuku. "Senryo kara Ampo he," *Sekai* 502 (June 1987).

Fujimura Michio. "Futatsu no Senryo to Showashi," *Sekai* 427 (August 1981).

Hatano Sumio. "'Saigunbi' wo Meguru Seiji Rikigaku," *Nempo Kindai Nihon Kenkyu* 11 (1989).

Inoue Toshikazu. "Kokuren to Sengo Nihon Gaiko," *Nempo Kindai Nihon Kenkyu* 16 (1994).

Ito Masanao. "Dodge Line Zengo no 'Keizai Keikaku' to Koki Senryo Seisaku," *Keizaigaku Ronso* 62-2 (July 1996).

Kan Hideki. "Amerika no Ajia ni okeru Shudan Anzen Hosho Koso to Nihon Saigunbi 1948-51," *Kitakyushu Daigaku Gaikokugo Gakubu Kiyo* 62 (March 1988).

Kataoka Tetsuya. "Yoshida/Makkasa no 'Mitsuyaku'," *Bungei Shunju* 61-1 (April 1983).

Kitaoka Shinichi. "Yoshida Shigeru ni okeru Senzen to Sengo," *Nempo Kindai Nihon Kenkyu* 16 (1994).

Koseki Shoichi. "Kempo Seitei heno Kodawari," *Shiso no Kagaku* 468 (August 1990).

Miyajima Hideaki. "'Zaikai Tsuiho' to Shin Keieisha no Tojo," *Will* (July 1991).

Miyazaki Koji. "Dai Sanji Yoshida Shigeru Naikakuki no Seiji Katei," *Chiba Daigaku Hogaku Ronso* 3-1 (1988).

Murakawa Ichiro. "Kowa wo Meguru Daresu-Yoshida Shokan," *Chuo Koron* 106-2 (February 1991).

Nakamura Masanori. "'Gyaku Kosu' to Senryo Kenkyu," *Sekai* 427 (June 1981).

Nakanishi Hiroshi. "Sengo Ajia Taiheiyo no Anzen Hosho Wakugumi no Mosaku to Nihon," *Nempo Kindai Nihon Kenkyu* 16 (1994).

Ohtake Hideo. "Yoshida Naikaku ni yoru 'Saigunbi'," *Hogaku* 50-4 (October 1986).

Okonogi Masao. "Chosen ni okeru 'Fujikome' no Mosaku," *Kokusai Seiji* 70 (1982).

Shibahara Yoshio. "Saisho Yoshida Shigeru Ron, 1-3" *Jiyu* 34-12, 35-1, and 35-2 (1992-93).

Shichisawa Mikiko. "Tai Nichi Baisho Seisaku no Saikento," *Seiji Keizai Shigaku* 318 (December 1992).

Takemae Eiji. "Kades Nihon Senryo Kaikoroku," *Tokyo Keidai Gakkaishi* 148 (November 1986).

Takemae Eiji. "Moto GHQ Minseikyoku Jicho Kades ni Kiku," *Chuo Koron* 102-6 (May 1987).

Toyoshita Narahiko. "Yoshida Gaiko to Tenno Gaiko," *Sekai* 615 (November 1995).

Toyoshita Narahiko. "Yoshida Dokutorin to 'Shocho Tenno'," *Rekishi Chiri Kyoiku* (October 1997).

Wada Haruki. "Chosen Senso ni tsuite Kangaeru," *Shiso* 795 (September 1990).

Yoshikawa Hiroshi and Okazaki Tetsuji. "Sengo Infureshon to Dodge Line," *Bijinesu Review* 39-2 (1992).

Index of Persons

Index